Horror as Racism in H. P. Lovecraft

Horror as Racism in H. P. Lovecraft

White Fragility in the Weird Tales

John L. Steadman

BLOOMSBURY ACADEMIC
NEW YORK • LONDON • OXFORD • NEW DELHI • SYDNEY

BLOOMSBURY ACADEMIC
Bloomsbury Publishing Inc
1385 Broadway, New York, NY 10018, USA
50 Bedford Square, London, WC1B 3DP, UK
29 Earlsfort Terrace, Dublin 2, Ireland

BLOOMSBURY, BLOOMSBURY ACADEMIC and the Diana logo are trademarks of
Bloomsbury Publishing Plc

First published in the United States of America 2024

Copyright © John L. Steadman, 2024

Cover design: Eleanor Rose
Cover image: gremlin / Getty Images

All rights reserved. No part of this publication may be reproduced or transmitted in any form or by any means, electronic or mechanical, including photocopying, recording, or any information storage or retrieval system, without prior permission in writing from the publishers.

Bloomsbury Publishing Inc does not have any control over, or responsibility for, any third-party websites referred to or in this book. All internet addresses given in this book were correct at the time of going to press. The author and publisher regret any inconvenience caused if addresses have changed or sites have ceased to exist, but can accept no responsibility for any such changes.

Library of Congress Cataloging-in-Publication Data
Names: Steadman, John L., author.
Title: Horror as racism in H. P. Lovecraft : white fragility in the weird tales / John L. Steadman.
Description: New York : Bloomsbury Academic, 2024. | Includes bibliographical references and index. |
Identifiers: LCCN 2023025308 (print) | LCCN 2023025309 (ebook) | ISBN 9798765107683 (hardback) | ISBN 9798765107690 (paperback) | ISBN 9798765107706 (epub) | ISBN 9798765107713 (pdf) | ISBN 9798765107720 (ebook)
Subjects: LCSH: Lovecraft, H. P. (Howard Phillips), 1890–1937–Political and social views. | Lovecraft, H. P. (Howard Phillips), 1890–1937–Criticism and interpretation. | Racism in literature. | LCGFT: Literary criticism.
Classification: LCC PS3523.O833 Z866 2024 (print) | LCC PS3523.O833 (ebook) | DDC 813/.52–dc23/eng/20230607
LC record available at https://lccn.loc.gov/2023025308
LC ebook record available at https://lccn.loc.gov/2023025309

ISBN: HB: 979-8-7651-0768-3
PB: 979-8-7651-0769-0
ePDF: 979-8-7651-0771-3
eBook: 979-8-7651-0770-6

Typeset by Newgen KnowledgeWorks Pvt. Ltd., Chennai, India
Print and bound in Great Britain

To find out more about our authors and books visit www.bloomsbury.com
and sign up for our newsletters.

Again, and always, to my beautiful wife, Pamela, and my beautiful daughter, Ligeia.

CONTENTS

Introduction 1

Part I Beginnings
1. Privilege Lost 13
2. The Pattern of Loss and Failure 21
3. Racist Influences 35
4. Racist Writings 45

Part II Humankind against Hybrid, Degenerative Monsters
5. Lovecraft's Early Weird Tales 63
6. Arthur Jermyn (1920) 67
7. Herbert West—Reanimator (1922) 77
8. The Lurking Fear (1923) 87
9. The Rats in the Walls (1924) 99
10. The Horror at Red Hook (1925) 111
11. Critical Commentaries 123

Part III Humankind against the Cosmic Slave Masters
12. Lovecraft's Later Weird Tales 135
13. *The Case of Charles Dexter Ward* (1927) 139

14	The Whisperer in Darkness (1930)	151
15	The Shadow Over Innsmouth (1931)	161
16	*At the Mountains of Madness* (1931)	171
17	The Shadow Out of Time (1934)	183
18	Critical Commentaries (II)	195
19	Conclusion	207

Appendix—Lovecraft, Lovecraft Country, *and Afrofuturism* 217
Notes 227
Bibliography 239
Index 243

They were the Great Old Ones that had filtered down from the stars when the Earth was young ... before the true life of earth had existed at all. They were the makers and enslavers of that life.

H. P. LOVECRAFT

(At the Mountains of Madness)

Introduction

Robin DiAngelo, in *White Fragility: Why It's So Hard for White People to Talk about Racism* (2018), defines white fragility as a process that can occur when a white person's racial worldviews are challenged. As she describes it,

> We [white people] become highly fragile in conversations about race. We consider a challenge to our racial worldviews as challenges to our very identities as good, moral people. Thus, we perceive any attempt to connect us to the system of racism as an unsettling, and unfair moral offense. The smallest amount of racial stress is intolerable—the mere suggestion that being white has meaning often triggers a range of defensive responses. These include emotions such as anger, fear, and guilt and behaviors such as argumentation, silence, and withdrawal from the stress-inducing situation.[1]

The purpose of these responses, DiAngelo further argues, is to repel the challenge, to return to racial comfort, and maintain dominance within the racial hierarchy.

In terms of this definition, H. P. Lovecraft (1890–1937), the great New England horror writer and notorious racist, could easily have served as the poster child for the fragile, white male in his generation. Indeed, in his adult life, whenever Lovecraft was forced to consider the hated, non-Anglo-Saxon races or, heaven forbid, engage in actual contact with them, he exhibited all of the defensive reactions that DiAngelo identifies as characteristic of white fragility: extreme discomfort, anxiety, psychotic rage, and anger. Lovecraft's fragility, however, did not stem from challenges to his racial views—his family and friends, in fact, never seriously challenged those views, though many of them felt that they were extreme, even for the early twentieth century when racist views were the status quo and freely expressed by a majority of Americans and Europeans. Lovecraft's fragility, instead, was latent in his childhood and early youth. In 1904, Lovecraft lost his privileged lifestyle; his grandfather Whipple Phillips died suddenly when Lovecraft was only twelve years old and he along with his mother was forced to leave their palatial family home. This event "activated" Lovecraft's white fragility and brought it out in the open. The Lovecrafts moved into rented rooms three blocks from their previous home and the gravy train, such as it was, abruptly ended. As Lovecraft puts it in a letter to J. V. Shea in 1934, "for the first time I knew what a congested, servantless home—with another family in the same house—was."[2] But this event was much more than a merely uncomfortable change of venue, as it would have been for most teens; it was literally a psychological and psychic trauma, and for the first time in his life (but not the last), Lovecraft seriously considered suicide.

Lovecraft's loss of his privileged lifestyle led to two other unfortunate outcomes. First, it triggered a general pattern of loss and failure that rose directly out of his tendency to experience extreme nervous disturbance in reaction to stressful, childhood situations, a pattern that repeats in his later life as he attempts to reconcile himself to his loss of privilege and seek compensations for his economic and social diminishment. A second negative outcome from the loss of privilege was, as DiAngelo suggests in her book, an intensification of his racist feelings, which often occurs when a fragile white person is thwarted when it comes to a denial of his or her presumed God-given right to superior status and economic dominance. Or, to put it simply, Lovecraft's racist attitudes toward members of the nonwhite races, especially African Americans—which up until then had been relatively mild and paternalistic—grew increasingly harsh and vitriolic. Even worse, Lovecraft could not avoid recognizing that members of the supposedly inferior races were not so inferior to him after all, at least economically. And it became painfully obvious to him as well that many of these nonwhite Americans owned homes and *were* economically self-sufficient, unlike he and his mother, and able to take care of themselves and their families.[3]

In Part I of this study, I delve into the Lovecraft biography in some detail. In Chapter 1, I examine the fall of Lovecraft's privileged lifestyle and show exactly how traumatic this event proved to be. Following this, in Chapter 2, I study key examples of the pattern of loss and failure that characterized Lovecraft's life from that moment onward. In Chapters 3 and 4, I shift my attention to Lovecraft's racism. I look at the roots of his racial hatred and the documents that he used to intellectually justify it. I then focus on Lovecraft's nonfictional works—his correspondence, essays, and poetry—and trace firsthand the foundation that Lovecraft provides for the racist elements that appear in the fictional works. These two latter chapters will likely offend some of my readers, who may end up wondering how any man, especially a man as intelligent and philosophically sophisticated as Lovecraft was, could think and write such things. But he did think and write these things, and in order to understand the man and where he was coming from, we must look at them clearly and unflinchingly.

***

Lovecraft began writing fiction while still living in the protected bubble of his privileged lifestyle and continued to do so after the privilege had ended. Over time, he created a remarkable body of work which, though relatively small, ended up placing him among the foremost horror and sf (science fiction) writers in the world. As we might expect, racism runs rampant throughout both the early and later weird tales. The basic horrors underlying Lovecraft's tales are the "Others," a term derived from the Latin word "alius," or "alien." There are various types of Others in Lovecraft's fiction. In the early tales, they are creatures that were originally human but subsequently transformed or else devolved into hybrid, degenerative monsters. In the later tales, the entities are either extraterrestrial aliens from outer space or, in one case, terrestrial aliens that came about due to divergent evolutionary streams on Earth. When it comes to the hybrid, degenerative monsters, Lovecraft uses *racist images* in his depiction of their physical or phenomenological aspects. These images are drawn from Lovecraft's observations of members of the nonwhite race that he most despised and abhorred, that is, African Americans, especially as he observed them in the slums of his hometown Providence, Rhode Island, and at close quarters during his brief residence in the Red Hook district of New York. Lovecraft focuses on the simian and ape-like characteristics that he insisted on seeing in the faces and forms of the locals and then simply projects these onto his monsters. He does this in a very conscious and deliberate manner in order to enhance the horror and the repugnance that hybrid, degenerative monsters inspire in the minds of his readers (or, at least, so Lovecraft presumed).

In addition, in the early weird tales, Lovecraft uses a racist narrative that I am referring to in this study as the *miscegenation narrative*, which holds that sexual liaisons or intimate, nonsexual associations between members of different races, or species, pose a threat for Anglo-Saxon whites. In Lovecraft's view, miscegenation always debases the white partner—male or female—and it can lead to the production of mixed-race children, who are, in effect, not only an abomination against natural law but also a threat to the longevity of the white race and to the survival of Western civilization in general. As a further elaboration of this narrative, there are two types of miscegenation narratives: first, there is *miscegenation by blood*; in these cases, the relationship between the two parties is always sexual, and hybrids are produced. Second, there is *miscegenation by association*; in these cases, no sexual contact occurs; the danger, thus, arises merely from the contact between the partners. As we will see in Part II, the miscegenation narrative is central to all of the early weird tales.

In the later tales, the racist images and the miscegenation narrative continue. But Lovecraft moves beyond these as he creates Others that are more complex and multifaceted than his hybrid, degenerative monsters. The Others in his mature tales include extraterrestrial aliens such as the Mi-Go, who are five-foot-long crustaceous creatures; the Elder Things, who are eight-foot-long, barrel-shaped things with membranous wings; and the Great Race, who resemble immense, ten-foot rugose cones, with tentacles and eyes at the end of distensible stalks. Entities such as these are too alien in appearance to sustain the kinds of racist images Lovecraft uses for the hybrids. Likewise, the extraterrestrial entities are radically different from humans in terms of their sexual or reproductive practices, and so, miscegenation is not possible. Thus, Lovecraft devises a second racist narrative that runs parallel with the plots of the later tales. This is the *slave master/slave narrative*, which is drawn from Lovecraft's knowledge of the Atlantic slave trade in colonial times. Lovecraft uses the slave master/slave narrative to promote the practice of slavery. He holds up the alien astronaut civilizations, all of whom enslaved weaker races, as ideal civilizations—the highest, most advanced civilizations in the cosmos, in fact. Since these civilizations kept slaves, or so the argument goes, the Anglo-Saxon race should feel no compunctions about doing likewise. The slave master/slave narrative is central to nearly all of Lovecraft's later tales, especially "The Whisperer in Darkness," *At the Mountains of Madness*, and "The Shadow Out of Time"; these tales will be examined in Part III.

Lovecraft's slave master/slave narrative serves another purpose in his mature fictional works. Lovecraft's friend and *Weird Tales* colleague Robert Bloch identifies this purpose in his introduction to the Del Rey Books edition *The Best of H. P. Lovecraft* (1982):

> In "Supernatural Horror in Literature" ... Lovecraft intended to present an explanation of why horror fiction appealed to certain types of readers. And in so doing he unconsciously revealed his own reasons for writing—as attempts to come to grips with a lifelong fear of the unknown. What he said about the readers of fifty years ago is still valid. In a time of turmoil there is a widespread intimation—not based on hereditary impulse but on today's realities—that the evils abroad in the world may come from without as well as from within ourselves. While we may consciously reject his cosmology as absurd, a part of us finds in it a chilling confirmation of secret fears.[4]

Evils abroad that come from without. This is at the root of humankind's paranoid fears about the future and Lovecraft taps into these fears in his later works as he develops a frightening image of Earth as a veritable plantation planet. Before humankind evolved on the Earth, starting as early as 1,000,000,000 BCE, cosmic slave masters such as the Elder Things, the

Mi-Go, and the Great Race established colonies on Earth and enslaved competing alien races. When human beings finally appear around 350,000 BCE, the cosmic slave masters are long gone. And yet, members of these races as well as some of their former slaves remain behind in hidden cities buried underground or in frozen wastelands, and Lovecraft makes it clear that humankind, though currently free, is still living unbeknownst on a plantation planet, since there is a strong likelihood that one or more of the alien races will return en masse in the near future and humankind will end up as physically enslaved as the extraterrestrial slaves had been in the distant past.

***

In this book, I argue that Lovecraft uses racist images and narratives in his weird tales to advocate for his two central political beliefs: (1) Western civilization is in a state of decline due to unrestrained immigration, miscegenation, and hybridism; and (2) slavery is not only endemic but also justifiable among superior civilizations, especially the white, Anglo-Saxon civilizations. As a secondary thesis, I argue that the pattern of loss and failure that defines Lovecraft's personal and professional life is reflected in his fiction as well, such that a similar pattern of loss and failure is evident in the lives of Lovecraft's main characters, his "privileged protagonists," as I am referring to them in this book—though, for these characters, the loss is much more catastrophic than merely a diminishment in class status or economic want. In the early tales, the main characters—Arthur Jermyn, Herbert West, Thomas Delapore, and Thomas Malone—find themselves confronting ancient curses, reanimated corpses, deformed cannibals, and hideous, devolved bipeds, and they end up frozen by fear and existential angst, which, in turn, drives them to suicide, insanity, and death. In the later tales, Lovecraft projects his personal pattern of loss and failure out into the universe itself and the pattern becomes macrocosmic in scope. Characters such as Charles Dexter Ward, Henry Wentworth Akeley, Robert Martin Olmstead, William Dyer, and Nathanial Wingate Peaslee (many of whom are modeled on Lovecraft himself) suffer the same fates the privileged protagonists do in the early tales. But they also represent humankind in general in conflict with the Other. Lovecraft's protagonists, thus, can be read as metaphors for humankind itself decimated psychologically and physically by outside forces beyond their control.

This book is an academic book and, as such, my primary audience consists of individuals who live or work in academia, ranging from university and college professors to research scholars, postgraduate students, graduate students, and undergraduates. Since the 1990s, Lovecraft's significance as an object of study among academics has grown steadily, perhaps even exponentially, and, as of 2024, shows no sign of diminishing. Over this same period of time, due to the fact most of Lovecraft's work is now in the public domain, the full extent and range of Lovecraft's racist beliefs have also become known. This has caused Lovecraft's reputation to become tarnished to a certain extent outside of academia: the kerfuffle over the awarding of the "Howie" award—a bust of Lovecraft at the World Fantasy Awards for 2014—being a case in point. Because of this, one might have expected that Lovecraft's notoriously extreme brand of racism would also have eroded his literary reputation in academia and led to his demise at the hands of the so-called cancel culture. However, it has had quite the opposite effect. For, in fact, those who occupy the higher spectrums of academia continue to embrace Lovecraft all the more and refuse to let him go. Indeed, his racism almost seems to serve as a spur to even greater intellectual acuity, as academics continue to wrestle with his toxic views and try to understand his works and how they can best be "read," not merely as products of Lovecraft's own times but as artifacts that have managed to linger on to become part of our own. These Lovecraft scholars and instructors by their actions, likewise, convey to their students that it is important to do the same thing and this, in turn, helps foster an attitude in academia that pushes back against cancel culture, telling those who wish to cancel Lovecraft (or any great thinker or individual, for that matter) to keep away. Nevertheless, we must recognize that there is no simple consensus on this issue and that, moreover, since academia cannot help but reflect the larger culture and diversity outside of the academy, there will likely always be those both inside and outside academia who might feel inclined to "toss Lovecraft out" sooner or later, in contrast to those (a larger group, I hope) who will continue to keep the Lovecraft connection going as long as possible. I will have more to say about these matters in the conclusion.

Before commencing this study, it is necessary to clarify what Lovecraft meant by the terms "humanity" or "human being." After all, "humans" are envisioned as being in conflict with nonhumans. Thus, we must define exactly what human beings are in Lovecraft's view. Naturally, they are *Homo sapiens*. But for Lovecraft, as shown in his nonfictional writings, the category of *Homo sapiens* was limited only to white, Anglo-Saxon men and women or, in certain cases, to the nonwhite races that could be assimilated into Western culture and society—such as Jews and Italians, for example. When it came to African Americans, Lovecraft believed that they could never be assimilated under any circumstances and so, they are not to be included among the members of this elite group and, consequently, are not human. The view of Blacks as less than human was, of course, common among white people in Lovecraft's day. Lovecraft lived in the period of American history known by historians as the Segregation Era, and the nonwhite populations were, in fact, kept at arm's length from whites—the Jim Crow laws stipulated "separate but equal" services, facilities, and institutions for Blacks and whites. In addition, there was a strong color line enforced between the two races in public places and elsewhere. Blacks lived in separate neighborhoods;

they shopped in separate stores (or separate places in the same stores); they ate at separate counters and tables in restaurants; and they were expected to keep to themselves and associate with their own kind.[5]

In Lovecraft's early tales, then, the humans who confront hybrid, degenerative monsters are white, Anglo-Saxon men and women. Likewise, in the later weird tales, humankind against the cosmic slave masters means simply white, Anglo-Saxon humans against the cosmic slave masters. Thus, it is the white races that are (or will be) the slaves who inhabit the plantation planet. Interestingly, this places African Americans and the members of Lovecraft's other hated races who are not able to assimilate in the rather unique position of alignment, if not outright collusion, with cosmic forces that threaten the existence and continued presence of white human beings in the universe. This is hardly an enviable position, however; in Lovecraft's work, whether the characters are white, Black, or of any other race on Earth, the Others have no compunctions about exterminating them if they interfere—either deliberately or otherwise—in the working out of the Others' agendas.

* * *

Up until the late twentieth century, scholars have largely ignored or downplayed Lovecraft's racial hatred, and they remained mostly silent when it came to his white fragility and the ill effects of his loss of privilege, preferring to focus on interpretations that were less politically charged and, certainly, less embarrassing to write about. However, twenty-first-century scholars are in the process of taking a closer look at these issues and over the last two decades or so, Lovecraft criticism has evolved away from being merely a "cottage industry" consisting of foundational work enacted by a small coterie of scholars led by S. T. Joshi, Donald Burleson, and others into a full-fledged academic "takeover," which effectively moved Lovecraft into the limelight of twenty-first-century thought and philosophy. As a consequence of this, the amount of books, essays, articles, and monographs devoted to Lovecraft in recent years has proliferated. Indeed, Carl H. Sederholm searched the MLA International Bibliography with "Lovecraft" as the keyword in 2015 and found over 500 hits, including 374 journal articles, 100 book chapters, and 33 monographs or edited collections.[6] A search of this same database in 2024 would likely show double or even triple the number of hits in each category.

Naturally, I utilize a generous portion of secondary sources throughout the course of this study on a chapter-by-chapter basis as I defend my theses and develop my arguments. However, there is so much recent material that I have decided to add two "critical commentaries" chapters to the book in which I engage directly with key contemporary "voices" and thinkers who, like me, are committed to making sense of Lovecraft's racial hatred and understanding how it relates to his weird tales. I have placed these two chapters strategically at the ends of Parts II and III, depending on whether the essays focus on the hybrid, degenerative monsters or the cosmic slave masters. In my selections, I have chosen essays whose ideas run contrary to my own; this will, I think, not only highlight important differences between my ideas and those of my colleagues but also show the reader exactly where I am gaining traction for my views. I think, also, that the reader will find the ideas and issues raised in these chapters interesting to contemplate in their own right—rather startling, too, and often delightfully "against the grain." For example, David Simmons in "A Certain Resemblance: Abject Hybridity in H. P. Lovecraft's Short Fiction" argues that Lovecraft's narrators' relations with the hybrid, degenerative monsters in such tales as "Arthur Jermyn" and "Imprisoned with the Pharaohs" are not wholly a horror show, but represent a "multifaceted engagement with ... the non-western *Other*, a stance that is attracted to that which it is simultaneously repulsed by."[7] Similarly, Jed Mayer, in "Race, Species, and Others: H. P. Lovecraft and the Animal," argues (and also very much against the grain) that Lovecraft's narrators feel an "essential racial and biological universality within humanity" and that, in turn, "they encounter a sense of kinship where once they knew only difference."[8] And, most spectacularly "out there," Patricia MacCormack, in "Lovecraft's Cosmic Ethics," argues that Lovecraft's work "offers entryways into feminism, ecosophical, queer, and mystical ... configurations of difference."[9]

In a study of this nature, it is legitimate for the reader to ask: *how does the book build on the work of others and contribute to current debates in the field?* The best way to answer the first part of this question is to frame it in the context of material drawn from Stephen Shapiro and Philip Barnard's *Pentecostal Modernism: Lovecraft, Los Angeles, and World-Systems Culture* (2017). Here, the authors argue that Lovecraft's entire body of work is "predominately colored" by the history of the Atlantic slave trade: as they put it: "the matter of slavery is fundamental in Lovecraft's fiction" and "the horrible legacy of slavery lurks in nearly all Lovecraft's Miskatonic tales."[10] This is the slave master/slave narrative that I have identified previously as the second of Lovecraft's racist narratives and it is, indeed, central to Lovecraft's works, *but this only applies to the later works*. In order to comprehend the scope and complexity of Lovecraft's use of his racial hatred throughout the entirety of his fictional canon, we must study Lovecraft's miscegenation narrative in conjunction with the slave master/slave narrative, since the former is central to the early tales. Thus, in this book, I build on the work of Shapiro and Barnard by giving equal weight to *both* of Lovecraft's racist narratives, and this, in turn, provides a fully nuanced and more balanced analysis of what Lovecraft was trying to accomplish in his fictional works.

As for current debates in the field of Lovecraft scholarship, there is *one* that I want to engage with—the most important one, in my opinion—and it is a debate that I think all Lovecraft scholars need to consider, particularly the generation of scholars that will be coming after us. This debate is defined succinctly by Carl H. Sederholm and Jeffrey Andrew Weinstock in the introduction to *The Age of Lovecraft* (2016). In referring to the MacCormack essay identified above, they write:

> Asking not what Lovecraft's stories mean but how we can "use" them today, MacCormack concludes that Lovecraftian horror can be rethought as a "vitalistic, activist, and wonderous celebration of otherness." Responding to the approach of MacCormack and others who seek to liberate Lovecraft's fiction from the author's odious beliefs is W. Scott Poole, who ... clearly gives voice to his "historian's refusal to allow the material conditions that informed Lovecraft's work to dissipate amid philosophical appropriations that ignore the author's own interests and ... beliefs." Together, MacCormack and Poole stage an important debate: With the "critical controversy" over Lovecraft's racism in mind, to what extent can his fiction be used ... to advance more progressive political causes?[11]

Central to this debate is the work of speculative realist Graham Harman, author of *Weird Realism: Lovecraft and Philosophy*. Poole, in "Lovecraft, Witch-Cults and Philosophy," argues that Harman does, indeed, use Lovecraft to advance his own "cause," which, in this case, is to promote his philosophical school of object-oriented ontology. As Poole lays out his specific critique of Harman, it quickly morphs into a more general, widespread critique of scholars who cannot leave their philosophies or politics at the door when they venture into Lovecraft territory. Since I am examining the Poole and MacCormack essays in the second of my critical commentaries chapters, I will add Harman to my analysis in that chapter as I weigh in on the debate identified above.

Shapiro and Barnard, finally, raise another issue that will be addressed in this book: *Was Lovecraft, at any time in his life or literary career, aware of the damaging effects of his racist beliefs on his "psyche" and did he feel any remorse about those beliefs, or feel the need to atone for them?* Shapiro and Barnard, in *Pentecostal Modernism*, answer this question definitely in the affirmative. They acknowledge that Lovecraft's use of "racializing and racist perspectives" is extreme. Yet, they speak of Lovecraft's "yearning to be unburdened" from his racism, and they write: "The heart of Lovecraft's fictional racism ... rarely beats without some degree of awareness, no matter how tortured, of the (self-inflicted) damage entailed by compensatory bigotry, fear, and hatred."[12] Shapiro and Barnard bolster their claim by suggesting that Lovecraft, in *At the Mountains of Madness*, recognizes the damaging effects of racism on advanced civilizations and that, in "The Outsider," Lovecraft shows that he felt a certain degree of shame about his racist beliefs.

Admittedly, Lovecraft did, indeed, "color" his work with an excess of racist imagery and he did link the plots in all of his weird tales to racist narratives—tracing these images and narratives will comprise a large part of this study, in fact. But there is no evidence that Lovecraft felt any need to "testify" as to his racial hatred and bias for cathartic or for any other reasons. And certainly, he was not interested in "unburdening" or purging his psyche of unwholesome matter, either consciously or unconsciously. Quite the contrary, in fact. Lovecraft *liked* unwholesome matter—it was his stock in trade. As for his correspondence and the published recollections of colleagues, friends, and family members, these show that Lovecraft embraced his racial hatred and held onto it tenaciously right up to the moment of his death, unwilling to let go of it. His racism seems to have been inextricably linked to his white fragility and privilege. And as we will see, Lovecraft coldbloodedly makes literary fodder out of his racial phobias, as he does with all of his other phobias (such as his well-documented aversion to extreme cold temperatures and his dislike of seafood) and uses them to further his literary purposes. Lovecraft wastes nothing and, in many ways, he was a remarkably transparent writer. With Lovecraft, it is almost always the case that what you see is what you get.

NOTE: Popular author Matt Ruff, in his Afrofuturistic novel, *Lovecraft Country* (2016), blends Lovecraftian horror with the horrors of mid-twentieth-century bigotry and, in the process, links Lovecraft directly to Afrofuturism—a subgenre of speculative fiction that reimagines African American history in the context of the future. *The New York Times* and other media outlets have praised *Lovecraft Country* for its use of Lovecraft's subject matter and tropes. But the novel can be challenged on the basis that it isn't really Lovecraftian at all and, in fact, has little relevance to either Lovecraft or his work. In the appendix, I will assess the validity of these criticisms and examine Lovecraft's connection to the Ruff novel. I will also take a look at the writings of Afrofuturist scholars and artists Mark Dery, Kodwo Eshun, and Greg Tate to determine if there is, indeed, a viable link between Lovecraft and Afrofuturism.

PART I

Beginnings

1

Privilege Lost

In a very real, tangible sense, H. P. Lovecraft's early life, from the moment of his birth to the age of fourteen, exuded white privilege. If it could be claimed for any young person, Lovecraft started out as the perennial golden child with a silver spoon in his mouth—he even had long, curling blonde hair, like Little Lord Fauntleroy, from three to six years of age. Lovecraft was born into the entitled New England gentry on August 20, 1890, in his grandfather Whipple Phillips' stately mansion on Angell Street, in Providence, Rhode Island. His mother had come back to her father's house during her pregnancy, which was common among upper-class girls at the time—a stint at the hospital for a woman in the "family way" was decidedly bourgeois. Immediately after Lovecraft's birth, his parents left the Phillips mansion and returned to Massachusetts, where they were in the process of laying down roots. His father was Winfield Scott Lovecraft, a Rochester commercial traveler for Gorham Silversmiths and his mother was Phillips' second daughter, Sarah Susan Phillips (known as "Susie"). They lived from November 1890 to May 1892 in Dorchester, Massachusetts; vacationed in Dudley for a few weeks starting June 1892; and then resided in Auburndale, first as boarders with the poet Louise Imogen Guiney and her mother from mid-June to July 1892 and finally in a rented house from August–April 1893.

Lovecraft's memories of these early years paint a very idyllic, charming picture. In particular, he remembers his experiences when they were boarding with the Guiney's.

> At the home of Miss Guiney, I probably saw more celebrated persons than I have ever seen since; for her poetical standing is very high. Dr. Oliver Wendell Holmes was a not infrequent caller ... I was nicknamed *Little Sunshine* by Mrs. Guiney, mother of the poetess ... In appearance, I was vastly different then. My hair was yellow, and allowed to curl over my

shoulders in ringlets much like those of the periwigs I am so fond of drawing. This gold mane was another cause of the nickname.[1]

Lovecraft also recalls how quiet and shady the neighborhoods were in Auburndale, and how he had learned to recite Mother Goose nursery rhymes—Miss Guiney would often take him up in her lap and request that he repeat some of them, to herself and to her other guests.

The family's life in Massachusetts was abruptly cut short when Winfield had a mental breakdown in April 1893 while on a business trip to Chicago and ended up being committed to Butler Hospital, a sanitarium in Providence (where he died, in fact, only five years later). Winfield was staying in a hotel and he rushed from his room, shouting that the chambermaid had insulted him and that, furthermore, his wife was being raped in the room above his own (his wife was back in Auburndale at the time). On the death certificate, Winfield's death was attributed to general paresis, which was caused by tertiary syphilis, though the two illnesses were not known to be linked until 1911. Susie Lovecraft and her seven-year-old son wasted little time in promptly moving back into the Phillips mansion. As we have seen, Lovecraft had been petted and flattered by Louise Imogen Guiney and other adoring adults in Auburndale, but of course, at his grandfather's house, there were even more people to spoil and pamper him. There was not only his mother, grandfather, and maternal grandmother Robie Phillips but also his two aunts, Lillian Delora Phillips (later Mrs. Clark) and Annie Emeline Phillips (later Mrs. Gamwell), both of whom were still unmarried. The patriarch of the family, Whipple Van Buren Phillips, was a very rich businessman at this time; he had established the Owyhee Land and Irrigation Company in Owyhee County, Idaho; this was later incorporated under the name Snake River Company in 1884, with Whipple serving as president and his nephew Jeremiah W. Phillips as secretary and treasurer. The company had been set up to create and maintain a dam over the Bruneau River, a tributary of the Snake River—this, of course, provided irrigation for the surrounding farmlands. The dam was washed out by high waters in 1890, but a new dam was constructed in 1891 and was up and running by 1893. In addition to his irrigation company, Whipple Phillips also purchased the Henry Dorsey Ferry just before the troubles with the dam and established a town near the ferry along the Snake River, naming it himself as Grand View.

The Phillips mansion had been built in 1881 and Lovecraft describes it in loving, elegiac detail.

> [It was] one of the handsomest residences in the city—to me, *the* handsomest—my own beloved birthplace! The spacious house, raised on a high green terrace, looks down on grounds which are almost a park, with winding walks, arbours, trees, & a delightful fountain. Back of the stable is the orchard, whose fruits have delighted so many of my

> ... childish hours ... and best of all, its proximity to the dreaming fields and mystic groves of antique New-England ... which the young sage's [i.e. himself] vibrant imagination peopled with every conceivable sort of unreal presence.[2]

This last statement was, as it turns out, quite literal. When Lovecraft was seven or eight years old, as he tells us, he was deep in the study of Greek and Roman mythology, as many children are at that age, and one twilight evening in autumn, he kept vigil beside the woods and fields, hoping to see dryads or satyrs. He ended up actually seeing what he took to be "sylvan" creatures dancing in the moonlight. He referred to this vision in his later correspondence as a "kind of religious experience," though how serious he was about such a claim is debatable.

Lovecraft was intellectually precocious, and his burgeoning literary interests were stimulated by the vast amount of books and tracts that were kept not only in the library but also hidden away in a windowless, third-story attic room (which it didn't take Lovecraft long to discover).

> It was then that the mellowed tomes of the family library became my complete world—at once my servants and my masters. I flitted hither & thither amongst them like a fascinated moth, taking supreme joy in the old English volumes of the Lovecrafts, sent to my mother for me when my father was paralyzed ... I read everything, understood a little, & imagined more ... at four, the *ars legendi* became [mine] ... Within the next few years I added to my supernatural lore the fairy tales of *Grimm* and the *Arabian Nights* ... I had chanced on Hawthorne's *Wonder Book* and *Tanglewood Tales*, and was enraptured by the Hellenic myths even in their Teutonised form. ... by the time I reached the end I was for evermore a Graeco-Roman.[3]

Whipple Phillips had traveled extensively in his youth throughout Europe and had a taste for the weird: there were editions of the famous gothic writers of the eighteenth and nineteenth centuries, Ann Radcliffe, Matthew "Monk" Lewis, Charles Robert Maturin, William Beckford, and Charles Brockden Brown. There were also Edgar Allan Poe's works and the weird tales of Joseph Sheridan LeFanu. These books served as the basis for Lovecraft's later interest in writing weird fiction, an interest that his grandfather would have avidly supported and likely even financed if he had lived longer.

The young Lovecraft also became interested in science and astronomy, an interest underwritten, naturally, by his grandfather. Susie, always worried about the health of her precious boy, had reservations about chemical experiments being conducted in the house—fearing, perhaps, that her son might blow himself up or, at the very least, suffer some kind of major injury. But she acquiesced in his plans, as she always did.

> The science of chemistry. ... first captivated me in the Year of Our Lord 1898. ... Chemical apparatus especially attracted me, and I resolved (before knowing a thing about the science!) to have a laboratory. Being a "spoiled child" I had but to ask, and it was mine. I was given a cellar room of good size, and provided by my elder aunt (who had studied chemistry at boarding school) with some simple apparatus, and a copy of *The Young Chemist*—beginner's manual by Prof. John Howard Appleton of Boston—a personal acquaintance.[4]

In February 1903, Lovecraft was presented with his first telescope; this was a simple affair with papier-mâché tubes. But a few months later, his mother bought him a 2.25-inch device with 50- and 100-power eyepieces (he purchased his third telescope in 1906, which was a three-inch refractor for $50—this device was found among his personal effects after his death). Lovecraft's interest in science led him to write youthful articles, mostly for himself, but some for various local outlets as well. He wrote a six-series volume of scientific works simply entitled *Chemistry* in the early 1900s, selling each installment for sums between 5 and 15 cents—only four of these have survived. He created *The Rhode Island Journal of Astronomy* that ran from 1903 to 1907 (well after the end of his privileged lifestyle). He even wrote astronomy columns for two local papers, the *Pawtuxet Valley Gleaner* and the *Providence Tribune*; these articles all started in the summer of 1906. Though all of these productions were only minor, barely competent efforts and they plagiarized information from other technical and scientific publications of the day, nevertheless, they helped Lovecraft hone his developing writing skills and led to his lifelong interest in cosmology and physics, which ultimately served as the foundation for his own, unique philosophical and scientific views later on.

In terms of toys and playthings, Lovecraft's collection was literally unlimited. The coachman at the Angell Street mansion built a summerhouse for Lovecraft to use and he constructed miniature villages, town, and cities filled with tiny people that acted out scenes based on historical events. As Lovecraft describes it to his correspondent J. Vernon Shea in a letter dated November 8, 1933:

> My favourite toys were *very small* ones, which would permit of their arrangement in widely extensive scenes. My mode of play was to devote an entire table-top to a scene, which I would proceed to develop as a broad landscape ... I had all sorts of *toy villages* with small wooden or carboard houses, & by combining several of them would often construct *cities* of considerable extent and intricacy. ... Toy trees ... even *forests*. ... Certain kinds of blocks made walls and hedges, & I also used blocks in constructing large public buildings ... My mode of play was to construct some scene as fancy—incited by some story or picture—dictated, &

then act out its life for long periods—sometimes a fortnight—making up events of a highly melodramatic cast as I went. ... Sometimes I would try to depict actual historical events & scenes—Roman, 18th century, or modern—& sometimes I would make everything up. Horror—plots were frequent ... There was a kind of intoxication in being lord of a visible world (albeit a miniature one) & determining the flow of its events. I kept this up till I was 11 or 12.[5]

The tendency to work out intricate plots and themes in his play-scenarios served Lovecraft later when he constructed plots and themes for his weird tales, particularly tales such as *At the Mountains of Madness* and "The Shadow Out of Time"—both of them meticulously crafted and designed with a precise, almost painstaking attention to detail.

Lovecraft's life from two and a half to nearly fourteen was, thus, as perfect an example of a privileged, white, upper-class upbringing as could be imagined and one cannot help but wonder what Lovecraft would have become as a man and as a citizen of the commonwealth of Rhode Island if his ideal childhood and youth had continued on into adulthood and he had remained an entitled member of the gentry. Perhaps, he would have been so comfortable and satisfied that he felt no need to become a writer at all! In any case, the extravagances and the perks at this period in Lovecraft's life seemed to be unending and L. Sprague de Camp is correct to say that Lovecraft's childhood was the happiest time in his life.[6] It was a veritable Garden of Eden on Earth. But of course, Edens tend to fall and certainly, there were enough snakes in Lovecraft's own personal Eden to bring it to ruin. There were warning signs in the household that things might be taking a turn for the worst. When the Lovecrafts moved into the mansion, there had been four servants, a coachman, and three horses, but by 1900, the coachman had left, the horses were gone (presumably sold), and the number of servants dwindled down to none. Yet, though he could not help but see these changes, Lovecraft remained blissfully oblivious to the impending sword of Damocles that inevitably seems to hang over the life of those who are blessed with a silver spoon in their mouths. And that sword was about to fall.

* * *

Lovecraft's life of privilege and entitlement came crashing down in 1904 when Whipple Phillips' primary source of income, his Owyhee Land and Development Company, failed due to flood damage. Whipple Phillips was naturally devastated—he was seventy years old at this time and though he had overcome losses in his younger years, this time around he didn't have the stamina for it; he suffered a stroke and died on March 28, 1904. At this time, only Lovecraft and his mother were living at the mansion; the two aunts had married in the interim and so, it was only just the two of them (Robey

Phillips, Whipple's wife, had died long before). Whipple's estate was less than mother and son could have hoped for: it was valued at only $25,000. These proceeds were divided between the surviving members of the family; Susie Lovecraft received $5,000 and Lovecraft himself $2,500. The rest of the money went to offset business losses. Since only two people remained in the mansion and neither one of them was earning any income, Susie and her son were forced to move out and put the estate up for sale. Susie found a small duplex at 598–600 Angell Street (they occupied the western side), only a block or so from the location of the Phillips mansion. Obviously, the gravy train, such as it had been, was entirely derailed. The loss of his beloved home proved to be the most traumatic event in Lovecraft's entire life, and it is safe to say that he never got over it. As Lovecraft describes it in a letter to J. Vernon Shea, dated February 4, 1934:

> My mother & I moved into a 5-room-&- attic flat two squares farther east ... & for the first time I knew what a congested, servantless home—with another family in the same house—was. There was a vacant lot next door ... which I promptly exploited as a landscape garden & adorned with a village of piano-box houses, but even that failed to assuage my nostalgia. I felt that I had lost my entire adjustment to the cosmos—for what indeed was HPL without the remembered rooms & hallways & hangings & staircases & statuary & paintings ... & yard & walks & cherry-trees & fountain & ivy-grown arch & stable & gardens & all the rest? How could an old man of 14 (& I surely felt that way!) readjust his existence to a skimpy flat & new household programme & inferior outdoor setting in which almost nothing familiar remained?[7]

S. T. Joshi implies that this traumatic event (and deeply traumatic it was, as the above passage shows) was second only to Lovecraft's trauma over his mother's death in 1921.[8] I would argue, however, that the loss of his home was *the* most traumatic event in his life, superseding even the death of his mother. It must be understood that Lovecraft was always more sensitive to *places* than persons. As we will see in the next chapter, Lovecraft was so sensitive to hospitals that he refused to visit his mother inside Butler hospital, even after she underwent a life-threatening operation. Similarly, he was so attached to Providence that he had no compunction about abandoning his wife in New York City and returning alone to his hometown, even given the fact that she was trying in a weakened, physical state to support them both—he even declares pompously: "I am Providence" when he got back home. Places, thus—the Phillips mansion, the College Hill neighborhood, Providence itself—were always more important to Lovecraft than people, even the people closest to him.

Indeed, the loss of the mansion and the lifestyle that went along with it had such a pernicious effect on Lovecraft, psychologically as well as spiritually, that he contemplated suicide. Even more remarkably, he goes so far as to meditate on the best methods for ending his life.

> It seemed like a damned futile business to keep on living. ... Oh, hell! Why not slough off consciousness altogether? The whole life of man & of the planet was a mere cosmic second—so I couldn't be missing much. The *method* was the only trouble. I didn't like messy exits, & dignified ones were hard to find. Really good poisons were hard to get—those in my chemical laboratory ... were crude & painful. Bullets were spattery & unreliable. Hanging was ignominious. Daggers were messy unless one could arrange to open a wrist-vein in a bowl of warm water—& even that had its drawbacks despite good Roman precedent. Falls from a cliff were positively vulgar in view of the probable state of the remains. Well—what tempted me most was the warm, shallow, reed-grown Barrington River down the east shore of the bay. I used to go there on my bicycle & look speculatively at it. (That summer, I was always on my bicycle—wishing to be away from home as much as possible, since my abode reminded me of the home I had lost.) How easy it would be to wade out among the rushes & lie face down in the warm water till oblivion came. There would be a certain gurgling or choking unpleasantness at first—but it would soon be over. Then the long peaceful night of non-existence ... what I had enjoyed from the mythical start of eternity till the 20th August, 1890.[9]

This is strong stuff, and doubly so when we consider that these are the thoughts of a fourteen-year-old boy. How many youths of comparable age, even those who are suicidal, go so far as to weigh the pros and cons of such a litany of dreadful options?

Undoubtedly, living as the son of a single mother in rented rooms, Lovecraft's situation was growing steadily worse, not just psychologically but also economically. Neither Lovecraft nor his mother were self-sufficient and Lovecraft remained dependent on the income from the estate right up to the time of his mother's death in 1921; afterward, his aunts took over the role of Lovecraft's main financial support. During this especially stressful time in his life, however, Lovecraft's sense of white privilege never diminished for a moment, even in the midst of all his failures and setbacks. Indeed, it seems to have only gotten stronger and this contributed, in part, to the increasingly venomous nature of Lovecraft's racial hatred and the development of the pattern of loss and failure that ended up defining the course of his future life, both professionally and personally, as he tried to make his way in the world.

2

The Pattern of Loss and Failure

The pattern of loss and failure, as I refer to it, can be traced to Lovecraft's early childhood tendency toward "extreme nervous disturbance" in response to stress in the family circle. S. T. Joshi, commenting on Lovecraft's relationship with his mother, links this tendency to the pattern of loss and failure itself by identifying Lovecraft's extreme nervousness as a pattern in its own right.

> It is obvious that Lovecraft felt very close to his mother, however much he may have failed to understand her or she to understand him. I have no warrant for saying that his response to her illness is pathological; rather, I see it as part of a pattern whereby any serious alteration in his familial environment leads to extreme nervous disturbance. The death of his grandmother in 1896 leads to dreams of "night-gaunts";[1] the death of his father in 1898 brings on some sort of "near-breakdown"; the death of Whipple Phillips and the loss of his birthplace in 1904 cause Lovecraft seriously to consider suicide.[2]

Here, in brief, are the two elements necessary for working out the pattern of loss and failure that we will see later in Lovecraft's life: (1) Lovecraft finds himself facing some kind of major crisis that requires either direct action on his part or, at the very least, an immediate response; (2) Lovecraft feels overwhelming stress and anxiety and is unable to take the action or give the response. Instead, he chooses to remain in a state of stasis—withdrawn, frozen, shut down.

The initial pattern of loss and failure in the Lovecraft biography was, of course, brought about by the loss of the Phillips mansion. This single event proved to be the most profoundly traumatic event that Lovecraft had ever experienced up until this time. As described in Chapter 1, Lovecraft reacts to this crisis by simply doing nothing. He speaks to a correspondent about riding his bike frequently that summer so that he doesn't have to spend too much time at the duplex; he cannot bear his new home because it reminds him of what he had lost. He considers suicide. And he goes as far as to declare that he might be able to recapture what he lost in the future: "Life from that day has held for me but one ambition—to regain the old place and reestablish its glory," but then, in the same sentence, he adds: "a thing I fear I can never accomplish."[3] Here, he has already thrown in the towel before the struggle can even begin! Lovecraft's other actions, likewise, back up his defeatist attitude. In the middle of his psychological angst, he never once considers the possibility of getting out into the world and being productive while preparing for his final year in high school. Most fourteen-year-old boys would consider a part-time job, perhaps, especially if they had a parent who was struggling financially, as Susie Lovecraft was. But not Lovecraft. He remained withdrawn and immobile.

As a part of my general theses in this book, I will be examining the pattern of loss and failure as it relates to Lovecraft's fictional protagonists, both in the early weird tales and especially in his mature tales. Characters such as Arthur Jermyn, Herbert West, Thomas Delapore, Charles Dexter Ward, Henry Wentworth Akeley, Robert Olmstead, and Nathaniel Wingate Peaslee find themselves facing unique crises in their lives and they end up in stasis, much as Lovecraft did after his first major crisis. Even as their circumstances worsen and the negative outcomes start to pile up, the characters remain remarkably passive—again like Lovecraft—though in all cases, the negative outcomes are much more severe than those that Lovecraft experiences. We will get to these characters in Parts II and III. But before turning to the tales, I want to take a closer look at four of the most significant incidents of loss and failure in Lovecraft's adult life. These will, I think, give the reader a sense of how eerily similar Lovecraft's life was to those of his characters and how the pattern of loss and failure in the tales is, in a sense, a playing out of Lovecraft's personal tragedies on a greater canvas.

The Crisis of Lovecraft's High School Graduation

From 1907 to 1908, Lovecraft was in his third year at Hope Street High School. Despite a minor nervous breakdown in 1906, his high school career so far had been promising. During his first year (1904–5), he took elementary algebra, botany, English, ancient history, and Latin and received passing grades in all these classes. In his second year (1906–7), he took intermediate algebra, drawing, English, plane geometry, Greek texts, Latin grammar, Latin texts, and physics and, again, received passing grades, all of them above 85 with the exception of algebra, where he received 75. In the third year, Lovecraft only took three classes: intermediate algebra, chemistry, and physics; his grades were 85, 95, and 95, respectively—again, passing all subjects. He had decided to retake the algebra class because he felt that his original grade of 75 was too low; by this time, he had decided to enroll as an undergraduate at Brown University following his graduation and pursue a BS in astronomy, which requires proficiency in math. He was, in fact, on track to do exactly as he had planned, and he would have, indeed, been able to attend Brown after one more year of high school studies. But inexplicably, when he finished the semester, he withdrew from Hope Street High School and never returned to complete his final year.

The crisis that precipitated this action is not immediately apparent. Lovecraft was, as I have noted, passing all of his classes and he had managed to improve his math grade. But he provides a clue about what was on his mind at the time. In a letter to Reinhardt Kleiner, dated November 16, 1916, he states:

> Having resolved at the age of twelve to become an astronomer, I of course deemed it needful to perfect myself in algebra, geometry, trigonometry & calculus, but discovered at high school that my old hatred of *arithmetic* extended even into the loftier regions of mathematical research. The first year I barely passed in algebra, but was so little satisfied with what I had accomplished, that I voluntarily repeated the last half of the term.[4]

S. T. Joshi rightly associates the crisis at this period in Lovecraft's life with his recognition that he "hated" the study of higher mathematics and, thus, he knew deep down that he was not capable of achieving his dream of becoming an astronomer. As Joshi writes:

> My feeling, therefore, is that Lovecraft's relative failure to master algebra made him gradually awaken to the realisation that he could never do serious professional work in either chemistry or astronomy, and that therefore a career in these two fields was an impossibility.[5]

This then was the crisis that led to Lovecraft's withdrawal from school— he was afraid that he was not intelligent enough to master quantitative subjects and would therefore be unable to pursue a career in an essentially quantitative field. Lovecraft himself confirms that this is, in fact, the crisis behind his decision to leave school in a later letter to Robert E. Howard, dated March 25–28–29, 1933:

> It was *algebra* which formed the bugbear. ... I was then intending to pursue *astronomy* as a career, and of course advanced astronomy is simply a mass of mathematics. ... It was clear to me that I hadn't brains enough to be an astronomer—and that was a pill I couldn't swallow with equanimity. But it's just as well to have one's ego deflated early.[6]

Lovecraft's reaction to the crisis was similar to his response after losing the Phillips mansion and here, the pattern of loss and failure kicks in again. S. T. Joshi considers this as a "full-fledged nervous breakdown" and perhaps it was.[7] But Lovecraft embraces his presumed limitations here with a willful passivity that almost becomes a self-fulfilling prophecy; he seems entirely willing to become a high school dropout and remain so for the remainder of his life. There were, of course, options that he might have pursued at the time. He could have taken remedial math courses and buckled down, forcing himself by harder work to master algebra, chemistry, and the other sciences. Or, he could have stayed in school and gotten his diploma; after all, all of his grades were passing grades and so, he would have been able to graduate at the end of his senior year. And then, he could have enrolled in Brown University and pursued a different major, perhaps a degree in English or history instead of a technical degree. But he simply gave up. It was, as before, the same old story: passivity, immobility, and defeat.

It is worth noting that Lovecraft was so embarrassed about this early failure that he misrepresents what had actually occurred on a number of occasions to his correspondents. In letters to Maurice Moe (1915), Reinhart Kleiner (1916), Bernard Austin Dwyer (1927), and Helen Sully (1935), Lovecraft states that he was unable to attend Brown University due to his poor health. But that is all that he claims; he conveniently leaves out the fact that he wouldn't have been able to attend the university even if he had been in excellent health because he didn't have a high school diploma. Eventually, however, Lovecraft became reconciled to his loss and provided a more accurate description of what had taken place.

> Of my non-university education, I never cease to be ashamed; but I know, at least, that I could not have done differently. ... I shunned all human society, deeming myself too much of a failure in life to be seen socially by those who had known me in youth, & had foolishly expected such great things of me. From then to now, I have been practically unknown save to a very few old acquaintances. I am a complete disappointment, having accomplished absolutely nothing during my 26 futile years of existence.[8]

The Crisis of Susie Lovecraft's Decline and Death

When Lovecraft left high school, he and his mother Susie had been living at 598 Angell Street for approximately four years. Susie had always been what was known as a "high-strung" woman in those days, which was the term usually reserved for extremely nervous women, and she had become even more "nervous" since the horrific death of her husband in 1898. It certainly didn't help matters that she now had a high school dropout on her hands. For, in fact, neither one of them were wage earners and they were living off the small bequests from the Phillips estate and an unsteady income stream of mortgage payments from the Providence Crushed Stone and Sand Company, which was managed by one of Whipple Phillips' former tenants, Mariano de Magistris—these payments were very small, averaging less than $40 biannually. Not surprisingly, Susie's mental health began to decline significantly. Around 1911, neighbor Clara Hess visited Susie at the duplex and had this to report:

> One day after many urgent invitations I went in to call upon her. She was considered then to be getting rather odd. My call was pleasant enough but the house had a strange and shut up air and the atmosphere seemed weird and Mrs. Lovecraft talked continuously of her unfortunate son who was so hideous that he hid from everyone and did not like to walk upon the streets where people could gaze at him. When I protested that she was exaggerating and that he should not feel that way, she looked at me with a rather pitiful look as though I did not understand about it. I remember that I was glad to get out in the fresh air and sunshine and that I did not repeat my visit.[9]

Susie's comments about her son's appearance here were clearly an exaggeration, but only in part; Lovecraft looked normal enough, despite his long face and prominent chin, but to Susie, his hideousness really stemmed from the simple fact that he was doing nothing but hanging around the house and not contributing to household expenses—that was "hideous" indeed. Susie's decline sharpened around 1919 and Clara Hess reported (in a 1948 letter to August Derleth) that Susie was hallucinating:

> I remember that Mrs. Lovecraft spoke to me about weird and fantastic creatures that rushed out from behind buildings and from corners at dark, and that she shivered and looked about apprehensively as she told her story. The last time I saw Mrs. Lovecraft we were both going "down street" on the Butler Avenue car. She was excited and apparently did not know where she was. She attracted the attention of everyone. I was greatly embarrassed, as I was the object of all her attention.[10]

In March 1919, Susie Lovecraft broke down completely and was admitted to the Butler Hospital; ironically, this was the same hospital that her husband had died in twenty-one years ago. Winfield Townley Scott, a distant relative, examined Susie's hospital records and confirms that the primary cause of her mental breakdown was her son, toward whom she had an unhealthy love–hate attitude. His unwillingness to work appears to have been the major bone of contention between them.

> She suffered periods of mental and physical exhaustion. She wept frequently under emotional strains. In common lingo, she was a woman who had gone to pieces. When interviewed, she stressed her economic worries, and she spoke ... of all she had done for "a poet of the highest order;" that is, of course, her son. The psychiatrist's record takes note of an Oedipus complex, a "psycho-sexual contact" with the son, but observes that the effects of such a complex are usually more important on the son than on the mother, and does not pursue the point. It was presumed that Mrs. Lovecraft was suffering from an "insufficiency complex." This had been brought about by the increasingly perilous state of her finances, complicated by the fact that neither she nor her son was a wage earner. However she adored him, there may have been a subconscious criticism of Howard, so brilliant in promise but so economically useless. Or perhaps not; perhaps she would not have changed him any more than she could have changed herself, and so, distraught and helpless, she at last collapsed.[11]

As we will see later, these last two sentences could also apply to Lovecraft's wife Sonia Haft Greene later on, who also gained first-hand experience of Lovecraft as an "economically useless" person for whom she nevertheless cherished adoration. But Sonia was of stronger stuff than Susie and got rid of Lovecraft when she reached the end of her resources.

The crisis that triggered the pattern of loss and failure was Susie Lovecraft's death in the hospital on May 24, 1921, just over two years after she had been admitted. She did not die of nervous exhaustion, as we might expect, but rather from a gallbladder operation that resulted in complications. Lovecraft's immediate reaction is similar (if not equivalent) to the kinds of reactions that we have seen when Lovecraft faced the loss of the Phillips mansion and the fading of his college ambitions: extreme nervous disturbance, immobility, stasis, and even hints of suicide. As Lovecraft describes it in a letter to Anne Tillery Renshaw dated June 1, 1921.

> I am answering letters promptly these last few days, because I lack the will and energy to do anything heavier. The death of my mother on May 24 gave me an extreme nervous shock, and I find concentration and continuous endeavour quite impossible. I am, of course, supremely unemotional; and do not indulge in any of the lugubrious demonstrations of the vulgar—but the psychological effect of so vast and unexpected a disaster is none the less considerable, and I cannot sleep much, or labor with any particular spirit or success. ... The result is the cause of wide and profound sorrow, although to my mother it was only relief from

nervous suffering. For two years she had wished for little else—just as I myself wish for oblivion. ... For my part, I do not think I shall wait for a natural death; since there is no longer any particular reason why I should exist. During my mother's lifetime I was aware that voluntary euthanasia on my part would cause her distress, but it is now possible for me to regulate the term of my existence with the assurance that my end would cause no one more than a passing annoyance—of course my aunts are infinitely considerate and solicitous, but the death of a nephew is seldom a momentous event.[12]

The colossal egotism and smugness of this letter cannot be overstressed. What caused his mother's "nervous suffering" was not the possibility of her son killing himself; it was the simple fact that she was living with a person who was too inept to go out and get a job and help support the family. As usual when it came to his descriptions of personal matters such as this, the focus is almost entirely on Lovecraft himself: his feelings, his desires, his needs, at the exclusion of everyone else.

The crisis, also, appears to have included the period of Susie's confinement at the hospital, since Lovecraft's passivity and emotional immobility were clearly at work before Susie's death. There were two indications that tend to confirm this. The first of these is Lovecraft's unwillingness to visit his mother inside the hospital itself; he was content to meet her on the grounds and then take strolls with her, but he didn't actually enter the building. The second was the incredible fact that Lovecraft was not present during her operation, nor did he appear on the day of her death. As Winfield Townley Scott writes:

> [Lovecraft] used to visit his mother at the hospital, but he never entered the buildings; always she met him on the grounds, usually at "the grotto," and they would stroll together through the Butler woods above the river. To other patients she spoke constantly and pridefully of her son, but they never saw him. And in her final illness, when she was confined to her bed, he apparently did not visit her.[13]

This passage, along with the citation from the Renshaw letter, tells us exactly what we need to know about Lovecraft's feelings for his mother. Perhaps he loved her, but if so, it was an odd, unemotional kind of love. S. T. Joshi and a few other critics have tried to justify Lovecraft's behavior here, arguing that he had a phobia about hospitals and that this alone kept him away from his mother. Maybe so. But what sort of son who really loves his mother would avoid visiting her inside the hospital, especially when she is facing a serious operation? His love for his wife, too, proved to be equally odd and emotionless.

The Crisis of Lovecraft's Marriage

Lovecraft met his future wife Sonia Haft Greene at a National Press Association convention in Boston in 1921. She was a little older than him, but much more of a dominating, vibrant person—a "Junoesque," sexy, busty woman who had gotten through an unhappy first marriage and, yet, managed to come out on top. She wasn't highly educated—she'd only completed extension courses at Columbia University (though technically, she was more academically trained than Lovecraft himself, at least on the college level). She ran a very successful women's clothing shop, Ferle Heller's, on 36 West 57th Street in New York and was paid $10,000 a year, which was a "princely sum," as S. T. Joshi puts it—much better than many men could boast of in the 1920s. Following their first meeting, Lovecraft and Sonia became correspondents over the next three years; they also exchanged visits—she came to Providence on at least one occasion and met Lovecraft's aunts, while early in their relationship, she let Lovecraft and his friend Samuel Loveman stay at her apartment when they came to New York to visit some of Lovecraft's other correspondents. Lovecraft had a lot of friends who lived in New York or close by, among whom were Frank Belknap Long (who stayed with his well-to-do parents on the Upper West side of Manhattan), Reinhart Kleiner, who lived in Brooklyn, and George Kirk, a Manhattan bookseller. These men, who called themselves the Kalem Club, got in the habit of holding weekly meetings at each other's homes and the meetings provided solace for Lovecraft when he eventually relocated to the city. Over the course of their three-year acquaintance, Sonia fell in love with Lovecraft; she admired his intellect and his writing abilities (she had literary pretensions and he helped her revise her fiction for *Weird Tales* magazine). However, Sonia didn't find him sexually appealing, at least initially—as she writes in her 1948 memoir "Lovecraft as I Knew Him," "I admired his personality but, frankly, at first not his person."[14] She knew all about his academic and employment problems but she had come to believe that if she married and nurtured him, she could help him along the path to emotional maturity and economic self-sufficiency; as she put it, "I had hoped in time to humanize him further. ... that my embrace would make of him not only a great genius but also a lover and husband."[15] So, Sonia broached the subject of marriage, probably just a little over two years into their friendship. No doubt, Lovecraft was surprised, but he didn't object to the proposal and there was an understanding between them that they would, indeed, get married in the near future. As we might expect, Lovecraft's "love" for Sonia was similar to his love for his deceased mother. Nowhere in his correspondence does he declare that he felt love for Sonia at any time in their lives together (at least in their *extant* correspondence; Sonia burned all of his letters after the divorce). Lovecraft's motives for marrying appear to have been twofold: he was interested in getting out of his shell and taking a stab at life in the big city; in the back of his mind, also, he no doubt liked the idea of marrying a relatively well-off woman who had enough money to support both of them easily if his plans didn't work out. Thus, Lovecraft and Sonia set the date for the wedding just over a month before the ceremony took place. They told no one about their plans, not even Lovecraft's aunts; Lovecraft simply boarded a train with his valise and went to New York as he had done many times before and he and Sonia were married on March 3, 1924, at St. Paul's Chapel in lower Manhattan. After the ceremony, the Lovecrafts immediately went back to Sonia's Flatbush apartment.

At first, Lovecraft and Sonia felt the customary period of euphoria that newlyweds commonly experience when they first set up their household, though with the added excitement on Lovecraft's part of actually residing in a big, glamorous city. Lovecraft promptly set out putting in job applications at publishing houses and bookseller establishments, while Sonia went back to her shop, selling hats and women's clothes. But unfortunately, the grace period didn't last very long. In February 1924, Sonia lost her job at Ferle Heller's and then attempted to start her own millinery business. This didn't work out for her and she was out of work for the rest of the year. She managed to find jobs in the Midwest and went through a succession of them, but none of them lasted very long. Lovecraft's income was almost nonexistent; he did some revisionary work for David Van Bush, a pop-psychology author and lecturer around this time, but the income from this was very small. He also received a few checks from his contributions to *Weird Tales*, but again, this was only a trickle—nothing even close to what Sonia could pull in when she was fully employed. Lovecraft redoubled his job-hunting efforts, but he was woefully incompetent when it came to drafting query letters and filling out applications and his lack of a high school diploma and experience in the workforce were constant thorns in his side. On October 20, Sonia had stomach spasms and Lovecraft took her to Brooklyn Hospital. These symptoms were due to stress over their worsening financial condition—this is, of course, reminiscent of Susie Lovecraft's nervous disorders over finances when she and Lovecraft were living at the duplex. At this time, Lovecraft finally condescended to visit a loved one *inside* the hospital, something that he was not willing to do for his mother. It seems incredible that Lovecraft was not able to make the connection between the nervous symptoms that his wife was experiencing in 1924 and the symptoms that his mother had experienced when she had been admitted to the Butler Hospital in 1919. Or even more incredible was that he didn't perceive that he himself was the common factor behind both sets of symptoms. When Sonia came out of the hospital, she was forced to relocate to the Midwest for a new job prospect; thus, the expensive apartment at 259 Parkside had to be given up (her jobs at this time and after were sporadic—at one point, in March 1925, she took a rest cure at Sarasota Springs by herself). Lovecraft moved alone into a one-room apartment at 169 Clinton Street, Brooklyn Heights, which was, in the early 1920s, a fairly inexpensive area to live in.

Obviously, the crisis that precipitated Lovecraft's loss and failure in New York was the decline of Sonia Lovecraft's fortunes (and his own). But in a sense, this crisis was similar to what had happened when he was preparing to graduate from Hope Street High School; the loss and failure itself wasn't an actual event that had occurred as yet; it was Lovecraft's fears of what *might* occur. Indeed, Sonia's fortunes could have started to improve at any time and Lovecraft could have at last landed a job that was proportionate to his skills and expectations. However, Lovecraft was afraid in advance that he wasn't going to make a success of it in New York after all. Indeed, the magnitude of his fears is revealed by a statement made by Lovecraft's friend, Samuel Loveman, concerning Lovecraft's mental state at this time. He had gotten in the habit of carrying around a bottle of poison so he could "regulate the terms of his existence," as he had put it in the letter to Renshaw five years previously. As L. Sprague de Camp describes it:

> By the winter of 1925–26, Lovecraft began hinting broadly that he would like to be asked back to Providence. ... By this time, according to Sam Loveman, Lovecraft was carrying a bottle of poison. When he talked of suicide, he was probably not bluffing. Frank Long's mother wrote to the aunts, warning them that anything might happen if something were not done about Lovecraft's mental condition.[16]

De Camp speculates as to why Lovecraft didn't simply return to Providence even without an invitation and concludes (rightly I think) that he had too much pride to do so, at least at this time.

Predictably, Lovecraft's response to the crisis follows the same pattern that we have been observing throughout this chapter. Lovecraft did what he always did; he shut down and simply gave up. He did nothing useful to secure a job. He didn't offer to move to the Midwest along with his wife and help her in her struggles to secure financial stability for both of them. He simply stayed put in Brooklyn. Admittedly, this turned out to be a good thing for his writing career. He wrote "The Horror at Red Hook" (see Chapter 10) and began work on his great essay "Supernatural Horror in Literature" (1927). But more than anything else, Lovecraft wanted to return to Providence. As de Camp notes above, he was hoping that his aunts would formally invite him to come home. He was a desperately unhappy man and he didn't feel that he belonged in New York any longer. Also, he was growing even more disgusted and repulsed by the racially diverse immigrant populations in Brooklyn, particularly in the nearby Red Hook district. Finally, in March, his aunt Lillian did indeed invite him to return to Providence; she held forth the tantalizing lure that she could get a good set of rooms for both of them on 10–12 Barnes Street, which was just three blocks north of the Brown University campus. He would be occupying half of the duplex and she would occupy the other.

Naturally, Lovecraft jumped at the chance to return to his beloved hometown. On the train back home, as he wrote a reply to his aunt, he was quite literally delirious, even ecstatic. As he describes it in a letter to Frank Belknap Long, dated May 1, 1926:

> [I had] some notion of having boarded a train somewhere. A blur of stations follow'd ...
>
> Who am I? What am I? Where am I? I—a corpse—once lived, and here are the signs of a resurrection! ... Then at last a still subtler magick fill'd the air—nobler roofs and steeples ... Intoxication follow'd—Kingston—East Greenwich with its steep Georgian alleys climbing up from the railway ... Auburn—just outside the city limits—I fumble with bags and wraps in a desperate effort to appear calm—THEN—a delirous [sic] marble dome outside the window—a hissing of air brakes—a slackening of speed—surges of ecstasy and dropping of clouds from my eyes and mind—HOME—UNION STATION—PROVIDENCE!!!! Something snapped—and everything unreal fell away. There was no more excitement; no sense of strangeness, and no perception of the lapse of time since last I stood on that holy ground. ... There *is* no other place for me. My world is Providence.[17]

In reading this cheerful missive, it must be remembered that Lovecraft was in the process of deserting his wife. But as usual, his feelings and his needs took precedence over Sonia's. He simply needed to get out of a difficult situation and did exactly that.

The Crisis of Lovecraft's "Divorce"

Sonia wasn't about to give up her husband easily. They were separated, but she still aggressively chased after him. In Spring 1928, she invited him to visit her in New York and to help her set up a millinery shop in Brooklyn; the store duly opened on the 28th and it seemed like a perfect business venture for her, but like most of her other ventures, it did not succeed. Lovecraft stayed through the summer, but never resumed "conjugal relations" with his wife (as he put it) and spent most of his nights hanging out with the members of the now-defunct Kalem Club, only coming back to Sonia's Brooklyn flat in the early morning hours. Lovecraft was perfectly happy to continue being married to Sonia, as long as they didn't have to live together and, certainly, as long as he could reside permanently in Providence. He was, in short, content to have a long-distance marriage: separate residences; separate cities; no sex.

Finally, Sonia came up with an interesting compromise (and one wonders why neither of them had thought about this before, given Lovecraft's nearly pathological attachment to Providence). Sonia decided that she should buy a house in Providence and then open up her millinery shop right there in the city. Then, she and her husband could live together in her new house as husbands and wives ought to do.

Sonia went to Providence to discuss the proposal with Lovecraft and his two aunts. But as we might expect, the results were considerably less than satisfactory. As Sonia describes it in her memoir:

> Eventually we had a conference with the aunts. I suggested I take a large house in Providence, hire a maid, pay the expenses, and we all live together; our family to use one side of the house, I to use the other for a business venture of my own. The aunts gently but firmly informed me that neither they nor Howard could afford to have Howard's wife work for a living in Providence. That was that. I knew then where we all stood.[18]

This is rather macabre and what makes it even more so is that Lovecraft was sitting in the same room; yet he wasn't making any comments at all—he was letting his aunts do all the talking, allowing Sonia and the aunts to fight over him, in effect, as though he were some sort of prize. Lovecraft was an adult man in his thirties who could not take care of himself or anyone else and the aunts were now deliberately undercutting the possibility of economic security for both him and themselves. In addition, as L. Sprague de Camp bluntly points out, the aunts were acting hypocritically here; they acquiesced in Lovecraft's status as a "kept man" while he was living in New York, but in Providence, where he and the Phillips family had social standing, it simply wouldn't do for Lovecraft to be supported by his wife.[19] This was another crisis in Lovecraft's life—the last major crisis, in fact, before his death—and once more, we see him passively acquiescing in loss and failure. He silently defers to his aunts and allows them to decide his fate. It is not surprising that Sonia gave up the fight after this meeting was over and began pressuring Lovecraft to file for a divorce, though, of course, he botched the job as he usually did when it came to business matters and the divorce was never finalized.

* * *

From the foregoing analysis, Lovecraft's choice to hunker down by himself in Providence following the separation from his wife and concentrate on his writing, limiting his personal contacts with his two doting aunts and face-to-face interactions with only a select circle of correspondents, was probably the wisest choice. His hard work on his tales and novels—and he did work hard at it, despite his general ineptitude when it came to seeking out more lucrative, gainful employment—ultimately gave him a solid literary reputation that has, so far, stood the test of time. Unfortunately, the posthumous fame that Lovecraft has garnered since his death also led to the exposure of his racist beliefs and practices, and it is to this topic that we must now turn.

3

Racist Influences

Lovecraft's loss of privilege led to an increase and intensification of his racist beliefs; this is, as Robin DiAngelo notes, a common outcome when a white, Anglo-Saxon male's white fragility is challenged. As a child of the early twentieth century, Lovecraft naturally imbibed the standard beliefs and mores characteristic of his class and upbringing, including racism, which, though widespread in the United States at this time, tended to be mild and rather indulgent; the victim races were perceived as childlike in terms of their mentality and rarely suffered verbal or physical assault, thought they were very obviously segregated from white society and constantly aware of their second-class status in Providence and elsewhere. The members of the victim races at this stage in Lovecraft's life were the obvious ones: African Americans, Native Americans, and Jews. Lovecraft, who adored cats all of his life, had a black cat as a pet in his childhood that he named Nigger Man; this name, more than anything else, indicated Lovecraft's view of African Americans; they were like pets, not human like white people, but not to be treated harshly either and, perhaps, worthy of being cherished and, on occasion, even loved, within certain limits. Later, Lovecraft praised Alice, a Black maid who worked for Elizabeth Toldridge, one of his correspondents, for her efficiency as a worker. And yet, he could not resist referring to the maid as the "dusky Alice" and makes it clear that she was only a servant and not to be considered an equal to Toldridge or, indeed, to any Anglo-Saxon white woman. When his aunt Lillian Clark praised her own Black maid Delilah, Lovecraft referred to Delilah as a "valuable nigger" and joked that she would bring a fair price in a slave auction in Savannah.

As Lovecraft found himself increasingly isolated—increasingly fragile as it were—and as he grew to manhood, his racist views sharpened and transformed into an unusually virulent, aggressive hate that was very uncharacteristic of his time and class. Lovecraft's racism, in fact, expanded exponentially beyond the racism shared by his family members, friends, and acquaintances. The list of races and cultural groups that Lovecraft detested grew to inordinate numbers, and it almost begs one to ask: who exactly *didn't* Lovecraft hate, apart from Anglo-Saxon, Nordic white people? Besides African Americans, Native Americans, and Jews, Lovecraft hated Middle Easterners, mostly Syrians. He hated East Indians. He hated Asians, whom he described as "loathsome Asiatic hordes trail[ing] their dirty carcasses over streets where white men once moved." He hated Italians, Portuguese, and French Canadians ("scarcely less desirable Latins—low-grade Southern Italians & Portuguese, & the clamorous plague of French- Canadians"); the Irish ("who, in a highly unassimilated state, are the pest of Boston"); the Polish ("the hideous peasant Poles of New Jersey & Pennsylvania are absolutely unassimilable save by the thinnest trickling thread"); and Hispanics ("whilst the Mexicans—half to three-quarters Indian—form a tough morsel in the southwest"). This is quite a list, and it is demoralizing to think that Lovecraft could express sentiments like this within the parameters of a single letter written to his aunt Lillian Clark in January 1926, while he was living in his one-room apartment in Brooklyn Heights, New York.[1]

There were two literary influences that fostered the intensification of Lovecraft's racist views in his early adulthood, and both of them can be blamed equally for contributing to the kind of person that he ultimately became. First, Lovecraft read and studied Houston Stewart Chamberlain's popular and influential book *The Foundations of the Nineteenth Century* (1899); this provided an "intellectual" basis and rationale for his beliefs and led him, in turn, to uncritically adopt the Aryan myth and all that it implied. Second, Lovecraft read Oswald Spengler's *The Decline of the West* (1923) and he adopted Spengler's belief that Western civilization was in a state of decline and that the cause of this was the influx of immigrants from other countries into the United States and Europe, especially immigrants of different races and cultures. In Lovecraft's estimation, this influx (or "invasion," as he tended to see it) would ultimately lead to the downfall of Western civilization and the destruction of all the things that he held dear— art, literature, science, philosophy, and political institutions, to name a few.

The Aryan Myth

The term "Aryan" has as its root the word "Arya," or "noble," which was used as a self-designation by Indo-Iranian people in India as an ethnic label for themselves; it referred to the noble class as well as the geographic region known as Āryāvarta, where Indo-Iranian culture is based. "Arya" is also the etymological source of the name Iran. The original Aryans lived during the Vedic period in India, around 150 BCE. From the beginning, "Aryan" actually referred to religious, cultural, and linguistic factors, not racial. The Aryan myth was based on misinterpretation of material in the Rig Veda, an Indian holy text, and was popularized by the French aristocrat Arthur de Gobineau, who in his book *Essai sur l'inégalité des races humaines* (The Inequality of the Races), written around the middle of the nineteenth century, argued that aristocrats like himself were the descendants of the Germanic Franks, members of the original Aryan race, who had conquered the Roman province of Gaul (500 CE), while ordinary French people were the descendants of racially inferior Latin and Celtic peoples. Gobineau, fascinated by Hindu mythology, studied East Indian epics like the Vedas and the Upanishads and, along with other nineteenth-century scholars, found a reference in these texts to the "light ones," which he interpreted to mean the Aryans—that is, the light-skinned ones. This misreading was, in effect, the basis of the Aryan myth. Nevertheless, the view that "Aryan" was a racial category and not a cultural designation was readily adopted by racist scholars of the early twentieth century.

* * *

Lovecraft was convinced that the Aryan race was a viable concept not by Gobineau but by Chamberlain's *Foundations*, which had originally been published in Germany at the end of the nineteenth century under the title *Die Grundlagen des neunzehnten Jahrhunderts*. The book is a pseudo-scientific "racial history" of humanity from the emergence of the first civilizations in the ancient Near East to the year 1800. Chamberlain's argument is that all of the "foundations" of the current century are the works of the Aryan race. The book was the first volume of a projected three-volume history of the West—the second and third installments would have continued the narrative into the nineteenth century, but Chamberlain never wrote these latter volumes. Lovecraft read *Foundations* when it was translated into English and published by John Lane at the Bodley Head in London in 1912.

Chamberlain was born in Southsea, Hampshire, England, in 1855, the son of Rear Admiral William Charles Chamberlain, Royal Navy, and Eliza Jane, daughter of another prominent Navy officer. Chamberlain grew up as a privileged member of Victorian society and believed in Britain's greatness as a world power and in the tenets of democracy and capitalism. However, unlike his father, Chamberlain, in poor health, did not pursue a military career. He went to Geneva in his twenties and studied botany, geology, astronomy, and, later, anatomy and physiology, at the University of Geneva. Around this time, inspired by Wagner's music, Chamberlain started to become a Germanophile; he admired Wagner so much that the admiration spread to the German culture. This laid the seeds for Chamberlain's later embracing of German culture and nationalist values, and when Chamberlain settled in Dresden (he was now twenty-nine) in 1884, we see the first anti-Semitic and racist statements to appear in the letters to his parents back home.

During his time in Dresden, Chamberlain read *Essai sur l'inégalité des races humaines* and he accepted Gobineau's reading of the Hindu texts. He was himself likewise fascinated by Hindu mythology and legend; he even took it upon himself to study Sanskrit so he could read these texts in their original language. Chamberlain agreed with Gobineau that the Aryans did, indeed, conquer Rome and that ancient Aryan heroes conquered the Indian subcontinent as well. Indeed, the Indian caste system, for Chamberlain, confirmed the Aryan link; it seemed to reflect the ideal way to deal with lesser races; a world governed by such rigid societal distinctions would keep racial inferiors firmly locked into their place. These ideas fermented in Chamberlain's mind as he evolved his ideas of Teutonic superiority. From 1889 to 1909, Chamberlain lived in Vienna; Vienna had a large Jewish population, and it has been suggested that Chamberlain's encounters with Jews at this time represented his first fact-to-face contact with Jews. Obviously, he didn't like what he saw; Chamberlain's observations of the activities and living conditions of the Jews in Austria transformed his previously mild disapproval of the Jewish people to actual distaste and disgust.

Finally, in 1909, Chamberlain moved to Bayreuth, Germany; he realized that the "Fatherland" was his spiritual home and he quickly became an important member of the "Bayreuth Circle" of German nationalist intellectuals. At this time, he had written his influential book and he viewed himself as a missionary for Aryan supremacy and discrimination against non-Aryans. He genuinely believed that the rise of Germany and racial purity would represent an important step toward curing modern world cultures from the "spiritual ills" caused by capitalism, industrialization, materialism, and urbanization. At the time of the Boer War, Chamberlain supported the Boers against the British, and he expressed much regret that two white peoples should be killing each other at a time when he believed that white supremacy around the world was being threatened not only by Jews but also by Asians—here, Chamberlain used the same kinds of arguments that we will see Lovecraft using in "The Crime of the Century" (see Chapter 4). Chamberlain's influence and reputation, though as lurid as it was, spread throughout Europe as well as in Germany; *Foundations* sold very well—a hundred thousand copies had been sold worldwide by the outbreak of the First World War and a little over a quarter of a million copies by 1938. Chamberlain was praised by Kaiser Wilhelm II, who distributed copies of *Foundations* among the conservative elites and the German Army and even went so far as to require the book to be standard reading in the public schools. Chamberlain did not live to see the blossoming of the Third Reich, though he had befriended Adolf Hitler as the latter slowly became a growing political figure in Germany. Indeed, Hitler visited Chamberlain on at least two separate occasions, once in 1923 and in 1926, the year before his death.

Chamberlain makes several key arguments in *Foundations*, all of which Lovecraft accepted as fact: (1) all European peoples—Germans, Celts, Slavs, Greeks, Latins—are part of the Aryan race; however, the most important

Aryans have always been the Teutonic peoples, who, in Chamberlain's estimation, had preserved the Aryan blood in its purist form; in France and Russia, however, the purity of the Aryan blood had been diluted by too much admixture with non-Aryan races (Mediterraneans and Asians, respectively); (2) the Aryan race is responsible for the best things in the Western world—art, culture, philosophy, political institutions, scientific discoveries, and so on; Chamberlain himself determined which groups are to be considered descendants of the Aryan race and thus, he was free to claim whomever he wished as a member of this select club and to decide which cultural contributions were the "best"; (3) the Jews, in contrast to the Aryans, served as an inverse or anti-Aryan race, undermining and negating all of the positive advances made by the Aryans and using the "law of blood" (Jewish women marrying Gentiles, but Jewish men not doing so, thus keeping the male line untainted, or "spotless," as Chamberlain called it) to ensure the continued survival of the Jewish race; (4) miscegenation, specifically between Aryans and Jews, led to the destruction of many great civilizations in the past, such as Rome; and finally, (5) the goal of the Jewish race was to become the only pure race in Europe; all of the other races would be hybrids and thus, by definition, degenerative physically, mentally, and morally. In addition, the domination of the Jews would mean economic domination, aided and abetted by democracy and capitalism, both of which promoted the illusion of universal human equality. The only solution to this outcome, in Chamberlain's view, would be Aryan world domination, which would, in turn, keep the Jewish bloodline separate from the Aryan bloodline, with the goal of eventually purging the Jewish "virus" from the national bloodstream.

S. T. Joshi, in *Lovecraft: A Life* (1996), states that "even a cursory examination of the specific tenets of Chamberlain's racism shows that Lovecraft's beliefs are very different."[2] But this is wrong; Lovecraft did accept the above "tenets" at least until 1932 or 1933, though he was at odds with Chamberlain over the more inconsequential details, such as Chamberlain's exaltation of Christianity (which Lovecraft quite frankly detested) and the importance of Rome as a political, unifying force in the ancient world— Lovecraft saw Teutonic superiority in Rome demonstrated solely by the artistic and cultural productions of the Romans. There is another striking similarly between Chamberlain and Lovecraft as well; they tend to use terms like "Aryan," "Indo-European," "Indo-Teutonic," "Celtic," "Slavic," "Teutonic," and "Anglo-Saxon" interchangeably and indiscriminately, and this, in turn, lends to their racist writings a kind of pseudo-universality, suggesting that the Aryan race had (and still has) a widespread, pervasive presence across the world. As Chamberlain writes:

> It was Teutonic blood and Teutonic blood alone (in the wide sense in which I take the word, that is to say, embracing the Celtic, Teutonic and

Slavonic, or North European races) that formed the impelling force and the informing power [as creators of a new culture]. ... "Indo-European" or "Aryan" is admissible and advantageous when we construct it from the sure, well investigated, indisputable facts of Indianism, Eranianism, Hellenism, Romanism, and Teutonism. ... Teutons with their virtues alone. ... [and] their own right to rule, would have won the victory, no one will have the audacity to assert, but everyone must admit that in the very places where they were most cruel—as, for instance, the Anglo-Saxons in England, the German Order in Prussia, the French and English in North America—they laid by this very means the surest foundation of what is highest and most moral.[3]

There are several outright falsehoods in this passage. Anglo-Saxons inhabited Great Britain from the fifth century onward; they were made up of divergent racial types and dominated in Europe during the Norman invasion, but they were not believed to be predominately Germanic in origin until the eighth century. The Teutons, also, were classified as a Germanic tribe, though they had roots in Denmark and in Celtic Ireland. The belief that any one of these groups were "pure," or that they represented the high water mark of the Aryan race, is simply not correct; the idea of being an "Aryan," from the start, was based on religious, cultural, and linguistic factors, not racial categories. And yet, Chamberlain persisted in his belief in the Aryan race and Lovecraft, following Chamberlain, concurred.

The Decline of Western Civilization

Lovecraft's views about the decline of Western civilization and his intellectual justification for those views, at least in part, were derived from Spengler's *The Decline of the West* (*Untergang des Abendlandes* in German, which translates as "The Downfall of the West"), a two-volume work published in its entirety in 1923 in Germany. Oswald Arnold Gottfried Spengler (1880–1936) was a German historian and philosopher of history and definitely not a racist scholar; thus, Lovecraft had little compunctions about admitting freely that he used Spengler's work as a source in formulating his own views of civilization (compunctions that may have been in play when it came to Chamberlain's book). As Lovecraft writes to his friend August Derleth on March 26, 1927: "Have you read Oswald Spengler's now celebrated work *The Decline of the West,* whose first volume was lately translated into English? You will find there much sound and bitter sense regarding the slackening of the cultural fibre of the dominant Aryan race during the last century or less."[4]

Oswald Spengler did not argue for a race-based interpretation of civilization, nor did he believe in the Aryan myth. Rather, he saw civilizations as organisms, made up of different aggregates of races, cultures, and the like; there have been, in his view, eight "high" cultures in human history so far—Babylonian, Egyptian, Chinese, Indian, Mayan/Aztec, Greek/Roman, Arabian, and Western or European—and each had, at one time, reached the point of becoming a civilization. However, civilizations are not permanent; each high culture has (or will have, in the case of the Western/European culture) only a life span of about a thousand years, in which they dominate in the world, followed by a "fall," which takes place over roughly the same period of time. When it comes to the issue of race, Spengler did not think this was based on blood, physical characteristics, or ethnic identity. Instead, race is only a "race feeling" among people living together for a long time in a certain area. A race, thus, includes any number of different people—white, Anglo-Saxons, Blacks, Jews, Asians, and so on, all of whom are united in a particular area due to mainly their outlook. In developing this view, Spengler uses the analogy of a plant that lays down roots in an area; the plant itself is the race; the individual members vary, like buds on the plant, and here, by way of the buds, biological issues enter into the equation. But the plant analogy breaks down a little when Spengler discusses the tendency of human beings to migrate and move around (buds, certainly, cannot migrate away from the plant). But his analogy still expresses very well what race feeling actually means.

> A race does not migrate. Men migrate, and their successive generations are born in ever-changing landscapes; but the landscape exercises a secret force upon the extinction of the old and the appearance of the new one. ... Science has completely failed to note that race is not the same for rooted plants as it is for mobile animals, that with the micro-cosmic side of life a fresh group of characteristics appear and that for the animal world it is decisive. Nor again has it perceived that a completely different significance must be attached to "races" when the word denotes subdivisions within the integral race "Man." With its talk of adaptation and inheritance it sets up a soulless concatenation of superficial characters, and blots out the fact that here the blood and there the power of the land over the blood are expressing themselves—secrets that cannot be inspected and measured, but only livingly experienced from eye to eye. Nor are scientists at one as to the relative rank of these superficial characters ... Comradeship breeds races ... Where a race-ideal exists, as it does, supremely, in the Early period of a culture ... the yearning of a ruling class towards this ideal, its will to be just so and not otherwise, operates. ... towards actualizing this ideal and eventually achieves it.[5]

Lovecraft takes Spengler's idea that the Western, European civilization was in a state of decline, but distorts it, arguing that the decline is not simply a natural thing, brought about by internal issues, such as migration to and from the area in which the civilization had flourished, or differing opinions and needs on the part of the individuals who comprise the civilization, but due to the presence of alien races and the negative effects that their inferior, biological status have brought to the purity of the original cultural strain.

Indeed, Lovecraft hardly needed Spengler to bolster his racist interpretations of the migrations in Western culture that Spengler was referring to. Lovecraft was quite clear in his thinking as to the effects of the migrations of Blacks, Jews, Asians, and other hated races into the United States. During the course of his formative years, Lovecraft gradually noticed the increasing influx of immigrants, even in his beloved Providence. He noted that they looked different than the Anglo-Saxon Americans that he was accustomed to seeing; they sounded different and acted different. Then, too, though they were assimilating to American culture, it seemed to him that this was an entirely too slow of a process, and that immigrants still retained enough of their original cultures even after they had supposedly completed the assimilation process. Thus, it was only logical in his mind to assume that increasing numbers of immigrants might represent a threat to Providence and the New England way of life, and to America overall; they might, in fact, alter how America in the future might end up looking and sounding, and how the texture of Anglo-Saxon culture in the West might be drastically altered. Lovecraft's beliefs in the decline of Western civilization were only confirmed when, as we have seen, Lovecraft relocated to New York after marrying Sonia Greene. In New York, he got a close, first-hand look at a city that had hosted immigrants for a much longer period of time than Providence and he didn't like what he saw. Thus, his personal observations and experiences (such as they were) seemed to "prove" that Spengler's arguments were justified and that Western civilization was in a slow process of decay and decline.

Of particular interest for Lovecraft was the issue of hybrids and hybridism. Spengler had no problem with miscegenation (which he likely would have argued was a natural result of differing groups of people occupying the same area), but Lovecraft, following Chamberlain, had a particularly violent aversion to hybrids, seeing them as a major factor in the decline of the West. As Lovecraft writes, in a letter to J. Vernon Shea, dated July 30, 1933:

> As for the negro question—I think that intermarriage ought to be banned in view of the vast number of blacks in the country. Illicit miscegenation by the white male is bad enough, heaven knows—but at least the hybrid offspring is kept below a definite colour-line & kept from vitiating the main stock. Nothing but pain & disaster can come from the mingling of black and white, & the law ought to aid in checking this criminal folly. Granting the negro his full due, he is not the sort of material which can mix successfully into the fabric of a civilized Caucasian nation. Isolated cases of high-grade hybrids prove nothing. It is easy to see the ultimate

result of the wholesale pollution of highly evolved blood by definitely inferior strains. It happened in ancient Egypt—& made a race of supine fellaheen out of what was once a noble stock.[6]

Lovecraft's low opinion of hybrids, as we will see in Part II, reaches such a level of dislike and revulsion that it can only be described as psychotic. And it fueled his first racist narrative, the miscegenation narrative.

4

Racist Writings

The most that can be said for H. P. Lovecraft's racial hatred is that Lovecraft was an equal opportunity racist: he impartially hated all races that were not Anglo-Saxons (and, during periods of high stress, such as his brief residency in Brooklyn, "nearly everybody [else] got on his nerves," as L. Sprague de Camp notes).[1] We will be examining Lovecraft's nonfictional writings in this chapter and his poetry; in Parts II and III, the focus will be on Lovecraft's fictional writings. It is important to recognize that there is racial hatred and bias scattered throughout *all* of Lovecraft's works, major as well as minor, and nonfictional as well as fictional. To the twenty-first-century reader, of course, this is unconscionable. But to individuals living at the turn of the last century, it was less so; the general reader of that time might have wondered at the intensity of Lovecraft's hatred toward different races, but he or she would have agreed that Lovecraft's beliefs were the proper ones. Lovecraft was a highly intelligent man, except for the blind spot that he nourished in his mind against the members of different races and cultures, and he was no fool; from the feedback that he had received from friends and from his wife, he realized that his particular brand of racism was unusual or, perhaps, even extreme. Yet, he did little to curtail the expression of those views at any time in his life, particularly in his correspondence. It has been suggested by admirers that Lovecraft felt remorse in later life for his racial hatred, which is why he wrote, in 1937, that he wished that he could go back and make alterations: "Yuggoth, but I'd pay blackmail to keep some of my essays & editorials of 20 or more years ago from being exhumed & reprinted."[2] But this passage shows no remorse; this is merely the statement of a person who has been caught in an embarrassing situation—with "his hand in the cookie jar," so to speak, and wishes that he could rectify it.

As a cautionary note to the reader, the following selections are often appalling and may make for difficult reading. I have decided to quote from Lovecraft's works on this topic at length because I think it is necessary to show exactly how intense Lovecraft's racism was; it is necessary for the reader to see this so that she can fully appreciate how this hatred is transformed and sublimated, in Lovecraft's later fiction, into the creation of compelling fantasy and horror. At the end of this study, of course, the reader will have to decide for herself what she ultimately thinks about Lovecraft's work, given the fact that it is rooted so deeply in racism and hate. Is the fantasy and horror sufficiently "compelling" to justify what may have helped inspire it? Does the fantasy and horror rise above its dark, festering roots? I tend to agree with Paul Rolland, Lovecraft scholar and author of *The Curious Case of H. P. Lovecraft* (2014), when he writes: "The deficiencies of the man do not, however, debase the quality of his best work. If anything, they invest it with a twisted passion that is missing from his more fantastic fiction."[3] The reader may agree, or not. But "twisted passion" is the perfect phrase to describe Lovecraft's work, both the racist and the nonracist works, and this part of my book is, at the very least, an attempt to study and understand exactly how passionate and twisted Lovecraft really was.

Essays

With the exception of "Supernatural Horror in Literature," "Something About Cats" (1937), and a few others, the bulk of Lovecraft's essays were written during the first two decades of the twentieth century and appeared either in his own self-published magazine *The Conservative* or else in the magazines (also self-published) of his amateur colleagues. Before his first professional sale to *Weird Tales* (in 1923) and during his literary apprenticeship, Lovecraft was invited to join the amateur journalism movement. The invitation was extended in 1914 by Edward F. Daas, a member of the United Amateur Press Association (UAPA). Lovecraft had come to Daas's attention from an exchange between Lovecraft and John Russell in the letters column of *Argosy* magazine (the two men were squabbling over the literary "merits" of popular *Argosy* author Fred Jackson). Daas thought that Lovecraft was a talented writer and he felt that Lovecraft would be a good fit for amateur journalism. Daas was right, more right than he knew. For at this stage in his young life, Lovecraft had just lost his family home and his grandfather and had suffered his first nervous breakdown; thus, he needed to emerge from his self-imposed shell and amateur journalism helped him do so. After joining the UAPA, Lovecraft gained immediate access to a wide range of potential friends and colleagues; many of them, such as Samuel Loveman, Rheinhart Kleiner, James Morton, and Edward D. Cole, in fact, became lifelong friends. Lovecraft immediately began to send out his essays, poetry, early fiction, literary reviews, and fugitive news items to *The United Amateur*, the official organ of the UAPA, and to the newsletters and magazines of the other UAPA members. Lovecraft, also, involved himself in the operation of the UAPA;

he held offices at various periods in his relationship with the association—president in 1917; chairperson in 1918; and official editor in 1920 until he finally left the UAPA in 1925.

Lovecraft's magazine *The Conservative* commenced its run in 1915. There were thirteen issues in total: Volume I, consisting of four issues—April, July, October 1915, and January 1916; Volume II, also four issues—April, July, October 1916, and January 1917; Volumes III, IV, and V, one issue each—July 1917, July 1918, July 1919, respectively; and finally, No. 12—March 1923 and No. 13—July 1923. Of the three essays that we will be examining in this section, the first and the third were published in *The Conservative*, while the second essay was published in *The United Amateur*. In these essays, Lovecraft develops his view of the Aryan myth and explains why the Teuton is superior to other racial groups. In making his points, Lovecraft takes a more moderate tone toward different races and cultural groups than he does in his letters, poetry, or fiction; there are, thus, none of the "rants" or hysterical tirades that we find elsewhere in his works. The reason for this isn't hard to understand; Lovecraft is seeking to convince his readers by arguments that his views are correct and this calls for minimal emotion—the approach of a philosopher rather than that of an advocate.

***

"The Crime of the Century" (1915) appeared in *The Conservative* 1, No. 1, pp. 2–3. This is a rather innocuous essay, despite how "notorious" some of Lovecraft's critics believe it to be; Lovecraft is merely rehashing and reworking the Aryan myth, as he got it from Chamberlain. The argument is a familiar one to those who have studied *Foundations of the Nineteenth Century*—England, Germany, Austria, Scandinavia, Switzerland, Holland, and Belgium are all at odds with one another in the First World War and are asserting their rights and dominance in Europe, and yet, these are all Teutonic nations. The Teuton, on the other hand, represents the "summit of human evolution," as Lovecraft puts it, and is responsible for the establishment of the highest civilization that the world has ever seen (or is likely to ever see)—the great Aryan civilization. Consequently, the so-called "crime of the century" is that these Teutonic races are all fighting against each other instead of uniting to ensure that the lesser racial groups do not gain a foothold on the way to their own aspirations toward global supremacy.

As the following passage makes clear, the Aryan myth is alive and well in Lovecraft's mind:

> The Teuton is the summit of evolution. ... we must cast aside the popular nomenclature which would confuse the names "Teuton" and "German," and view him not nationally but racially, identifying his fundamental stock with the tall, pale, blue-eyed, yellow-haired, long-headed 'Xanthochroi' as described by Huxley, amongst whom the class of languages we call

"Teutonic" arose, and who today constitute the majority of the Teutonic-speaking population of our globe. ... the languages and institutions of the other nominally Aryan races were derived alone from his superior speech. ... we can find no possible excuse for denying his actual biological supremacy ... In a world of diverse and hostile races the joint mission of these virile men is one of union and cooperation with their fellow-Teutons in defense of civilization against the onslaughts of all others.[4]

S. T. Joshi argues that Lovecraft's version of the Aryan myth, especially as it is articulated here, was *not* derived from Chamberlain, but rather from two of Thomas Henry Huxley's essays, "On the Methods and Results of Ethnology" (1865) and "On the Aryan Question" (1890). In these essays, Huxley describes the Xanthochroi, a blonde, pale race, which is clearly Huxley's version of the Aryans and which, he claimed, proliferated in key areas of Europe (excluding the Mediterranean and the Middle East). Because Lovecraft uses the word "Xanthochroi" in the above passage, therefore, as Joshi argues, Lovecraft must have gotten the idea of the Aryan myth from Huxley rather than Chamberlain.[5] There is a problem with Joshi's argument, however. Huxley's essay doesn't just deal with a single great race; Huxley argues that there were *two* equally great races, one dark-haired (the Melanochroi) and the other light (the Xanthochroi), and that *both* were instrumental in the rise of Western civilization and languages. Lovecraft, on the contrary, is claiming that there was only the *one* master race—the Aryans. Lovecraft's use of the word "Xanthochroi" does prove that he had read Huxley's essays, but that is all it proves.

Joshi's motives in identifying Huxley as Lovecraft's source here and in discounting the Chamberlain connection are, I think, clear; Joshi would prefer that readers believe that Lovecraft was inspired by a writer who does not have a reputation for extreme racism rather than by a writer who does, and that this, in turn, makes Lovecraft seem more "reasonable" in his choice of sources. Nevertheless, the parallels between specific passages in Chamberlain's work and passages from "The Crime of the Century," are, in fact, quite striking, and in the latter essay, it is quite obvious that Lovecraft follows Chamberlain's views closely. Indeed, if we collate *Foundations* with "Crime," we are forced to conclude, as does L. Sprague de Camp, in *Lovecraft: A Biography* (1975), that "The Crime of the Century," at times, "almost reads like a paraphrase of passages from Chamberlain."[6]

***

"Americanism" (1919) appeared in *The United Amateur* 18, No. 6 (July 1919), pp. 118–20. "Americanism" is Lovecraft's attempt to transplant the Aryan myth to the New World, bringing it to the colonies along with the colonists, some of whom were Anglo-Saxon Teutons, but most of whom were not. The essay starts out like a standard philosophical essay with a preliminary identification of the terms that will be proven, refuted, or displaced in the text that follows. Lovecraft tells us that he is interested in pinning down a concrete definition of "Americanism," since this word is often sentimentalized or else cloaked in vague, abstract language, such that it has become merely a synonym for the "American spirit," or "opportunity," or the principles of "liberty," "democracy," and "freedom of speech." There are three components to Lovecraft's argument: (1) the British nation was founded by Anglo-Saxons, and the Anglo-Saxons are essentially Teutonic, racially and culturally; (2) the American nation is an extension of Britain; the early colonies established in Massachusetts and Virginia are, to all intents and purposes, British colonies; (3) thus, the American colonies represent an expansion of Anglo-Saxonism into the New World and, therefore, an expansion of the Teutonic race as well.

As Lovecraft elaborates on these points, he is careful to note that America's greatness stems from its roots in Anglo-Saxon culture, not merely from its origins in Europe, and that the Teuton, both in Britain and the New World, is the "highest" race and the most successful in implementing the principles of democracy that all Americans cherish.

> "Americanism" is expanded Anglo Saxonism. It is the spirit of England, transplanted to a soil of vast extent and diversity, and nourished for a time under pioneer conditions calculated to increase its democratic aspects without impairing is fundamental virtues ... It is the expression of the world's highest race under the most favourable social, political, and geographical conditions. Those who endeavour to belittle the importance of our British ancestry, are invited to consider the other nations of this continent. All these are equally "American" in every particular, differing only in race-stock and heritage; yet of them all, none save British Canada will ever bear comparison with us. We are great because we are part of the great Anglo-Saxon cultural sphere; a section detached only after a century and a half of heavy colonization and English rule, which gave to our land the ineradicable stamp of British civilization.[7]

Looking at the qualifying remarks that Lovecraft inserts into this passage (and other passages) in "Americanism"—that is, "differing only in race-stock," for example—the reader suspects that Lovecraft would have issues with the "melting pot" principle that has been an important, even defining, characteristic of America from the start—as important as the other principles that Lovecraft refers to at the beginning of his essay. This proves to be the case. Lovecraft argues, as we might have expected, that the melting pot notion is "dangerous" and "fallacious." Then, he makes the same point he will make repeatedly in the letters that follow, that only the Teutonic and Celtic races are capable of fully assimilating into English and American populations; a mixture of "really alien blood or ideas" with Anglo-Saxon blood and ideas, on the contrary, can only cause harm to America.

* * *

"In a Major Key" (1915) appeared in *The Conservative* 1, No. 2, pp. 9–11. Lovecraft, in this rather minor essay, is essentially picking a fight with another amateur writer, Charles D. Isaacson, who self-published his own journal, *In a Minor Key*. Isaacson was a proponent of toleration toward different races, including Blacks; he was also an admirer of Walt Whitman; Lovecraft, as an aggressive racist, naturally took issue with Isaacson's views on racial toleration and the purpose of "In a Major Key" is, thus, to refute those views. Lovecraft, in passing, also reprints a stanza that he wrote years before on Whitman, accusing the latter of "licentiousness" and indecency.

The so-called refutation is rather weak; there are no arguments—not even specious arguments; Lovecraft is merely uncritically repeating the racist beliefs that he articulates in the former essays and in the letters and the poems that follow:

> Mr. Isaacson's views on racial prejudice, as outlined in his *Minor Key*, are too subjective to be impartial ... a man of his perspicuity should be able to distinguish this illiberal feeling [resentment against Jews], a religious and social animosity of one white race toward another white and equally intellectual race, from the natural and scientifically just sentiment which keeps the African black from contaminating the Caucasian population of the United States. The negro is fundamentally the biological inferior of all White and even Mongolian races, and the Northern People must occasionally be reminded of the danger which they incur in admitting him too freely to the privileges of society and government. ... Race prejudice is a gift of Nature, intended to preserve in purity the various divisions of mankind which the ages have evolved.[8]

Here, as Lovecraft seems to imply, for any intelligent, cultivated white man, the inferiority of the Black race should be obvious and hardly needs to be defended by rigorous analysis or reasoning.

Letters

Most critics would agree that Lovecraft is one of the greatest epistolarians in the history of American and English literature. L. Sprague de Camp estimates that Lovecraft wrote a hundred thousand letters over the course of his lifetime, starting with a note to his mother, dated November 30, 1911, and ending with a long letter to his old friend James F. Morton, unfinished and found in his desk after he had been taken to the hospital where he died shortly thereafter on March 15, 1937. Whatever the final estimate, however, it certainly is close to de Camp's figure. August Derleth and Donald Wandrei, in the *Preface* to the first volume of Lovecraft's *Selected Letters*, describe Arkham House's project to publish as many Lovecraft letters as they could get their hands on—including the many letters that they themselves possessed from Lovecraft. They proceeded to contact all of Lovecraft's known correspondents, requesting them to send any Lovecraft letters that they had and, over the next few years that followed, Derleth and Wandrei were literally inundated with letters.

> We received parcels and bundles of letters in such quantity as to require the full time service of a stenographer merely to copy the portions edited from them. It became obvious that virtually every individual who had ever had occasion to write to Lovecraft had prized and preserved his letters and postcards. … The work of compiling, arranging, and re-editing the letters continued for a full quarter-century. Eventually, more than fifty typescript-volumes, each of approximately a hundred pages of single-space typing, were copied from the Lovecraft letters alone, apart from countless postcards that he sent out from various sites of his antiquarian explorations into Colonial America.[9]

S. T. Joshi suggests that Lovecraft's letters "may equal, and perhaps surpass, his fiction as the quintessence of [his] literary expression" at some distant period in the future of Lovecraft scholarship.[10] It would be nice to think that this might happen. But the likelihood seems doubtful. As I have noted in the introduction, Lovecraft's fictional works are now readily accessible to a vast audience, including the racist components of those works—all courtesy of the internet and social media—and this has, in turn, caused harm—perhaps even irreparable harm—to Lovecraft's current and continuing literary reputation. Because Lovecraft's letters are filled with more racism and racial hatred than any of his other works, Lovecraft's possible fame as a great epistolarian may, thus, end up becoming something of an infamy instead.

In this study, I will be examining the letters that deal specifically with the Aryan myth; there are more of these than one might suspect, and in them, Lovecraft develops as fully as he can his interpretation of the myth, as well as his views on assimilation, the differences between Aryan culture and the Aryan race, and the role that the Black race plays in the natural scheme of things in Europe and America. The other elements of Lovecraft's racism—the decline of Western civilization, hybridism, miscegenation, and such—are also addressed by Lovecraft in his letters—these have been examined and cited, when relevant, in the previous chapter.

The reader may wonder why Lovecraft was willing to write so freely about his racial hatred in his correspondence, especially in such a transparent, open manner, but it must be remembered that these letters were mostly private documents, intended for the recipients only. Lovecraft had no reason to think that they would be read by anyone other than their recipients unless the latter circulated them on a limited basis (which they did sometimes). This explains why Lovecraft is so honest, unrestrained, and emotional in articulating his views on race, white supremacy, and other controversial or unpopular subjects. In these letters, we will see Lovecraft constructing arguments, of course, and we will see him attempting to use logical reasoning as he develops his ideas. Likewise, he attempts to maintain as objective of a stance as he is able to manage, given the nature of the subject matter. But most definitely, the kid gloves are off and Lovecraft's passion, intensity, and, unfortunately, his hate come through loud and clear, as the following examples will show.

***

Lovecraft, in a letter to his friend Reinhardt Kleiner, dated November 25, 1915, articulates the Aryan myth as he saw it, in terms similar to those he uses in "The Crime of the Century" and "In a Major Key" (both of which were written during the same year as this letter). The Aryan, or Teutonic race, is the superior race and this preeminence has been predetermined by nature; thus, there is nothing that anyone can do about it—the other races need to merely accept their subordinate status and not dispute it. We will see Lovecraft making a similar argument in the poems that follow.

> As to races, I deem it most proper to recognize the divisions into which Nature has grouped mankind. Science shows us the infinite superiority of the Teutonic Aryan over all others, and it therefore becomes us to see that his ascendancy shall remain undisputed. Any racial mixture can but lower the result. The Teutonic race, whether in Scandinavia, other parts of the continent, England, or America, is the cream of humanity, and its wanton and deliberate adulteration with baser material is even more repulsive to consider than the elaborately staged racial suicide now being conducted, wherein Germanic and Britannic Teutons are striving to annihilate each other instead of uniting against the Mongol-tainted Slav or menacing Oriental.[11]

An important point, as indicated in comment made about "adulteration with baser material," is that the actual *blood* of the Teuton can be more easily debased by contact with "alien blood," even if this is only a mere drop—much more readily, in fact, than can the blood of other races. Thus, "racial combinations" engender "chemical reactions" that transform the Aryan into something that is no longer purely Aryan. As we will see, the results of such chemical reactions are, in part, the subject of certain key Lovecraft tales—"Arthur Jermyn" and "The Shadow Over Innsmouth," for example.

Much later, in a letter to James Ferdinand Morton, dated November 6, 1930, Lovecraft breaks up the Aryan "heritage," as he puts it, into separate subset heritages and then views them all as "layers" that should not be "detached" from one another.

> Of course, our heritage comes in layers of different intensity, each being more vital and potent as it comes closer to our immediate individuality. We have an Aryan heritage, a Western-European heritage, a Teuton-Celtic heritage, an Anglo-Saxon or English heritage, an Anglo-American heritage, and so on—but we can't detach one layer from another without serious loss—loss of a sense of significance and orientation in the world. America without England is absolutely meaningless to a civilised man of any generation yet grown to maturity.[12]

This idea about "layers of different intensity" is interesting. It is, in fact, comparable to Lovecraft's concept of the cosmos as a succession of layers. There are five distinct layers: (i) the cosmos itself; (ii) the universe; (iii) the galaxies; (iv) the solar system; and, finally, (v) the Earth. The four latter components are subsets of the larger set of the cosmos as a whole and they lead to "something"—not a god, or even an impersonal first cause—but just a something that proves to be "incommensurable," that is, beyond human comprehension. The layers in Lovecraft's racist cosmology, also, lead to a "something," and this is equally incommensurable. One can presume that this "something" in the first instance is, perhaps, cosmic law, while the "something" in the second case is natural law, and this latter, in turn, dictates that the Aryan is supreme among all of the other racial groups—I will explore the distinction between cosmic law and natural law in greater detail in Chapter 11.

As we might expect, the assimilation of non-Anglo-Saxons into Anglo-Saxon cultures was, for Lovecraft, a rather tricky affair. Assimilation by blood was, of course, prohibited; the mixing of bloods, he insists, only weakens the dominant race. But assimilation via culture was acceptable. There was one important caveat, however. Non-Anglo-Saxon races that wished to become part of any Aryan culture must be willing to capitulate utterly to the dominant culture; they must give up their own cultural mores, practices, and beliefs and adopt the culture, mores, and so on of the nation into which they are assimilating.

> I am *not* prepared to admit that the essentially exotic and Oriental culture-stream of the Hebraic tradition has any legitimate place in a Western and Aryan civilisation. We can gradually absorb such Jewish elements that are dominantly Nordic or even Mediterranean in their biological composition—keen, gray-eyed, white-skinned German Jews ... or ascetic Portuguese-Jewish types like those whose blood has already

tinctured to a great extent the body of the Spanish people. But this absorption absolutely postulates a complete cultural surrender on their part—an acceptance of our own Aryan point of view, loyalties, religion, and heritage. In other words, they must throw themselves wholly into the main stream and utterly forget their own individual past; else they will engender unpleasant cross-currents of taste and feeling which will continue to make them socially distasteful.[13]

Here, Lovecraft confesses that he is uneasy about assimilating Asians since they are too "exotic" for Aryan civilizations. There is, however, one race that is not able (and never will be) to assimilate into Teutonic-based nations and that race is, not surprisingly, the Black race. Lovecraft is very firm in his view that Blacks are not a part of the human race any more than apes or higher primates and mammals are human, and thus, they are barred from becoming human due simply to their biological roots. Lovecraft's viciousness in stating this belief is staggeringly unpleasant:

As with the negro, there is only one thing we can do as an immediate expedient to save ourselves; *Keep them out of our national and racial life.* With the negro the fight is wholly biological ... We are Aryans, and our only future as a self-respecting stock lies in our resistance to anything like an Alexandrian mental hybridisation.[14]

As Lovecraft grew older, we might expect that his extremist, hardline views on cultural heritage and assimilation would naturally soften, or at least tilt slightly more toward the conservative, as such views often do over time. In Lovecraft's case, there is some indication of a softening in his views from 1933 to 1935. In a letter to J. Vernon Shea, dated September 25, 1933, Lovecraft talks about keeping "the culture stream ... relatively undiluted by alien traditions" and he argues that any settled and "homogeneous" nation—such as the Teutonic/Anglo-Saxon nations—should not bring in too many members of alien races, since this may "bring about an actual alteration in the dominant ethnic composition" and "dilution of the culture-stream with emotional and intellectual elements alien to the original cultural impulse."[15] Here, Lovecraft is talking about cultural and ethnic issues rather than racial or blood purity issues.

Despite this, however, Lovecraft is still unable to relinquish his view that there is such a thing as Aryan or Teutonic blood, or Aryan languages, and near the end of the Shea letter, he actually praises the motives of Adolf Hitler to preserve racial–cultural continuity in Germany; Lovecraft even makes this remarkable, personal statement about Hitler—"I know he's a clown, but by God, I *like* the boy!"[16] And Lovecraft, as late as 1934, never wavered in his aggressive advocation for a strong color line dividing the white race from the darker races. He even goes so far as to state that this same color line needs to be imposed against East Indians as well.[17] As for the Black race specifically, Lovecraft's racial hatred remained as strong as it ever was. In a letter to Natalie H. Wooley, dated November 22, 1934, only three years before his death, Lovecraft gives us these edifying remarks: "Of the complete biological inferiority of the negro there can be no question—he has anatomical features consistently varying from those of other stocks, & always in the direction of the lower primates. Moreover, he has never developed a civilisation of his own, despite his ample contact with the very earliest white civilizations."[18]

Poetry

Like many great writers who matured into prose stylists in later years, Lovecraft began his writing career by focusing his energies on the composition of poetry. Lovecraft wrote an awful lot of poetry, the bulk of it between 1897 and 1925, and, generally speaking, it is awful indeed. Lovecraft possessed no genuine poetical feeling or any real ability to write verse that was capable of creatively expressing his inmost "psyche." He admired classical Augustan poetry, which included the works of Virgil, Horace, and Ovid. But in the majority of his own verse, he imitated the later Augustan poetry of the eighteenth century in England, specifically the poetry of Alexander Pope. King George, who ruled England at this period, liked to think of himself as an emperor, that is, an "Augustus," and so, the poetry of his time was labeled "Augustan" or, alternately, "Georgian." Late Augustan poetry tended to be didactic, political, satirical, and philosophical, as was Lovecraft's own work, so this type of verse was a good fit for Lovecraft. There are only a few of Lovecraft's poems that will stand the test of time in my opinion, and these are definitely *not* Augustan in tone or substance. These include "The Ancient Track" (1929), "The Messenger" (1929), and the *Fungi from Yuggoth* sonnet sequence (1929–30).

Lovecraft had no illusions about the quality of his poetry, as the following passage from a letter to his friend Elizabeth Toldridge makes clear. Apparently, Lovecraft's motives in writing verse were obliquely antiquarian; Lovecraft wanted to re-create an idealized version of the eighteenth century, a period that he himself loved, and then to bask in the illusion that he was living in that time and period.

> In my metrical novitiate I was, alas, a chronic and inveterate mimic; allowing my antiquarian tendencies to get the better of my abstract poetic feeling. As a result, the whole purpose of my writing soon became distorted—till at length I wrote only as a means of re-creating around me the atmosphere of my 18th century favourites. Self- expression as such sank out of sight, & my sole test of excellence was the degree with

which I approached the style of Mr. Pope, Dr. Young, Mr. Thomson. ... Dr. Johnson, & so on. My verse lost every vestige of originality & sincerity, its only core being to reproduce the typical forms & sentiments of the Georgian scene amidst which it was supposed to be produced.[19]

I am only examining two poems here; there are quite a few in the Lovecraft canon, of course, that contain racist comments or observations, but which do not develop racist arguments. The following poems, however, do exactly that, and they are important because they get at the "philosophical" rationale that lies at the heart of Lovecraft's hatred of the nonwhite races. Indeed, they are essential documents for the scholar who wishes to understand exactly why Lovecraft felt that it might be useful, if not justified, to deploy racist imagery and narratives in his fictional works.

**

"De Triumpho Naturae" (1905) has as its subtitle "The Triumph of Nature Over Northern Ignorance"—"Northern" here referring to the northern states that called for the abolition of slavery in the American south during the mid-1800s, an action that, in turn, led to the Civil War. Lovecraft dedicates the poem to William Benjamin Smith (1850–1934), professor of mathematics at Tulane University and author of *"The Colour Line": A Brief in Behalf of the Unborn* (1905), in which Smith, like Lovecraft, argues that Blacks were inferior biologically to whites. Obviously, Lovecraft had read and was impressed by Smith's "brief" before he wrote "De Triumpho Naturae"; as we have seen, Lovecraft, too, supported the enforcement of a strong color line between Blacks and whites throughout all US territories.

> The Northern bigot, with false zeal inflam'd,
> The virtues of the Afric race proclaim'd;
> Declar'd the blacks his brothers and his peers,
> And at their slav'ry shed fraternal tears;
> Distorted for his cause the Holy Word,
> And deem'd himself commanded by the Lord
> To draw his sword, whate'er the cost might be,
> And set the sons of Aethiopia free.
> First with the South in battle he engag'd;
> And four hard years an impious warfare wag'd,
> Then, deaf to Nature, and to God's decree,
> He gave the blacks their fatal liberty.
> The halls where Southern justice once had reign'd
> He now with horrid negro rites profan'd.
> Among the free in cursed mock'ry sate

The grinning Aethiop, conscious of his state.
But reckless folly can no further run;
The will of Nature must in Time be done.
The savage black, the ape-resembling beast,
Hath held too long his Saturnalian feast.
From out the land, by act of far'way Heav'n,
To ling'ring death his numbers shall be driv'n.
Against God's will the Yankee freed the slave
And in the act consign'd him to the grave.[20]

There are several features of interest in this poem. First, of course, the poem reflects the Aryan myth's contention that Blacks are an inferior race, meant to be slaves and, certainly, not to be understood as brothers and peers of the Teutonic race (notice that Lovecraft refuses to capitalize the word "negro" and yet, oddly, he has no problem capitalizing "Aethiop"—the two words are synonymous). Second, Lovecraft makes the point that the inferiority of the Black has been ordained by God ("God's decree") and thus, by trying to elevate the Black as an equal to the Teuton, Northern abolitionists and their supporters are demonstrating a willful "ignorance" and disregard of God's will, that is, acting contrary to "the Holy Word." This assertion might seem rather strange to readers; Lovecraft didn't believe in God or God's "decree," and yet, here he is invoking both to further his racial hatred.

In addition, Lovecraft asserts (as he did in his letters) that the natural world decrees that Blacks are inferior to whites. As we have seen, Lovecraft shares this view with Chamberlain. As far as Lovecraft was concerned, Blacks are subhuman; they are "ape-resembling" beasts and, thus, something of an anomaly in the natural world—not beasts in the strict sense and, yet, not human either. Lovecraft doesn't specify the exact position that Blacks occupy in the evolutionary scale (he will do so in the following poem); nevertheless, he makes it clear that the elevation of the Black to a position of equality with the Teutonic will end up having severe consequences not only for the white race but for the Black race as a whole. Blacks, in his view, are less intelligent and less capable than whites and, therefore, could never hope to compete with Anglo-Saxons either in the workforce or elsewhere. This is, of course, a rather ironic observation; as we have seen, Lovecraft himself was woefully incapable of competing with his own Anglo-Saxon peers economically or academically, much less capable, indeed, than even moderately educated "Aethiops."

***

"On the Creation of Niggers" (1912) is Lovecraft's most notoriously racist poem. By the time that Lovecraft wrote "Creation," he had read and assimilated Chamberlain's *Foundations*. Chamberlain declares that the inferiority of the Black is due to divine fiat; it is not merely "natural fiat," so to speak (as Lovecraft argues in the preceding poem), and Lovecraft picks up on this by uncharacteristically invoking a creation myth in the first few lines of the poem. But interestingly, Lovecraft interprets the first cause in terms of the pagan pantheon of gods and goddesses (the "Olympian host") as opposed to the Christian mythos.

> When, long ago, the Gods created Earth,
> In Jove's fair image Man was shap'd at birth.
> The beasts for lesser parts were next design'd;
> Yet were they too remote from humankind.
> To fill this gap, and join the rest to man,
> Th' Olympian host conceiv'd a clever plan.
> A beast they wrought, in semi-human figure,
> Fill'd it with vice, and call'd the thing a NIGGER.[21]

Here, Lovecraft clarifies exactly what Blacks are, in his estimation. The Black is a vicious beast, an ape-like beast, in fact, that looks more like human beings than the other beasts. Yet, his outward appearance is deceptive, since he really isn't human at all; he is a separate species, just as the animals are. There were, consequently, three components to the creation of life: humans were initially created in "Jove's fair image"; then, beasts, apes, and other animals were created; and lastly, Blacks were created. But of course, as noted previously, Lovecraft was an atheist and didn't believe that Jove or, indeed, any other God existed. And so, we must interpret Lovecraft's above reference to "creation" to mean "evolution," since Lovecraft *did* accept Darwin's theory of evolution, as articulated in *On the Origin of Species* (1859) and *The Descent of Man* (1871), both of which Lovecraft read.

Lovecraft, thus, is doing something rather remarkable in this small, seemingly minor poem. *Essentially, he is upending Darwin's theory by suggesting that there were three separate evolutionary processes at work here that resulted in the current existing higher life forms.* First, all higher animals, including apes, were derived from an ancient marsupial animal, which, in turn, was the end product of a long line of diversified forms that likely originated from an amphibian-like creature or possibly even a reptile. Second, humans, including the highest types of humans—white Anglo-Saxons—evolved from some type of quadruped, complete with pointed ears and a tail, like its distant cousin the monkey. And lastly, Blacks evolved from apes, probably not the same quadrupeds that humankind evolved from; thus, humans, Blacks, and apes are all separate species. The Blacks, however, are close to humans—a lower, less perfect species in Lovecraft's view, but still, nearly equivalent—at least in terms of genetics, which, of course, explains why Blacks and whites can produce viable hybrid children. In the tales that we will be examining in Parts II and III, Lovecraft will carry this argument even further. He will suggest that when it comes to separate, but similar species such as Blacks and whites, there is a built-in genetic barrier that excludes members of the "lower" species from becoming members of the higher species. However, the reverse is *not* true—members of the higher species can move between the barriers and devolve if they so desire, but this will force them to leave their "humanity" behind.

* * *

Previously, Lovecraft wrote that members of the non-Anglo-Saxon races could only become viable American citizens if they essentially relinquished their native culture, values, and ethnic attributes and capitulated entirely to the dominant Teutonic culture. But as the above arguments make clear, the members of the Black race could never do so, no matter how hard they tried or how willing they were to relinquish their heritage. They are not human, as Lovecraft argues explicitly above, and thus, by definition, a nonhuman being cannot become a full-fledged member of a human civilization—*any* human civilization—especially as highly developed and intricately perfected of a civilization as that created by Anglo-Saxons.

Of course, Blacks had their place in America. They were slaves originally, which as far as Lovecraft was concerned had been their best chance for happiness in their relations with whites. As long as slaves performed their functions effectively and efficiently, and as long as they remained docile and subservient, they would be treated much like adored pets, to be cherished and even loved by their masters. But Blacks must behave themselves; they must keep to their place. We must recall, in this context, Lovecraft's condescending remarks about Elizabeth Toldridge's "dusky" maid Alice; Lovecraft acknowledged that she was an effective servant and pleasant to interact with. But certainly, Lovecraft didn't intend that she should attempt to be anything more than what she was; she shouldn't be attending college, for example, or competing with white women or white men for jobs, or even voting in elections. And under no circumstances should she marry a white man or bear interracial children.

There was a darker side to Blacks, however, that always simmered beneath the surface. According to Lovecraft, since Blacks are beasts, not human, even though they resemble human beings much more than apes, they are essentially wild animals deep down in the core of their nature. Consequently, there was always a potential that the wildness would come to the surface—that the "beast would out," so to speak. As a result, Blacks might end up resenting their subordinate, secondary status in America and violently rebel. Certainly, Lovecraft would admit, they had at least *enough* intelligence to do *that*. Thus, Blacks as a race could end up exterminating the white race if they had a mind to and this represented a continuing danger to the white race. As we will see later in our analysis of specific tales and novels (especially the later works that deal with alien entities), Lovecraft constructs fictional plots that reflect his apprehensions (fears?) about the Black race; two of these involve violent uprisings on the part of enslaved races against their cosmic slave masters. In the fiction, of course, the uprisings do not specifically refer to slave rebellions against humankind. But Lovecraft's hidden meaning is clear enough.

PART II

Humankind against Hybrid, Degenerative Monsters

5

Lovecraft's Early Weird Tales

In 1917, Lovecraft decided to concentrate his writing efforts on commercial fiction. He had grown disenchanted with amateur journalism, after having self-published at least a hundred poems, essays, and articles for the last two years in his own periodical *The Conservative* and in the periodicals generated by other members of the UAPA. At long last, Lovecraft realized that amateur journalism was not an avenue to literary recognition but, instead, a dead end. Due to his apprenticeship in the field of arts and letters, such as it was, he had developed the ability to write effective prose, and thus, many of his earliest tales turned out to be very competent work. Though he took a bit of a detour due to the influence of Edgar Allan Poe, a good mentor, and John Moreton Drax Plunkett, Lord Dunsany (1878–1957), a bad mentor, tales such as "Beyond the Wall of Sleep" (1919), "The Cats of Ulthar" (1920), "The Statement of Randolph Carter" (1920), and "From Beyond" (1920) are effective, if not exactly good, while one of them, "The Music of Erich Zann" (1921), is excellent and can be placed among Lovecraft's finest fictional works. Interestingly, in many of these earliest tales, we see Lovecraft setting up themes that he will use later on in his major weird tales.

For example, the theme of the lonely, scholarly elitist who encounters supernatural entities in isolated locales was first articulated by Lovecraft in "The Tomb" (1917). The protagonist, Jervas Dudley, is the prototype for much more fully developed characters in the mature fiction such as Charles Dexter Ward, Henry Wentworth Akeley, and Nathaniel Wingate Peaslee. Similarly, the theme of an alien astronaut race living on earth in the dim past first surfaced in "The Doom That Came to Sarnath" (1919). Before humans appeared on the earth, the extraterrestrial alien race known as the Thuum-ha came from the Moon to Ib, a city in the land of Mnar. Then humans colonized Mnar and built the nearby city of Sarnath. The men of Sarnath are repulsed by the appearance of the Thuum-ha—the aliens are greenish in color, with bulging eyes; thick, flabby lips; and "curious ears" (all racist images, for sure). Eventually, Sarnath rises up against the city of Ib and exterminates the entire population. But predictably, centuries later, the Thuum-ha return to earth and destroy Sarnath. When we study Lovecraft's "The Shadow Over Innsmouth" in Chapter 15, the parallels between the Thuum-ha and the Innsmouth mutants will become readily apparent.

The tales that I am examining in the next five chapters, which are among Lovecraft's best early weird tales, focus on the Other as hybrid, degenerative monsters. In the first of these tales, "Arthur Jermyn," these monsters are the Jermyn hybrids, who are the descendants of Sir Wade Jermyn, a British explorer in the eighteenth century who spent extensive amounts of time in the Congo region of Africa. Second, in "Herbert West-Reanimator," the monsters are the West menagerie, a collection of formerly living human corpses that have been reanimated and find themselves among the living again, though consigned to a type of life that is more along the lines of a death-in-life. Third, in "The Lurking Fear," the hybrids are the Martense cannibals, as I am calling them, the dwarfed, deformed, and cannibalistic descendants of Gerrit Martense, a reclusive New Amsterdam merchant who built a mansion in 1670 near Tempest Mountain in the Catskills. Next, in "The Rats in the Walls," the monsters are the Delapore clan, who are similar to the Martense cannibals; they are a family of degenerate, devolved subhuman creatures preying on the communities and environs surrounding their ancestral estate (this time it is Exham Priory in England instead of a manor house in the Catskills). Finally, in "The Horror at Red Hook," deemed by most Lovecraft scholars to be Lovecraft's most outrageously racist piece of prose fiction, the hybrid, degenerative monsters are the residents of the Red Hook district in New York, a swarthy, racially diverse group of immigrants who are, in turn, allied with supernatural creatures that dwell deep in the earth underneath the main protagonist's basement flat.

As I have noted in the introduction, Lovecraft uses racist images and his first racist narrative, the miscegenation narrative, to enhance the horror in these tales and to increase the reader's interest. Lovecraft assumed, of course, that his readers would be horrified by monsters that looked like Blacks and other members of the hated races, and that readers, likewise, would be outraged by the thought of miscegenation between Blacks and whites. Lovecraft shared this view with racist historian Houston Stewart Chamberlain, as we have seen in Chapter 3. The two writers also shared the view that hybrid, degenerative monsters are not human, even if they started out as humans, as did the West menagerie and the Martense cannibals. The issue of hybridism, of course, was always a touchy one with Lovecraft and in these early weird tales, Lovecraft, following Chamberlain, reveals a strong aversion to hybrids, seeing them as a major factor in the decline of Western civilization and the white, Anglo-Saxon race in general.

Superficially, the monsters in the following tales might strike the reader as similar to the zombie-like, walking dead monstrosities that were appearing in the work of the hack writers of Lovecraft's day—and in the work of hack writers of today as well—and one might be tempted to argue that Lovecraft had been inspired by the fictional compositions of his *Weird Tales* colleagues and by the stories that were featured in the Munsey chain of pulp magazines: *Argosy*, *All-Story Magazine*, and *The Cavalier*. To be fair, this argument is perfectly valid. Lovecraft's monsters do, indeed, seem conventional and even derivative to a certain extent. And yet, they are originally imagined and unique in their own ways, and, as we will see, each of them is a little different than the others and from the creations of other, competing horror writers.

One of the remarkable things about Lovecraft is that he never repeats himself in his fictional works. Each story, whether great, good, or indifferent, has a unique Other and thoroughly unique images and plots. The term "hack writer" can rightly be applied to authors such as Lovecraft's colleague August Derleth, who wrote reams and reams of formula-driven fiction, much of it, in fact, derived from Lovecraftian themes—if the reader doubts this assessment, I urge her to simply study Derleth's story collections published under the titles *The Mask of Cthulhu* (1958) and *The Trail of Cthulhu* (1962); as one reads each story in sequence, they quickly become monotonous and repetitive and one discovers that it is difficult to read more than two in a single sitting. But Lovecraft was never a hack writer—he couldn't have been a hack even if he tried. Lovecraft always puts a bit of himself, sometimes more, sometimes less, into each of the following stories, and invariably, he brings along something that is new and fresh—but of course, often deeply disturbing as well, not only on personal levels but on moral, philosophical, and metaphysical grounds.

6

Arthur Jermyn (1920)

Lovecraft's original title for this tale was "Facts Concerning the Late Arthur Jermyn and His Family," though it usually appears in print simply as "Arthur Jermyn." This is, in fact, the title used by August Derleth in the Arkham hardcover edition *Dagon and Other Macabre Tales* (1965), and Lovecraft himself, in letters to his friends, always uses the shortened title. The tale has been described as a blend of science fiction and horror, but this is a bit of an overstatement; there is plenty of horror, but little science in it. When Edwin Baird, the first editor of *Weird Tales*, published the tale in 1924, he decided to retitle it "The White Ape." This outraged Lovecraft, who immediately responded in a letter dated February 3, 1924:

> The sensation of gastric depression caused by the implication that *Arthur Jermyn* is going to press as *The White Ape*! I wish I could convert you to my point of view regarding the annoying literalness and flaccidity of that latter title ... but all I can do is say that it is the only title which I could never possibly have applied to that particular tale; that it is at war with the spirit and internal harmonies of the narrative, and clashes fearsomely with the effect of the opening paragraph. One thing—you may be sure that if I ever entitled a story *The White Ape, there would be no ape in it*. There would be something at first taken for an ape, which would not be an ape.[1]

Lovecraft is protesting too much here—"Arthur Jermyn" is a competently written story, but hardly so grand that Lovecraft should be speaking about its "internal harmonies" in such a pompous tone. And besides, the tale is, in fact, about a white ape that is not really an ape in the strict sense of the word—the white ape is a hybrid between the human and the anthropoid. Thus, when Lovecraft claims that there would be no ape in a story that he himself decided to call "The White Ape," then Baird is only following Lovecraft's own criteria in publishing it under that very title.

The plot of "Arthur Jermyn" is straightforward. Arthur Jermyn, an English baronet, ethnologist, and poet, has descended from a long line of nobles who have extremely simian physical characteristics and, at times, suffer from mental degeneracy as well. Jermyn decides to investigate his antecedents to find out the source of the degeneracy, which apparently originated after his great-great-great grandfather Sir Wade, an African explorer, returned from a visit to the Congo with a new wife, purportedly the daughter of a Portuguese trader, who was never seen by anyone. Arthur Jermyn outfits an expedition to the Congo and visits the Ongo and Kaliri country, which is the same district that Sir Wade visited. Arthur learns from an aged native that Sir Wade had discovered a lost city ruled by a white ape princess, but Arthur cannot visit the city because it had been destroyed by a warlike tribe in the interim.[2] Arthur also learns that the body of the white ape had been mummified and then removed from the city. Accordingly, he hires agents to track down the mummy and have it shipped to London. Eventually the mummy ends up in Sir Arthur's study, and upon inspecting it, he can see very clearly the root cause of the degeneracy that has plagued the Jermyn line; Sir Wade had married the white ape and thus, Arthur and the other Jermyn hybrids have ape DNA in their blood. Arthur's reaction is predictable: he screams, rushes out of the house like a madman, then rushes back in, dowses himself in oil, and rushes out again. On the moor, he sets himself on fire and ends the family curse. Later, members of the Royal Anthropological Institute acquire the mummy and conclude that it is, indeed, a remarkably grotesque specimen. But apparently, they share Arthur Jermyn's repugnance toward miscegenation, for they burn the mummy and pretend that Arthur Jermyn never existed.

***

Lovecraft claimed that his inspiration for "Arthur Jermyn" was Sherwood Anderson's *Winesburg, Ohio* (1919), a collection of twenty-two short stories set in the fictional town of Winesburg, Ohio, a place that was, in turn, modeled on the author's childhood memories of Clyde, Ohio. Anderson's characters are generally classified by critics as "grotesques," whose warped feelings and regressive natures give rise to feelings of isolation and loneliness. In crafting these characters, Anderson was making the claim (implicit though it was) that his grotesques may have come about due to Negro blood in their ancestry. And so, Lovecraft decided to up the ante by delving into deeper waters— apes rather than Negroes. Lovecraft writes, in a 1923 letter to Baird, as cited by Paul Rolland: "It occurred to me that I, in my weirder medium, could probably devise some secret behind a man's ancestry which would make the worst of Anderson's disclosures sound like the annual report of a Sabbath school. Hence, 'Arthur Jermyn.' "[3] Certainly, Lovecraft succeeds in this latter objective and he may, indeed, have been inspired to write his tale due to Anderson's influence. But the subject of hybrids was always important to

Lovecraft well before he had ever read Anderson. Lovecraft had a visceral hated and detestation of hybrids and hybridism. And, in fact, the underlying theme of "Arthur Jermyn" is nothing more or less than the anxiety and fear that Lovecraft believed was the natural result when white Anglo-Saxon men and women are confronted with miscegenation—an anxiety and fear that, as we have seen, Lovecraft expresses frequently in his nonfictional and poetic works and that he shared with Chamberlain.

Sprague de Camp identifies a more likely source for "Arthur Jermyn": the novels of Edgar Rice Burroughs. As de Camp writes:

> The story belongs to the lost-race sub-genre, very popular when "Arthur Jermyn" was written. ... Edgar Rice Burroughs used the idea over and over. Alas! the airplane has now been so perfected that hardly a square mile of the earth's surface has not been seen from the air. So the lost race and the lost city have dropped out of fiction, since there is no place left where they can plausibly hide.[4]

De Camp is correct about the lost city genre and also in associating Burroughs (1875–1950) with this genre, for lost cities proliferate in Burroughs's novels, especially in the Tarzan series, which ran from 1912 to 1947. For example, in *The Return of Tarzan* (1913), *Tarzan and the Jewels of Opar* (1918), and *Tarzan the Invincible* (1930), the lost city is Opar, an Atlantean outpost set up in Africa to harvest the dark continent for gold. After Atlantis sank beneath the ocean, Opar remained on the surface, but slowly degenerated over time. In *Tarzan the Terrible* (1921), the lost city is actually a lost land, Pal-ul-don, separated from the bulk of the African continent by a range of mountains and impenetrable morasses, inhabited by prehistoric creatures and humans. In *Tarzan and the Lost Empire* (1929), there are two lost cities: Castra Sanguinarius and Castrum Mare, both of them founded by the Roman empire shortly before the empire's decline and fall. These are just a few of Burroughs's lost cities and Lovecraft was likely aware of them all and drew inspiration from them when he envisioned the "forgotten" city of stone that Sir Wade visits in the Congo.

De Camp errs, however, when he makes his observation that the invention of the airplane made it impossible for lost cities to remain lost any longer, and that this was responsible for the demise of the lost city genre. Even in the twenty-first century, with our very sophisticated planes, drones, and black hawk helicopters, lost cities are still possible, provided that they exist *under* the surface of the earth. Thus, though most of Burroughs's lost cities would be accessible via the airplane, since they exist on the surface of the planet, nevertheless, Lovecraft's hidden cities would remain secure. The Deep Ones, which are featured in "The Shadow Over Innsmouth," dwell in metropolises that are deep under the oceans. In "The Whisperer in Darkness," the Mi-Go conduct their mining operations in hidden caverns inside the isolated hills of

Vermont, the entrances of which are concealed by the nearly impenetrable canopies of the trees. And the abandoned cites of the Great Race and the Elder Things are deeply buried under the shifting sands in Australia and in the frozen wastes of Antarctica. As for de Camp's contention that the lost city genre has disappeared from sf literature since Lovecraft's day, this, too, is not correct. The genre continued to flourish and is still going strong today, though most lost cities exist now in alternate dimensions of space and time or in parallel universes—places where no aircraft can reach them.

There is another, more important Burroughs connection to "Arthur Jermyn" that de Camp overlooks: this is Burroughs's concept of the half-human, half-ape hybrid. Burroughs developed numerous types of hybrids in the Tarzan novels. There are, first of all, the great apes themselves that rescue Tarzan as an infant after the death of his shipwrecked parents on the coast of Africa. The she-ape Kala is allowed by the ape clan to rear him (she had lost her own infant shortly before). These apes are a hybrid species, not gorillas or chimpanzees, and more intelligent than the other anthropoids. Second, there are the male priests and populace of Opar, who are stunted, hairy warriors, the result of cross-breeding between apes and humans; the women of Opar, including the city's high priestess La, are, on the contrary, tall, beautiful white women. A continuing plot theme in the Tarzan novels is La's unrequited crush on Tarzan and her unwillingness to marry one of the hybrid high priests, as she is required to do. Third, there are the white and Black races that live in Pal-ul-don, known as the pithecanthropi, which have tails and other simian traits such as long, tapering fingers with thumbs reaching to the first joints of the index fingers and feet whose great toes protrude at right angles from the rest of the appendage—both of these features make it easier for the pithecanthropi to travel through the trees as do monkeys and gibbons. And finally, there is a race of gorilla men who live in a country north of Opar that possess the intelligence of humans and periodically steal women from the Oparians to mate with. Undoubtedly, Lovecraft was influenced, if not exactly inspired, by all of Burroughs's hybrids and they must have been in his mind as he developed the female white ape that becomes Sir Wade Jermyn's consort and Arthur Jermyn's great-great-great grandmother.

* * *

There are seven hybrid, degenerative monsters in "Arthur Jermyn"—five of them identified by name and two left unnamed. The former include Philip, Sir Wade's son; Robert, Philip's son; Nevil, Robert's second son; Alfred, Nevil's son; and, of course, Arthur himself. The unnamed children, also males, are Alfred's siblings, both of whom, we are told, "were never publicly seen on account of deformities in mind and body."[5]

Up until the time of Sir Wade Jermyn, there had been no genetic abnormalities in the Jermyn family tree. As Lovecraft puts it, "the old family portraits in Jermyn House showed fine faces enough before Sir Wade's time."[6] Sir Wade, an African explorer, is convinced that a prehistoric white civilization exists somewhere in the Congo region. He writes a book, *Observation on the Several Parts of Africa*, articulating his views about the white civilization and his book is ridiculed by critics when it is released. On one of his expeditions, Sir Wade discovers his lost city in the Onga and Kaliri districts. Lovecraft's description of the city is strongly reminiscent of Burroughs's description of the city of Opar: "gigantic walls and pillars ... crumbling and vine grown, and of damp, silent, stone steps leading interminably down into the darkness of abysmal treasure-vaults and inconceivable catacombs."[7] In this city, the remnants of Sir Wade's white civilization still reside, though they are not quite what he had hoped for. They are half-white, half-ape hybrids, ruled by a white princess who is likewise half-ape. The princess becomes Sir Wade's consort and the two of them live together as king and queen of the city for a time until they have a son and then, Sir Wade takes his bride back home to England. The princess is kept in seclusion in the Jermyn mansion and her husband claims that she is the daughter of a Portuguese trader and does not like "English ways." Eventually, the two leave their son in the care of a "loathsome black woman from Guinea," as Lovecraft insists on remarking, and they return to the lost city for what proves to be Sir Wade's last visit to Africa. The princess eventually dies and Sir Wade has her body mummified and enshrined in a vast temple of stone in the lost city, where it becomes an object of worship and veneration.

The mummified white ape princess is eventually shipped back to the Jermyn house. Since the white ape is the genetic source of the subsequent Jermyn hybrids, the mummy bears full description here.

> The stuffed goddess was a nauseous sight, withered and eaten away, but it was clearly a mummified white ape of some unknown species, less hairy than any recorded variety, and infinitely nearer mankind—quite shockingly so ... the arms on the golden locket about the creature's neck were the Jermyn arms, and the jocose suggestion of M. Verhaeren about certain resemblance as connected with the shrivelled face applied with vivid, ghastly, and unnatural horror to none other than the sensitive Arthur Jermyn.[8]

The mummy is, indeed, a nauseous sight, withered and rotting. Be that as it may, however, Sir Wade had been attracted to the white ape princess when he first met her to the extent that he had married and then had a child with her. Thus, she must have been sexually appealing in life, and this thought, no doubt, horrified Lovecraft—imagine a white, Anglo-Saxon man—a European and a baronet at that—being sexually attracted to a half-human, half-ape hybrid woman! Over time, however, after Sir Wade returns to England, he broods over his past and, eventually, his mind becomes unhinged and he is committed to a barred room at Huntingdon asylum, where he dies three years later. Lovecraft doesn't tell us exactly *why* Sir Wade became unhinged, but the implication is strong that he meditated on his liaison with the princess and ultimately found his past behavior repulsive, so repulsive in fact that the thought of it drove him insane.

Sir Philip, Wade's only son, is the first of the Jermyns to show marked physical and mental anomalies due to the white ape's "tainted" DNA. Lovecraft refers to Philip as a "highly peculiar person," which is, admittedly, putting it very mildly.

> Despite a strong physical resemblance to his father, his appearance and conduct were in many particulars so coarse that he was universally shunned. Though he did not inherit the madness which was feared by some, he was densely stupid and given to brief periods of uncontrollable violence. In frame he was small, but intensely powerful, and was of incredible agility.[9]

Here, Philip is described as if he were a monkey, small, strong, and agile, and, of course, of subhuman intelligence, as monkeys are. After Sir Philip succeeds to the baronetcy, he marries the daughter of his gamekeeper, a person said to be "of gypsy extraction" (this is almost as bad as being a hybrid, in Lovecraft's mind). Then, Sir Philip joins the navy as a "common sailor"—certainly not as an officer, as would have been the usual course for a baronet. After the American war, Philip ships out on a merchantman ship in the African trade. Not surprisingly, he gains a reputation for feats of strength and climbing, taking advantage of his genetic heritage. He eventually disappears when the ship is off the coast of Africa and, one suspects, he has decided to return to the lost city and rediscover his true lineage among the savages.

Sir Robert, the son of Philip and the second of the Jermyn hybrids, is, as it turns out, almost entirely free from the tainted Jermyn DNA. Although we are told that he is proportioned "oddly," he has none of the simian traits manifested by his father and he becomes a scholarly researcher, just as his grandfather had been. It is Robert who collects much of the information about Sir Wade and his explorations that Arthur Jermyn will study later. Sir Robert is described thusly.

> Tall and fairly handsome, with a sort of weird Eastern grace despite certain oddities of proportion, Robert Jermyn began life as a scholar and investigator. It was he who first studied scientifically the vast collection of relics which his mad grandfather had brought from Africa, and who made the family name as celebrated in ethnology as in exploration. In 1815, Sir Robert married a daughter of the seventh Viscount Brightholme and was subsequently blessed with three children.[10]

Blessed is hardly the right word here. All three of these children have the negative Jermyn traits; the elder boy and the youngest, in fact, appear to have been too grotesque in appearance even by post-Sir Wade standards and had to be kept hidden in the mansion.[11] In 1852, Sir Robert is visited by a fellow explorer, Samuel Seaton, who calls at the Jermyn house with a manuscript of notes collected from the Ongas tribe in the Congo concerning the legends of the lost city. Apparently, this information reveals the truth about the relations between Sir Wade and the white ape, for Robert subsequently becomes mentally unhinged, and though he is an elderly man, he strangles Seaton and promptly kills all of his children. He then attempts to commit suicide but is restrained by his servants and ends up confined in an institution, much as Sir Wade had been—he finally dies of apoplexy in his second year of incarceration.

Sir Nevil, the third of the Jermyn hybrids, is only afforded a brief description by Lovecraft, though this is enough to let the reader know that Nevil has inherited the same types of degenerative traits as his progenitors: "Nevil, a singularly repellant person ... seemed to combine the surliness of Philip Jermyn with the hauteur of the Brightholmes."[12] Following in the path of his great-grandfather, Nevil leaves the ancestral mansion to seek his fortunes. He doesn't manage to get back to the African subcontinent, but nevertheless, he manifests the Jermyn inclination for foraging in low places and finds himself a bride suitable to his tastes—a "vulgar dancer," as we are told, and the two conceive a child. The dancer doesn't live very long and Nevil ends up a widower. He returns home with his infant and, initially, is welcomed back by Sir Robert. However, when Sir Robert has his mental breakdown, as described above, Nevil is killed along with his siblings. But before falling victim to his father's rage, Nevil manages to rescue his child.

This child, Alfred, is the sixth Jermyn hybrid and the father of Arthur. He succeeds to the baronetcy before he is four years of age. At no time in his life, even his childhood, do his "tastes match his title," as Lovecraft tells us. Lovecraft provides no details about the physical appearance or mental status of Sir Alfred; thus, we are forced to judge how much of the degenerative ape DNA might have been in play in the case of this particular Jermyn hybrid. At the age of twenty, Alfred joins a band of music hall performers and marries one of them; she bears him a child shortly after. By the time he turns thirty-six, Alfred deserts his wife and child and travels with an itinerant American circus. Among the animals in the circus, there is a huge bull gorilla "of lighter color than the average" and Alfred becomes fascinated by it. The gorilla is interested in Alfred as well and the ape and the hybrid begin to bond. Alfred is allowed to train the ape and he creates a boxing match act with the ape that turns out to be a popular crowd-pleaser. However, while Alfred and the gorilla are rehearsing the act in Chicago, the ape delivers a punch to Alfred that is more than usually forceful and Alfred's "dignity" is hurt. His reaction is what one might expect from a Jermyn hybrid.

> Of what followed, members of the "The Greatest Show on Earth" do not like to speak. They did not expect to hear Sir Alfred Jermyn emit a shrill, inhuman scream, or to see him seize his clumsy antagonist with both hands, dash it to the floor of the cage, and bite fiendishly at its hairy throat. The gorilla was off its guard, but not for long, and before anything could be done by the regular trainer the body which had belonged to a baronet was past recognition.[13]

Interestingly, in this short passage, Lovecraft identifies the three species central to his racist evolutionary theories: the white, Anglo-Saxons (i.e., the "regular trainer"); the hybrid, degenerative monsters (Alfred Jermyn)—a category that includes half-white, half-Black hybrids; and the anthropoids (the bull gorilla).

* * *

The life and career of Arthur Jermyn follows the pattern of loss and failure that most of Lovecraft's privileged protagonists face, though Arthur's initial loss of privilege is unique and comparable only to Thomas Delapore's and Robert Olmstead's loss of privilege in "The Rats in the Walls" and "The Shadow Over Innsmouth," respectively. Sir Arthur is lost from the start; the tainted DNA that runs through his veins automatically undercuts the benefits of his exalted birthright. Indeed, it can be argued that Sir Arthur's subsequent failures are nothing more than a working out of what has been predetermined all along, right from the moment that he took his first breath. From a physical standpoint, Sir Arthur is more strikingly degenerated than even Philip, Nevil, or Alfred, though Lovecraft doesn't provide as detailed of a description as he will do later in "Herbert West-Reanimator," for example, where he uses overtly racist images in his description of a Black hybrid, degenerative monster.

> Many would have disliked to live if possessed of the peculiar features of Arthur Jermyn ... Most of the Jermyns had possessed a subtly odd and repellent cast, but Arthur's case was very striking. It is hard to say just what he resembled, but his expression, his facial angle, and the length of his arms gave a thrill of repulsion to those who met him for the first time.[14]

It could not be any more obvious that Sir Arthur resembles a great, white ape—the references to his "facial angle" and the length of his arms are a telltale giveaway.

Sir Arthur's mind, however, is at odds with his exterior; he is highly gifted mentally. He graduates summa cum laude from Oxford and his scientific zeal is supplemented by a delicate, poetical temperament—this latter quality, no doubt, derives from his mother, who was a music hall performer. In

1912, Arthur embarks on a journey to Africa, determined to track down Sir Wade's lost city. Arthur learns that the city has been sacked in the interim by a warlike tribe, resulting in the annihilation of all the white hybrids and the disappearance of the mummy. Eventually, Sir Arthur finds the ruins of the lost city, but they tell him nothing that he doesn't already know. He meets M. Verhaeren, a Belgian agent, at a trading post in the Congo, who offers to track down the mummy and have it shipped back to England. Sir Arthur returns to the Jermyn mansion, apprehensively waiting for the mummy to arrive.

Arthur Jermyn's catastrophic fall happens rather quickly once the box containing the mummy is delivered in August 1913. Arthur's reaction is just as dramatic as Sir Robert's reaction had been when he was visited by the explorer Samuel Seaton, who likewise came bearing revelations, though this time around, Arthur doesn't harm anyone other than himself. Indeed, there isn't anyone else to harm; Arthur never married—due to his simian appearance, no doubt—so, there are no children. Truly, Arthur is the last of the Jermyn line. He has the box taken to the large room that houses Sir Wade's African collection, then dismisses all of his servants and opens it alone. The servants in the hall hear a sudden, bloodcurdling scream, then Arthur rushes out of the room, douses himself with oil from the basement, and then out the cellar door, disappearing into the adjoining moor. Presently, the servants see "a pillar of human fire" that reaches up to the heavens; Arthur has self-immolated himself, too traumatized by the sight of the mummy to continue living. This is the ultimate confirmation and apotheosis of his loss of white privilege.

But here, also, in Sir Arthur's response to the mummy, we see the same pattern that Lovecraft himself experienced in his own life when confronting a crisis. The crisis is, of course, the appearance of the mummy itself. Arthur can clearly see a resemblance between the face of the mummy, withered though it is, and his own face. As for the response, Sir Arthur freezes up and becomes passive, trying to process what he is seeing. This is confirmed by the fact that he does nothing at first. We are told that there is a long interval of time between the opening of the box and the moment when Arthur screams and then emerges from the room.[15] During this period, Sir Arthur is obviously in a state of temporary stasis, just as Lovecraft himself was after each of the crises he faced throughout his life. Of course, when Sir Arthur does get back into action, he promptly commits suicide; Lovecraft, on the contrary, doesn't go quite that far—as we have seen, he contemplates suicide on several occasions, but doesn't follow through.

***

The story of "Arthur Jermyn" consolidates Lovecraft's views of hybrids and hybridism for the first time in his fictional works and sets the stage for the tales that will follow. It is among Lovecraft's most troubling horror tales, but the horror is the horror of miscegenation or, specifically, miscegenation by blood. Sir Wade Jermyn is a privileged member of an exalted race, occupying the top of the racial totem pole. Yet, he encounters the white ape princess, who occupies a lower position on that same totem pole. And though Sir Wade is repulsed by her, at least intellectually and morally, he is also attracted to her. And ultimately, his sexual desire gets the better of him and he is willing to lay aside his high intellectual and moral standards and condescend to have sexual relations with her. Similarly, Lovecraft is suggesting, some whites are willing to do the same thing when it comes to members of the Black race. However, whether the consort is an ape, a hybrid, or an African American, in Lovecraft's view, miscegenation always debases the white partner of whatever gender and results in the production of hybrids, which are a violation of natural or divine law and which, invariably, suffer unpleasant, usually catastrophic outcomes. Thus, Sir Wade is driven insane and each of the Jermyn hybrids is punished in one way or another for his transgressions.

Even more troubling than the fate of Sir Wade or his family, however, Lovecraft is suggesting that his account of the Jermyn hybrids is not merely a localized, isolated incident. That is, "Arthur Jermyn" is more than a story about the decline and destruction of an entitled, English family. There is the strong implication in this tale (and, as we will see, in all of the tales examined in Part II) that miscegenation by blood—or, for that matter, miscegenation by association—is a significant, contributing factor in the decline of Western civilization. Thus, when white Anglo-Saxons have sexual relationships with Blacks and other members of the races on Lovecraft's "hit list" and hybrid children are produced, they are not only ruining themselves but contributing—even if only in a small way—to the destruction of the greatest civilization and culture in the history of humankind.

7

Herbert West—Reanimator (1922)

"Herbert West—Reanimator" is a six-part serial that Lovecraft wrote specifically for George Julian Houtain, a friend from his amateur journalism days, who had decided to launch a new magazine *Home Brew* in September 1921. Houtain asked Lovecraft to make the serial as "grewsome" and morbid" as he felt inclined to and Lovecraft certainly rose to the challenge. Lovecraft completed the first two tales in October and the third shortly after; then there was almost a five-month interval between those tales and the fourth; the last tale was finished in June 1921. The series ran eight months later, from February to July 1922. Each tale was roughly two thousand words in length and Lovecraft was paid only $5 for each installment, which netted him a grand total of $30; this translates into a quarter of a cent per word, which was, as has often been pointed out by critics, a "rock bottom" price. But at least Lovecraft was paid promptly—which was not often the case—and had the satisfaction of seeing his work finally published in a professional magazine. Up until then, his work had only appeared in amateur newsletters and journals. In letters to colleagues, Lovecraft described the Herbert West stories as "mechanical" and "unimaginative." However, when we examine these tales objectively, it becomes apparent that they are nothing of the sort. There is little that could be considered formulaic about any of the installments and the series as a whole is well-conceived and well-written. In addition, the overall plot is strong, which, no doubt, explains why the series was successfully adapted for the cinema in 1985 by director Stuart Gordon. Titled simply *Re—Animator*, the film was filled with plenty of sex, black humor, and gore, but is nevertheless a solid and faithful adaptation of the original text (a claim that cannot be made for most other Lovecraft adaptations). *Re—Animator* ended up doing very well at the box office and though it could not be described exactly as a runaway hit, it generated respectable profits and took first prize at the Paris Festival of Fantasy, Science Fiction and Horror. In fact, it was even awarded a special prize at the Cannes Film Festival for that season. The film was followed by two sequels: *Bride of Re—Animator* (1989) and *Beyond Re—Animator* (2003), both directed by Brian Yuzna; these films were less successful than their predecessor.

"Herbert West—Reanimator" follows the career of Herbert West, a brilliant young medical student at Miskatonic Medical School in Arkham, Massachusetts, and his unnamed assistant (who serves as narrator throughout the series). West has developed a chemical reagent to reanimate corpses, the only stipulation being that the bodies must be freshly dead—once the process of decomposition begins, the bodies can no longer be brought back. The goal of the experiments is to restore deceased humans to full human life, with the ability to speak, think, and reason. After the two students get their medical degrees, they continue their experiments off-campus. They are in practice during the typhoid epidemic in Arkham; in a working-class town near the city; as surgeons attached to a Canadian regiment in the Great War; and finally in an old house near a burial ground in Boston. They reanimate a succession of corpses, but in all cases, the corpses become monsters and must be incinerated after the experiments or else disposed of in other, unpleasant ways. Yet, a few of the monsters manage to escape and band together to take revenge against West for subjecting them to the reanimation process. Most of the monsters are mindless, but one or two are intelligent enough to lead the rest. Eventually, they track West down to the house in Boston and show up in the basement. They end up confronting West and literally tear him to pieces with their bare hands.

***

Lovecraft scholars have seen parallels between the West series and Mary Shelley's *Frankenstein* (1818), a novel that Lovecraft knew and admired. It might do well to examine this particular issue up front before getting down to our analysis of the tale since, superficially at least, the two works appear to be similar—that is, they both have a mad scientist; they both have laboratory-created monsters; and the monsters take revenge on their creators. When we read the Shelley novel and "Herbert West—Reanimator" together, however, it quickly becomes clear that they are very different from each other in two significant ways. First, Victor Frankenstein creates a single entity from a collection of disparate body parts taken from charnel houses, dissecting rooms, and cemeteries and then infuses it with life. In contrast, West reanimates a succession of freshly buried dead bodies; he does not really create anything. Indeed, the reanimation process is only possible if there is still a spark of life existing in the corpses. And interestingly, West is able to reanimate body parts as well. By the time we reach the fifth tale in the series, West experiments on reanimating both a headless torso and its severed head—"fractionally human" parts, as Lovecraft puts it.[1] This, of course, is something that never even occurs to Victor Frankenstein in the Shelley novel. The doctor respects the integrity of the human form and, to his credit, he tries hard to create an attractive creature: "His limbs were in proportion, and I had selected his features as beautiful." But the final result is less than satisfying, to say the least.[2]

A second, more important difference between *Frankenstein* and the West story is that Shelley's monster is capable of learning and evolving, unlike West's reanimated corpses. Once Dr. Frankenstein sees how hideous his creature is, he abandons him and the creature takes up his residence in the bordering woods. The creature sees his reflection in a pool of water and knows he looks frightening to humans. He hides out in an abandoned structure that is connected to a cottage and is able to study closely a family living there. Over a period of a few months, he learns to speak merely by listening to the cottagers converse. When a foreign visitor to the cottage appears, one of the cottagers teaches her to read and write in English and so, the creature likewise learns these skills. The creature's ability to read is augmented when he discovers a satchel of books. These are all works that were cherished by nineteenth-century romantic writers: Goethe's *Sorrows of Werter* (1779), Milton's *Paradise Lost* (1667), and Plutarch's *Parallel Lives* (circa 101–200 CE). These books inspire the Frankenstein monster and act as a spur to his intellectual growth. It could be argued, in fact, that the books give him a "soul," such as it is. The monster also identifies with Milton's Satan, who was cast out of heaven by God. Indeed, the monster feels himself in an even worse situation than Satan since the latter at least had the other fallen angels as companions to commiserate with. But the monster has no one to comfort him and Dr. Frankenstein refuses to create a mate for him, thinking (probably rightly) that this will lead to the generation of a new race of entities that will compete with humans. The creature's rage over his aloneness and his abandonment by his creator are the direct causes for the killings that he carries out in the latter half of the novel.

The monsters that comprise West's menagerie, by contrast, are not capable of the niceties of philosophical speculation that the Frankenstein monster indulges in. They cannot identify with literary prototypes such as Satan or, indeed, with any other fictional or living thing outside of themselves. They cannot bemoan their condition in life. And certainly, they cannot speculate about what they are or where they fit into the cosmic scheme, as does the Frankenstein monster. Likewise, they cannot read, or even speak—other than a few disjoined words at the beginning of the reanimation process. West's assistant, in fact, notes how *silent* the West menagerie are as they gather together to carry out the denouement in the final tale.

> There was no sound, but just then the electric lights went out and I saw outlined against some phosphorescence of the nether world a horde of silent toiling things which only insanity—or worse—could create. ... They were removing the stones quietly, one by one, from the centuried wall. ... Servants found me unconscious in the morning. West was gone ... Detectives have questioned me, but what can I say? ... They imply that I am a madman or a murderer—probably I am mad. But I might be not so mad if those accursed tomb-legions had not been so silent.[3]

Obviously, the West menagerie are of subhuman intelligence; they are not capable of evolving beyond the most rudimentary intellectual level.

***

Although West reanimates numerous corpses throughout the series, Lovecraft only describes five specific subjects—his prototypical hybrid, degenerative monsters. The term "hybrid" here is a bit of a misnomer; a hybrid is technically half-human and half something else, but the West menagerie are fully human—or at least, they *used* to be. Nevertheless, they are certainly degenerative and they are 100 percent monster, and Lovecraft uses these monsters as he does all of the hybrids in the early tales to suggest half-black, half-white hybrids. West's subjects include an unnamed, working-class youth; Dr. Allan Halsey, the dean of the Miskatonic University Medical School; Buck Robinson, an African American boxer; Robert Leavitt, a St. Louis businessman; and Major Sir Eric Moreland Clapham-Lee, a surgeon attached to a Canadian regiment during the Great War. In addition, there are also a constantly growing number of monsters, all left unnamed by Lovecraft, who have escaped from West over the course of his ongoing experiments and are in hot pursuit of him.

In the initial tale, "From the Dark," West and his assistant are graduate students finishing up their studies at Miskatonic University. Dr. Halsey has prohibited them from conducting their reanimating experiments on college grounds and so, the two men are forced to seek an alternate location for their laboratory. They choose the Chapman place, a deserted, isolated farmhouse past Meadow Hill on the outskirts of Arkham. Their first subject is an unnamed, "brawny young workman" who is the victim of an accidental drowning in Sumner's Pond. He has no family and is buried quickly at the town's expense without embalming and without a funeral. In his description of this "specimen," Lovecraft lets his readers know exactly what he thinks about young, working-class men—and this is a Caucasian at that, who has not even gone through the reanimation process.

> On an improvised dissecting-table in the old farmhouse, by the light of a powerful acetylene lamp, the specimen was not very special looking. It had been a sturdy and apparently unimaginative youth of wholesome

plebian type—large-framed, grey-eyed, and brown-haired—a sound animal without psychological subtleties, and probably having vital processes of the simplest and healthiest sort. Now, with the eyes closed, it looked more asleep than dead. ... Especially were we apprehensive concerning the mind and impulses of the creature.[4]

Lovecraft does not consider this man to be fully human—the pronoun "it" and the epithet "creature" underscore this. Also noteworthy is that this is a white, Anglo-Saxon man, and yet, Lovecraft still disparages him. This reveals the depths of Lovecraft's antipathy toward any individual who doesn't conform to his elitist views of what a human being should be.

The inhumanity of the dead man increases exponentially after West and his assistant reanimate him. The first injection of the reagent yields no results; it takes a second dose to do the trick. The corpse emits a series of bloodcurdling screams, causing the two doctors to abruptly flee from the laboratory; a lamp is overturned in the process. When they return the next day, they find that the farmhouse is burned to the ground and the hybrid, degenerative monster is gone. But as it turns out, this monster becomes the first member of the army of hybrid, degenerative monsters that will slowly grow over the course of the Herbert West series.

In Lovecraft's next tale, "The Plague-Demon," a typhoid epidemic has hit Arkham. Dr. Halsey, along with his colleagues at the university, volunteers to help treat townspeople who have contracted the disease. Although West and his assistant have by now graduated from the college and are bona fide physicians, free to set up practice wherever they please, nevertheless, they join in the effort and work side by side with their old mentor. Halsey succumbs to the disease in the late summer and predictably, West wastes no time in digging up Halsey's body and then reanimating it. Lovecraft's handling of this particular experiment is subtle; he doesn't actually tell us that West has obtained Halsey's corpse or that a reanimation has taken place; he merely suggests that this is what has occurred. West's landlady discovers West and his assistant lying unconscious on the floor of their room, bloodied up and mauled. Halsey's corpse is nowhere to be found. But later, an unnamed hybrid, degenerative monster goes on a killing spree and once it is captured, the authorities can see a physical likeness between this creature and Halsey.

As Lovecraft describes what the reanimated Halsey now looks like, racist images creep into the text.

A few persons had half seen it in the dark, and said it was white and like a malformed ape or anthropomorphic fiend. It had not left behind quite all that it had attacked, for sometimes it had been hungry. ... The thing was finally stopped by a bullet, though not a fatal one. ... it had been a man. This much was clear despite the nauseous eyes, the voiceless simianism, and the daemoniac savagery. They dressed its wound and carted it to the asylum at Sefton. ... What had most disgusted the searchers of Arkham was the thing they noticed when the monster's face was cleaned—the mocking, unbelievable resemblance to a learned and self-sacrificing martyr who had been entombed but three days before—the late Dr. Allan Halsey, public benefactor and dean of the medial school of Miskatonic University.[5]

Halsey in life was a distinguished looking white man; now, he is represented as a savage ape, reminiscent of the Jermyn hybrids.

The third tale, "Six Shots by Moonlight," provides full scope for Lovecraft's racial ire. West and his assistant have set up as general practitioners in Bolton, a factory town near Arkham. The sport of boxing has been outlawed in Bolton, but fights are still held surreptitiously. One evening, there is a match between an Irish boxer, Kid O'Brien, and a Black boxer, Buck Robinson, also known as "The Harlem Smoke." Robinson is killed and the organizers of the event, fearing police intervention, call in West to take the body away and dispose of it. West is only too happy to do so. Lovecraft unleashes a torrent of racist images in his description of Robinson even *before* Robinson transforms into a hybrid, degenerative monster.

> The negro had been knocked out, and a moment's examination shewed us that he would permanently remain so. He was a loathsome, gorilla-like thing, with abnormally long arms which I could not help calling fore legs, and a face that conjured up thoughts of unspeakable Congo secrets and tom-tom poundings under an eerie moon. The body must have looked even worse in life—but the world holds many ugly things.[6]

This is the most racist passage in the Herbert West series. But of course, given Lovecraft's opinion of African Americans, this should hardly surprise us.

The Harlem Smoke proves to be unresponsive to the reanimation process and West is forced to bury the corpse in an adjoining field. But Robinson is not dead and the next night, he digs his way out of his shallow grave and snatches a five-year-old child from its parents, then partially devours it. After this horrendous act, Robinson shows up on West's doorstep and West is forced to put six bullets in him, ending his brief half-life as a hybrid. Lovecraft's description of Robinson after the transformation is much more animalistic than his descriptions of the Caucasian members of the West menagerie.

> Looming hideously against the spectral moon was a gigantic misshapen thing not to be imagined save in nightmares—a glassy-eyed, ink-black apparition nearly on all fours, covered with bits of mold, leaves, and vines, foul with caked blood, and having between its glistening teeth a snow-white, terrible, cylindrical object terminating in a tiny hand.[7]

Robinson has devolved into a ghastly parody of a grinning, minstrel show Negro, chomping on a half-eaten arm rather than strumming a banjo.

In "The Scream of the Dead," the fourth tale, West and his assistant are still living in Bolton, eking out a living as general practitioners. West has developed a more powerful reagent serum, but he needs his next subject to be extra fresh: a living man, in short, and he plots on the best way to achieve this. The assistant is away, visiting his parents in Illinois and so, West is free to act as he chooses. By a lucky chance, Robert Leavitt, a traveling salesman, arrives in the town and stops at the West cottage to ask for directions to the Bolton Worsted Mills, where Leavitt has some business to transact. West, of course, sees this as "a heaven-sent gift."[8] Working alone, West overpowers the man, straps him to the operating table, and injects him with a special compound that puts him in a coma and keeps his body fresh until the assistant returns. Once the assistant is back home, West tells him that Leavitt had died from a heart attack, though Leavitt is still alive—but not for long. West deactivates the compound, smothers Leavitt, and then injects his body with the new reagent serum. At first, it looks as if the experiment might be successful; the subject wakes up and opens his eyes and, to the assistant, his eyes seem calm and he appears to be softly articulating words and phrases. But then, the situation changes for the worst.

> For that very fresh body, at last writhing into full and terrifying consciousness with eyes dilated at the memory of its last scene on earth, threw out its frantic hands in a life and death struggle with the air; and suddenly collapsing into a second and final dissolution. ... screamed out the cry that will ring eternally in my aching brain: "Help! Keep off, you cursed little tow-head fiend—keep that damned needle away from me!"[9]

As this passage makes clear, West's new experiment proves to be yet another failure, just as the others were, though now, West's assistant knows that his friend and partner—"the man with whom my professional fortunes were joined"—as the assistant puts it,[10] is actually a murderer.

In the fifth and second-to-the-last tale, "The Horror from the Shadows," West and his assistant are using an even stronger reanimating serum and this yields even more startling results than those with the body of the Bolton businessman. The physicians have decided to leave Bolton and they enlist in the Great War, attached to a Canadian regiment in Flanders, Germany. Their immediate supervisor is Major Sir Eric Moreland Clapham-Lee, DSO, a brilliant physician. During the course of their tour of duty, Clapham-Lee's plane is shot down and his body ends up decapitated. Such a circumstance might be considered as a deal breaker as far as the reanimation process is concerned, but West is undeterred. He, with the help of his assistant, reanimates Clapham-Lee's body and the trunk, dutifully, comes back to life.

But surprisingly, the detached head—which is being kept in a nearby vat—also reanimates.

> The body on the table had risen with a blind and terrible groping, and we had heard a sound. I should not call that sound a voice, for it was too awful. And yet its timbre was not the most awful thing about it. Neither was its message—it had merely screamed, "Jump, Ronald, for God's sake, jump!" The awful thing was its source. For it had come from the large, covered vat in that ghoulish corner of crawling black shadows.[11]

Here, Clapham-Lee is screaming out his final memories just before he died, just as the Bolton businessman did when he was reanimated, though this time around, West himself isn't implicated in the death of his subject.

* * *

The life and career of Herbert West is a nearly perfect illustration of Lovecraft's pattern of loss and failure, as worked out in his early weird tales, and it stands up well against his more mature treatments of the pattern in the later tales. Physically, West is almost a stereotypical white, Anglo-Saxon man—he could, in fact, be seen as an idealized member of the Hitler Youth organization set up by Adolf Hitler in 1933 for educating and training young males in Nazi principles. As the assistant describes him:

> West confided to me his resolution to get fresh human bodies. ... West was then a small, slender, spectacled youth with delicate features, yellow hair, pale blue eyes, and a soft voice, and it was uncanny to hear him dwelling on the relative merits of Christchurch Cemetery and the potter's field. We finally decided on the potter's field, because practically every body in Christchurch was embalmed; a thing of course ruinous to West's researches.[12]

This is an important description because it not only pins down West's physical appearance but gives us a glimpse into his psychological makeup as well. He is an apparently mild-mannered person and yet, he shows a reckless disregard for proper protocols when it comes to procuring specimens for his work. Also, he exhibits a fascination for the charnel house and for the darker aspects of his work.

In the first three installments of the series, West proves to be a serious, dedicated scientist, committed to overcoming the limitations and the finality of death. But when we get to the fourth tale, West's assistant begins to notice a change in his colleague. As he describes it, "West was more avid than I, so that it almost seemed to me that he looked half-covetously at any very healthy living physique."[13] As it turns out, West does more than merely look covetously at living people; as we have seen, he kills a living, healthy man in

Bolton. When West's assistant finds out about this, he begins to grow more and more afraid of his colleague. After the Bolton incident, while West and his assistant are serving in the Canadian regiment, West degenerates even further. And his assistant's fears have, correspondingly, also increased.

> Gradually, I came to find Herbert West himself more horrible than anything he did—that was when it dawned on me that his once normal scientific zeal for prolonging life had subtly degenerated into a mere morbid and ghoulish curiosity and secret sense of charnel picturesqueness. His interest became a hellish and perverse addiction to the repellently and fiendishly abnormal; he gloated calmly over artificial monstrosities which would make most healthy men drop dead from fright and disgust; he became, behind his pallid intellectuality, a fastidious Baudelaire of physical experiment—a languid Elagabalus of the tombs.[14]

Comparing West to Baudelaire, the nineteenth-century French poet and debauchee, and Elagabalus, a Roman emperor from 218 to 222 CE, noted for his sex scandals, illustrates that the assistant sees West as complicit in his own impending failure and downfall, just as Baudelaire and Elagabalus were. West is not more "sinned against than sinning," as will be the case for most of Lovecraft's later privileged protagonists, Nathaniel Wingate Peaslee, for example, in "The Shadow Out of Time," or Robert Olmstead, in "The Shadow Over Innsmouth." West, in fact, is much like Lovecraft himself; he appears to have been *psychologically predisposed* to bring about his own demise. Certainly, as I have shown in Chapters 1 and 2, Lovecraft was psychologically predisposed to the succession of losses and failures that he experienced after his privileged lifestyle fell apart. There is, however, one important difference between Lovecraft's case and West's; though both of their lives could be described as tragic, Lovecraft's loss was confined only to a decline in status and economic well-being, while West's loss—like the losses of most of the other privileged protagonists—is literally catastrophic.

The denouement of "Herbert West—Reanimator" is sudden and dramatic. This occurs in the final tale in the series, "The Tomb Legions." West and his assistant are living in an old house near a burying ground in Boston. For some time, they have had suspicions that a group of their previously reanimated subjects have been pursuing them. They see an article in the local newspaper describing a recent incident that occurs in the Sefton Asylum in Arkham, only fifty miles away from Boston. A group of silent men invade the asylum, beat and trample the attendants, then liberate Dr. Allan Halsey. The men are led by a menacing military figure whose head is made of wax with painted eyes—obviously, this is the decapitated body of Major Clapham-Lee. West is almost literally paralyzed by what he is reading; he has fallen into the same kind of stasis that Lovecraft himself experienced on the day his mother died (coincidentally, Lovecraft was working on this serial at the same time). In the evening, a box is left on his doorstep; it contains the actual head of the major. West finally rouses himself and goes down into the basement to incinerate the head. The assistant accompanies him. While they are doing this, the West menagerie suddenly break through the falling plaster of the walls. The assistant is knocked unconscious, but the monsters tear West apart with their bare hands, then carry off the fragments. West's head is taken by the major, and as it disappears into the darkness, the assistant notes: "I saw that the blue eyes behind the spectacles were hideously blazing with their first touch of frantic, visible emotion."[15]

Herbert West's response to the attack of the hideous menagerie that he created himself is disbelief, shock, and immobility. Here, once again, we see the culmination of the pattern of loss and failure. The crisis is sparked, naturally, by a basement full of bloodthirsty monsters, but West is too traumatized to put up a fight or to even consider trying to escape. As Lovecraft writes, "West did not resist or utter a sound."[16] He literally doesn't do a thing; he just gives up. In this, he is acting in a similar manner to Sir Arthur Jermyn, who likewise gives up the fight at the end of "Arthur Jermyn."

* * *

During the course of Herbert West's mental decline in the six installments of "Herbert West—Reanimator," Lovecraft's miscegenation narrative is in play: miscegenation by association, to be specific, in which a member of the white race associates closely with non-Anglo-Saxons and then, due to his or her proximity to these inferior races, the Anglo-Saxon slowly becomes less "pure" and ultimately succumbs to ruin. Herbert West's experiments, over time, have begun to tarnish him morally and, perhaps, *spiritually*. West becomes increasingly perverse, cold-hearted, and inhuman as the reanimations continue. His assistant recognizes this painful fact in the fourth installment of the series and the reader has no trouble doing so as well. Indeed, it is not difficult to pick up on Lovecraft's equating of the West menagerie with the non-Anglo-Saxon races and Lovecraft's equally obvious implication that a close connection to Blacks or "mongrel" races can likewise turn an Anglo-Saxon into a monster.

Lovecraft's concerns and fears about the decline of Western civilization are at the forefront of the West series. West's personal decline is, like Arthur Jermyn's, more or less a localized phenomenon, but it has wider implications as well. Anglo-Saxons who condescend to associate intimately with hybrids, Blacks, and the members of the other degraded, nonwhite races—even if the association does not involve miscegenation by blood—nevertheless risk personal loss and contribute to the decline and destruction of Western civilization. And, as in the case of Herbert West, the privileged white Anglo-Saxon is not protected by his privilege, his intellect, or his elite status; he will come to ruin in spite of these entitlements just the same.

8

The Lurking Fear (1923)

Barely a year after writing "Herbert West—Reanimator," Lovecraft wrote another serial for G. J. Houtain's *Home Brew*, which he entitled "The Lurking Fear." Apparently, the first series had been popular enough for the editor to request more of the same and Lovecraft was only too willing to comply. This time around, Lovecraft wrote four installments instead of six, each roughly around two thousand words or thereabouts. "The Lurking Fear" appeared in *Home Brew* in January 1923, February 1923, March 1923, and April 1923, respectively. In a letter to his fellow *Weird Tales* contributor, Clark Ashton Smith, dated December 2, 1922, Lovecraft disparaged the stories, calling them "frightfully wooden & mechanical."[1] As we have seen, he did the same sort of thing when it came to "Herbert West—Reanimator" in earlier letters to colleagues. But the new serial hardly warrants this criticism; given the natural limitations of the serial format, "The Lurking Fear" is, on the whole, very effectively written and suspenseful and it builds to an impressive conclusion.

The plot of the series is, of course, unbelievably turgid. The unnamed narrator comes to the deserted Martense mansion on Tempest Mountain in an isolated part of the Catskills, New York, to investigate the strange series of murders and disappearances among the squatter communities in the surrounding environs. These incidents have been happening periodically over the last two centuries, usually during the summer months and always when thunderstorms are raging. Exactly *what* is terrorizing the community is not known; the locals refer to it as the "lurking fear" and speculate wildly about what this is, but no one has observed it directly and thus, they can do little more than speculate. The narrator is accompanied by two friends and the three spend the night in the abandoned and partly ruined mansion. During the course of the vigil, the narrator falls asleep and wakes up suddenly due to a thunderbolt; he sees a strange shadow on the chimney, but his companions have disappeared. Later, he returns with another companion, who is killed horribly, though again, the perpetrator remains unknown. The narrator discovers finally that the lurking fear consists of a group of degenerate cannibals—the remnants of the Martense family—who live in the extensive network of caverns and tunnels that underpin the area around the mansion. They come to the surface during thunderstorms to attack and kidnap individuals from the squatter communities. The narrator, digging in the cellar of the mansion, finds a passageway that leads directly to the lair of the Martense cannibals. As another thunderstorm begins to rage, a large group of the creatures emerges and the narrator shoots one of them, then manages to escape. It takes him a week to recover from this traumatic experience. When he does, he returns with a posse of men, who dynamite the Martense mansion and the top of Tempest Mountain; the men also stop up entrances to the tunnels, making it impossible for any of the surviving cannibals to carry out future attacks.

* * *

"The Lurking Fear" explores the same subjects that we saw in "Arthur Jermyn" and the West series. There is, of course, the threat that hybrids and hybridism represent for white Anglo-Saxons and, by implication, white civilizations in general. Also, there is the threat of miscegenation, since this is, after all, responsible for the generation of the Martense cannibals in the first place. However, Lovecraft introduces two new plot motifs into his fiction in this new tale. First, he identifies what he calls the "swarm instinct" in hybrid, degenerative monsters, an instinct that is shared (at least in his mind) with the immigrant populations in New York City and elsewhere. Lovecraft "discovered" the swarm instinct when he took a walk through Chinatown in lower Manhattan early in May 1922, just a few months before he began working on "The Lurking Fear."

> Klei [Reinhardt Kleiner] ... proceeded to lead us into the slums, starting with "Chinatown" as an ulterior objective. My gawd—what a filthy dump! I thought Providence had slums, and antique Bostonium as well; but damn me if I ever saw the sprawling sty-atmosphere of N.Y.'s lower East side. We walked—at my suggestion—in the middle of the street, for contact with the heterogeneous sidewalk denizens, spilled out of their bulging brick kennels as if by a spawning beyond the capacity of the places, was not by any means to be sought. At times, though, we struck peculiarly deserted areas—these swine have instinctive swarming movements, no doubt, which no ordinary biologist can fathom. Gawd knows what they are ... a bastard mess of stewing mongrel flesh without intellect, repellent to eye, nose, and imagination—would to heaven a kindly gust of cyanogen could asphyxiate the whole gigantic abortion, end the misery, and clean out the place.[2]

In "The Lurking Fear," the Martense cannibals, likewise, seem inclined to "swarm"; and in the tales that follow, we will see this same swarming instinct among the members of the Delapore clan and the swarthy immigrants in the Red Hook district of Brooklyn.

As a second plot-motif, the Martense cannibals prefer living in underground places: caverns, catacombs, tombs, tunnels, grottos, or buried cities. In his very earliest fiction, Lovecraft shows a penchant for linking his horrors with these kinds of places—examples include "The Beast in the Cave" (1905), "The Statement of Randolph Carter" (1920), "The Outsider" (1921), and "The Festival" (1923). That Lovecraft retained his fascination with underground locales while he was beginning to plan "The Lurking Fear" is revealed in a passage that appears in an otherwise innocuous letter to his aunt Lillian (Mrs. F. C. Clark), dated September 29, 1922. Lovecraft was visiting an old Dutch Reformed Church in Brooklyn, New York, and his experience yielded the following impression:

> From one of the crumbling gravestones—dated 1747—I chipped a small piece to carry away. It lies before me as I write—and ought to suggest some sort of a horror-story ... who can say what *thing* might not come out of the centuried earth to exact vengeance for his desecrated tomb? And should it come, who can say what it might not resemble? At midnight, in many antique burying-grounds, shadows steal terribly about ... They have no voices, but sometimes do hideous deeds silently.[3]

In "The Lurking Fear," the Martense cannibals make effective use of the "centuried earth" to terrorize the squatter communities around Tempest Mountain; they come out of the various mounds that dot the landscape when storms are raging and then return the same way after they have completed their rampages. In "The Rats in the Walls" and "The Horror at Red Hook," the Delapore clan and the immigrant hordes also prefer to mount their attacks from below, doing their "hideous deeds" and then retreating back to their subterranean lairs. In his later, more sophisticated weird tales, the underground lairs morph into vast, extensive underground cities—the cities of the Great Race and the Elder Things, in "The Shadow Out of Time" and *At the Mountains of Madness*, to name just two, and even, in the case of the Innsmouth mutants in "The Shadow Over Innsmouth," vast *underwater* cities.

Critics have attempted to account for Lovecraft's obvious fascination with underground locales, and a number of them have concocted rather convoluted Freudian and/or Jungian explanations in an effort to explain this fascination. For example, Gavin Callaghan, in *H. P. Lovecraft's Dark Arcadia* (2013), argues that Lovecraft's underground locales are symbolic of the Dionysian, chthonian female principle—the Great Mother of antiquity—and that Lovecraft, in turn, feared this primal principle, identifying it with his mother.⁴ Similarly, Sara Williams, in "'The Infinitude of the Shrieking Abysses:' Rooms, Wombs, Tombs, and the Hysterical Female Gothic in 'The Dreams in the Witch-House'" (2013), following Callaghan, argues that Lovecraft's underground locales should be interpreted as wombs, or even vaginas dentata ("vaginas with teeth"); thus, Williams argues, Lovecraft is unconsciously expressing his fear and hatred of women, both his mother and other women in general.⁵ Both of these readings are certainly spirited, but there is little textual evidence in Lovecraft's fiction or correspondence to support them. Granted, Lovecraft was a bit of a misogynist and not particularly demonstrative in expressing his feelings toward either his mother or any other woman, but he certainly did not hate or fear them, and he didn't harbor any apprehensions about "the Great Inside of the mother's body," as Williams puts it.⁶ This is a problem, I think, with criticism that advances various so-called psychological analyses of Lovecraft; there is usually little empirical evidence for doing so. As for formal psychoanalysis, whether used for literary analysis or for probing the depths of the mind in the case of actual patients, Lovecraft had little use for it. Lovecraft's focus throughout his writings is never on humankind in terms of the "inner" man or woman; he couldn't have cared less about the Id, the Unconsciousness, the Subconsciousness, or what have you—they were to him as much chimeras as are the Christian God and the gods and goddesses of other religions.

Indeed, it is far more sensible to trace Lovecraft's fascination with underground locales to a simple childhood phobia—one of the many phobias that Lovecraft was subject to over the course of his life. In a letter to Harry O. Fischer, written in late February 1937, Lovecraft describes this phobia:

> Of the celebrated "phobias" of the modern psychologists ... I have only *one*; & that, amusingly enough, is one that I have never seen cited or named. ... I know about *claustrophobia* & *agoraphobia*, but have neither. I have, however, a *cross betwixt the two*—in the form of a distinct fear of *very large, enclosed spaces*. The dark carriage-room of a stable—the shadowy interior of a deserted gas-house—an empty assembly-room or theatre-auditorium—a large cave—you can probably get the idea. Not that such things throw me into visible & uncontrollable jittery spasms, but that they give me a profound & crawling sense of the sinister—even at my age. I'm not sure of the source of this fear, but I believe it must link up somehow with the black abysses of my infant nightmares.⁷

I have made the point several times in this study that Lovecraft was a cold-blooded literary artist who always uses elements from his life, including his phobias and fears (whether based on childhood dreams or not), as fodder for his literary works—thus, it should not be surprising to see him placing his monsters in environments that gave him the creeps when he was a child and, as he confesses above, still do so, that is, "even at my age."

* * *

In "The Lurking Fear," Lovecraft's hybrid, degenerative monsters are a clan of subhuman cannibals descended from a rich, elitist seventeenth-century American family known as the Martenses. In 1670, Gerrit Martense, a wealthy New Amsterdam merchant, decides to take up residence in the Catskills area of New York. This leads to the building of the Martense mansion on Tempest Mountain. Gerrit's rationale for choosing such an out-of-the-way place was that he disliked British rule in the colonies and wished to live a life independent from the political vagaries of the time. There is one ominous note, however; in the summer on Tempest Mountain there are an inordinate number of thunderstorms and Martense, as it turns out, has an aversion to these natural occurrences.

> The only substantial disappointment encountered in this site was that which concerned the prevalence of violent thunderstorms in summer. When selecting the hill and building his mansion, Mynheer Martense had laid these frequent natural outbursts to some peculiarity of the year; but in time he perceived that the locality was especially liable to such phenomena. At length, having found these storms injurious to his health, he fitted up a cellar into which he could retreat from their wildest pandemonium.[8]

I say this is ominous because it appears that right from the start, Gerrit Martense is resigned to living underground in the summer months, temporarily though it is. And this, in turn, serves as the basis for what eventually becomes a permanent thing in the lives of subsequent generations of Martenses.

The members of the Martense clan are characterized by a genetic peculiarity that first originated with Gerrit himself. As Lovecraft describes it, "All were marked by a peculiar inherited dissimilarity of eyes; one generally being blue and the other brown."[9] Over time, due to their isolation from the general cultural and economic flow of the rest of the country, the Martense descendants slowly degenerate.

> Their social contacts grew fewer and fewer, till at last they took to intermarrying with the numerous menial class about the estate. Many of the crowded family degenerated, moved across the valley, and merged with the mongrel population which was later to produce the pitiful squatters. The rest had stuck sullenly to their ancestral mansion, becoming more and more clannish and taciturn, yet developing a nervous responsiveness to the frequent thunderstorms.[10]

Here, we see the usual, racist scenario—the degeneration of the Martense family is due to intermarrying among the members of the "mongrel population." We see, too, that Gerrit Martense's aversion to thunderstorms has now become an inborn, genetic trait that is passed down from generation to generation. Eventually, the Martenses who have elected to remain in the mansion are ostracized by the rest of the outside world—even by the squatters. Finally, in 1810, nearly a hundred and fifty years from the time of the building of the mansion, the lights fail to appear in the windows and a party of investigators find the house partly in ruins and deserted. This, of course, marks the beginning of the Lurking Fear.

When it comes to describing his monsters, Lovecraft takes an entirely different approach in comparison to "Arthur Jermyn" and the Herbert West stories. Lovecraft does not offer specific descriptions of individual cannibals until the very last tale. In the first two tales, Lovecraft only gives the reader a glimpse of an oddly proportioned shadow and then a particularly harrowing image of one of the Lurking Fear's victims. In the third tale, the narrator sees only two eyes shining in the glow of his lamp, along with a claw. The reader, in fact, must wait almost to the end of the fourth tale before seeing specifically what the Lurking Fear actually is. We are given hints, of course, and the squatters have their theories; they come up with a number of wild speculations, including a giant snake, a bat, a vulture, a thunder-devil, and even a walking tree. The idea that the Lurking Fear is a wolf-fanged ghost is postulated as well.

In "The Shadow on the Chimney," the initial tale in the series, it is late summer, 1921, and the narrator and two companions, George Bennett and William Tobey, pay a visit to the Martense mansion. The narrator describes himself as a "connoisseur in horrors"[11]; and he and his friends have been brought to the area in response to newspaper accounts of a recent manifestation of the Lurking Fear. A village of squatters has been attacked and most of them killed, though twenty-five out of an estimated seventy-five have vanished, presumably taken away to serve as food for the cannibals—though, of course, the narrator doesn't know that at this early stage. The three friends search the mansion, but find nothing. At midnight, they camp out in a large room on the second floor. The narrator falls asleep between the others. Then, he is suddenly awakened by a flash of lightning. He sees that Tobey, who was on his right, is missing, but Bennett is still beside him on the left—or at least, he *thinks* that it is Bennett. Bennett leaps up and the narrator sees his shadow on the chimney. But it is not the shadow of his friend.

> That I am still alive and sane, is a marvel I cannot fathom. I cannot fathom it, for the shadow on that chimney was not that of George Bennett or of any other human creature, but a blasphemous abnormality from hell's nethermost craters; a nameless, shapeless abomination which no mind could fully grasp and no pen even partly describe. In another second

I was alone in the accursed mansion, shivering and gibbering. George Bennett and William Tobey had left no trace, not even of a struggle. They were never heard of again.[12]

What exactly happened here is not clear; obviously, the narrator's friends have been taken by the Martense cannibals, but the description almost suggests that Bennett had transformed into one of the monsters in the process. Or perhaps, Bennett had been taken before the narrator woke up and one of the monsters was lying beside him, getting ready to snatch him as well. In any case, the narrator doesn't get a direct look at the monster (or the monsters) that took his friends.

In the second tale, "A Passer in the Storm," Lovecraft gives us even less information about the Lurking Fear than he has previously. It is now October, about two months after the narrator's experiences in the Martense mansion. The narrator returns to the Catskills with a new companion, Arthur Munroe, one of the reporters still hanging around the scene of the recent destruction of the squatter village. The two men question some of the squatters, and Lovecraft insists on telling us that they found the squatters "curiously likeable in many ways. Simple animals they were, gently descending the evolutionary scale because of their unfortunate ancestry and stultifying isolation."[13] The narrator and Munroe comb over every inch of the decimated village, looking for clues as to the nature of the Lurking Fear, but find nothing. Though it is still day, the skies begin to darken and they can hear the rumble of a thunderstorm in the distance. When the storm hits, they take refuge inside one of the "least porous" cabins. The narrator sits on a rickety box as the storm rages, contemplating his future options. Munroe, on the other hand, stands by the window, watching the flashes of lightning and listening to the peals of the thunder. Gradually, the storm blows over and the sun begins to emerge from the clouds. The narrator prepares to leave, but oddly, Munroe doesn't move away from the window. Instead, he continues to look out. As the narrator tries to rouse him, Lovecraft gives us one of the creepiest passages to appear in his early work:

> I saw nothing to justify the interest which kept my companion silently leaning out the window. Crossing to where he leaned, I touched his shoulder; but he did not move. Then, as I playfully shook him and turned him around, I felt the strangling tendrils of a cancerous horror whose roots reached into illimitable pasts and fathomless abysms of the night that broods beyond time. For Arthur Munroe was dead. And on what remained of his chewed and gouged head there was no longer a face.[14]

It defies logic that this man's face could be so violently ripped from his head and yet, he continues to stand by the window. But there are no clues here as to what killed Munroe—whether snake, ghost, or something else.

In the third tale, "What the Red Glare Meant," it is now becoming clear to the narrator that the Lurking Fear is a clan of marauding cannibals. He should have figured this out much sooner, especially since he had observed right from the beginning all the strange mounds that are positioned all over the area—surely, bipedal things that can climb and run must be going into and out of them. It is November and the narrator is back at work near the Martense mansion, digging around in the grave of Jan Martense, one of Gerrit's sons. He discovers a tunnel that leads into a larger space and naturally, he decides to explore it. He ends up encountering a creature that is human shaped, though the narrator doesn't get a clear look—he can see only a set of eyes and a claw.

> I had been scrambling ... for some time, so that my [flashlight] battery had burned very low, when the passage suddenly inclined sharply upward, altering my mode of progress. And as I raised my glance it was without preparation that I saw glistening in the distance two daemoniac reflections of my expiring lamp; two reflections glowing with a baneful and unmistakable effulgence, and provoking maddeningly nebulous memories. ... The eyes approached, yet of the thing that bore them I could distinguish only a claw. But what a claw! Then far overhead I heard a faint crashing which I recognized. It was the wild thunder of the mountain, raised to hysteric fury—I must have been crawling upward for some time, so that the surface was now quite near. And as the muffled thunder clattered, those eyes still stared with vacuous viciousness.[15]

This strange creature quickly runs away. Obviously, it is one of the Martense cannibals. There is another one in the area as well, and this fact is confirmed later when the second monster attacks a family of squatters living in a nearby cabin. The neighbors set fire to the cabin (causing the "red glare" alluded to in the subtitle) and the monster is presumably burned alive—what, if anything, happens to the creature that the narrator saw is not disclosed.

Finally, in the last tale, "The Horror in the Eyes," Lovecraft gives us a clear description of what the Martense cannibals actually look like—no more shadows, glares, or reflections. A week or so after the events described in the previous tale, the narrator returns to the Martense mansion and decides to do some digging in the cellar near the base of the chimney. He unearths a tunnel and prepares to explore it. But then, as if on cue, a thunderstorm comes up and the narrator hides in a dim corner, reasoning that the storm will bring at least one of the monsters to the surface. The narrator gets more than he bargained for; a horde of the cannibals emerge and here, Lovecraft's racist images are fully unleashed. We see the same simian references that we saw in the descriptions of the hybrids in "Arthur Jermyn" and "Herbert West—Reanimator:" "God knows how many there were—there must have been thousands. ... When they had thinned out enough to be glimpsed as separate organisms, I saw that they were dwarfed, deformed hairy devils or apes—monstrous and diabolic caricatures of the monkey tribe."[16]

The narrator understandably feels threatened by this swarming horde of monsters and he shoots one of them. Presumably, the rest of them run away and he inspects the dead cannibal by the glow of his flashlight:

> The object was nauseous; a filthy whitish gorilla thing with sharp yellow fangs and matted fur. It was the ultimate product of mammalian degeneration; the frightful outcome of isolated spawning, multiplication, and cannibal nutrition above and below the ground; the embodiment of all the snarling chaos and grinning fear that lurk behind life. It had looked at me as it died, and its eyes had the same odd quality that marked those other eyes which had stared at me underground. ... One eye was blue, the other brown. They were the dissimilar Martense eyes of the old legends.[17]

The mummy of the white ape in "Arthur Jermyn" was equally "nauseous," "filthy," and "whitish." The Martense cannibals, thus, can take their rightful place beside this artifact or, for that matter, Dr. Allan Halsey or Buck Robinson, the Harlem Smoke. Though Caucasian, the Martense cannibals are as much a confirmation of Lovecraft's fears about the end result of miscegenation as is the image of any half-black, half-white hybrid in Lovecraft's work.

* * *

The narrator of "The Lurking Fear" is not quite as privileged of a white Anglo-Saxon as Arthur Jermyn or Herbert West; he is not a baronet nor is he an accomplished physician. Nevertheless, he appears to have a private income that allows him to travel independently around the country and investigate supernatural or paranormal events; he is, thus, an early twentieth-century version of a demon hunter, seeking out "strange horrors in literature and in life," as Lovecraft puts it.[18] The narrator, also, is apparently a very lucky man; he faces certain death on many occasions throughout the series and yet, always manages to survive. Indeed, he doesn't even get scratched or physically maimed in any way during the course of his visits to the Catskills. When he and his companions, George Bennett and William Tobey, hold a midnight vigil in the Martense mansion, the latter two end up disappearing—taken by the Martense cannibals, perhaps, as a late-night snack. But miraculously, the narrator is spared. Next, when the narrator returns to Tempest Mountain with Arthur Munroe, Munroe is killed when his face is literally ripped off, while the narrator is left alone—the narrator doesn't even see or hear anything when this horrible event takes place, though it is daytime and he is wide awake. The narrator's run of good luck continues when he returns to the community two more times. He is digging in the grave of Jan Martense and encounters one of the Martense cannibals—the set of eyes and the claw described previously—but this monster doesn't attack him. Nor is he molested by the monster's companion, who decides to invade a squatter family's cabin instead. And lastly, in the climactic scene that reveals finally what the Martense cannibals look like, the narrator finds himself facing down a swarming horde of the monsters and saves himself improbably by firing only a single shot, putting the rest of the cannibals to rout.

In spite of his entitlements and his luck, however, the narrator is subject to the same pattern of loss and failure that we have grown accustomed to seeing in the early weird tales. There is a separate crisis in each one of the tales—the strange shadow, the death of Munroe, the eyes and the claw, and so on—and each of these, in turn, sparks a negative effect. Gradually, the negative effects accumulate into a full-fledged, psychological trauma. The narrator lays "nervously exhausted" in his hotel room after the incidents in the first tale; he has "horrible" dreams; he tells us that his "mind was partly unhinged." By the time we get to the third tale, we are told that the horrors he has been experiencing have "grown to cataclysmic stature in [his] imagination."[19] After he sees the eyes and the claw, his brain "was as great a chaos as the earth" and he tells us that he "experienced virtual convulsions of fright."[20] This is, indeed, a trauma, which gradually intensifies over the course of the installments until it reaches the breaking point, signaled by the shooting of the cannibal. At this point, the narrator is forced to flee the district and ends up spending a week recuperating in a peaceful village well away from the Martense mansion and Tempest Mountain. When the narrator is sufficiently recovered, he hires men to dynamite both the mansion and the mountain, overseeing this project himself. Yet, he still wonders if these actions are sufficient to exterminate the Martense cannibals. And he even goes so far as to augment the effects of his trauma by indulging in the thought that similar monsters might lurk in other places throughout the world—"analogous phenomena" to the Lurking Fear—as he calls it.[21]

* * *

The overriding theme of "The Lurking Fear" is the same one that we have been studying in our analysis of the previous tales: the dangers of miscegenation and the threat that intermarriage between races poses for white Anglo-Saxons. Miscegenation by blood, in fact, is what nourishes the spawning of hybrid, degenerative monsters in "The Lurking Fear," and this is something that Lovecraft and his privileged protagonists cannot tolerate—the very thought of it causes them to experience extreme revulsion. As S. T. Joshi notes in *Lovecraft: A Life*:

> The theme of hereditary degeneration will be a significant one in Lovecraft's less openly "cosmic" tales. ... Here the evils of inbreeding

are exposed at their ghastliest. It would be easy to make an armchair Freudian analysis of this theme—involving such things as Lovecraft's general coolness toward sex, the frequency with which members of his own ancestry married their cousins, perhaps even his partial awareness of the cause of his father's death—but I think a racialist interpretation is perhaps more plausible. ... its social implications go well beyond the circumstances of his own life.[22]

Joshi is distracting us here a little by mentioning Lovecraft's well-chronicled aversion to sex and his knowledge—or lack of it—of the cause of his father's death, trying, I think, to downplay the real issue here, which is Lovecraft's racism. But Joshi is right; what is called for in this instance is, indeed, a "racialist" interpretation, and it couldn't be any clearer to the reader that, as far as Lovecraft was concerned, the Martense cannibals are only slightly more repulsive and degenerate than the squatter hordes that play host to them.

Lovecraft's thesis concerning the decline of Western civilization hovers like a deadly plague over "The Lurking Fear." But for the first time in his fictional works, Lovecraft takes his favorite theme to a higher—or, perhaps more appropriately, *lower*—level. The threat of hybrids and hybridism is now expanded out beyond the narrow confines that kept it localized in "Arthur Jermyn" and "Herbert West—Reanimator." Instead of seven hybrid, degenerative monsters, in the first case, and a dozen or so in the second, the Martense cannibals number in the thousands. The area infested by these monsters is expanded out as well; this is no longer the situation of a few hybrids living in an old, English manor, or a lab-based menagerie lurking about in various basement laboratories in and around Arkham. The contagion in "The Lurking Fear" originates in a mansion near the summit of Tempest Mountain in the Catskills and slowly spreads throughout the extensive countryside. Indeed, "The Lurking Fear" represents a first step on the part of Lovecraft's hybrid, degenerative monsters toward American towns and cities. The decline is now inching closer and closer to the great urban metropolises of Western civilization, a process that will reach its fruition in "The Horror at Red Hook."

9

The Rats in the Walls (1924)

"The Rats in the Walls" is among the best of Lovecraft's early tales—some critics argue, in fact, that it is *the* very best. I am not so sure that this claim is justifiable; the tale is undoubtedly an important one in terms of our analysis in this study; in it, Lovecraft offers an entirely different take on his theme of miscegenation (and this is part psychic, part supernatural). Yet, the next tale that we will be considering, "The Horror at Red Hook," is a much greater literary work—much richer, fuller, and more coherently developed, both in terms of plot and characterization. The French critic Barton Levi St. Armand, in a very perceptive, early study of Lovecraft's work, *The Roots of Horror in the Fiction of H. P. Lovecraft* (1977), agrees that "The Rats in the Walls" is of major importance in the Lovecraft corpus. However, for him, the importance doesn't lie so much in the quality of the tale itself but, rather, in the fact that it reveals a link between the early tales and the more mature tales. Barton argues, in fact, that Lovecraft's descent into the catacombs, caverns, and grottos of his imagination in this tale is nothing more or less than an instance of Lovecraft's cosmicism, only Lovecraft approaches the cosmic from the "other end," so to speak, from inside rather than outside—*horror* rather than *terror*, using the distinctions raised by gothic horror writer Ann Radcliffe in "On the Supernatural in Poetry" (1826).

> Yet the archetypal patterns that Lovecraft associates with fear apply most precisely not only to the springs of terror in his fiction (. ... the sublimity of the void) but to those roots of horror—especially traditional Gothic horror. ... For if terror expands the soul and leads to an overwhelming, potentially destructive, sense of cosmic outsideness in Lovecraft's later and longer science-fiction works, then horror is equally annihilating, but from a dramatically different direction. Horror overtakes the soul from the inside; consciousness shrinks or withers from within, and the self is not flung into the exterior ocean of awe but sinks in its own bloodstream,

choked by the alien salts of its inescapable prevertebrate heritage. ... horror is a species of de-evolution.[1]

It is arguable whether or not Lovecraft's cosmicism can be linked in this manner to "consciousness shrinking or withering from within." But nevertheless, I find this to be a more viable interpretation of Lovecraft's use of underground locales in his fiction than those posited by the Freudian/Jungian critics (see Chapter 8), since it rightly sees that Lovecraft's horrors are not rooted in such trite, humancentric things such as his relationships with his mother or with other women, or in his relationships with his male friends and colleagues. Instead, the horrors arise out of Lovecraft's own personal fears and psychological abnormalities. I like, too, St. Armand's phrase: "horror is a species of de-evolution." We have seen that this is, in fact, exactly the case when it comes to Lovecraft's hybrid, degenerative monsters.

Lovecraft wrote "The Rats in the Walls" over a two-month period, August to September 1923; he announced his completion of the tale in a letter to Frank Belknap Long, dated September 4 of that same year. The tale was published in *Weird Tales* in March 1924. Oddly enough, Lovecraft decided to first submit the tale to *Argosy All Story Weekly*, a competitor to *Weird Tales*, but it was rejected by the editor Robert H. Davis as being "too horrible for the tender sensibilities" of the public, as Lovecraft tells us. Edwin Baird, obviously, had the good sense not to worry about such silly things as this and the tale proved to be very popular among *Weird Tales* readers. Particularly appealing was the fact that this apparently gothic tale—with its ancient castle, secret passageways, and hidden chambers—had a modern and up-to-date setting. Lovecraft here was following Bram Stoker, who, in *Dracula* (1897), also updated the gothic, placing most of the action in the London of the 1890s. This "contemporaneousness," as S. T. Joshi labels it, became a "hallmark" of Lovecraft's later work and greatly increased its appeal, not only for readers of the early twentieth century but also for twenty-first-century readers.[2]

The tale is centered around the life and career of Thomas Delapore, a wealthy Virginia manufacturer who represents the American branch of the de la Poer family. The family had originally lived for centuries on the ancestral estate of Exham Priory in Anchester, England, until Walter de la Poer, the eleventh Baron Exham, killed all the members of his household and fled to the New World. Thomas Delapore is determined to regain the Priory; he does so in 1923. Curious about his family history, he searches extant documents and legends and finally traces the family line as far back as the first century CE. Apparently, his ancestors were leaders of a cannibalistic witch-cult, devoted to the worship of pagan gods and goddesses. They practiced their rites in the extensive underground vaults beneath the Priory. Thomas further learns that his grandfather

Walter, also, had discovered the existence of this cult and that members of his immediate family were still practicing the hellish rites; this is why Walter felt compelled to kill them. As the tale progresses, Delapore slowly degenerates, mentally if not physically. The process starts when he begins to hear the sounds of rats in the walls; other than the cats, only he can hear them. In conjunction with these sounds, Thomas has frightening dreams. Delapore and a friend of his deceased son, Captain Norrys, decide to investigate the nethermost regions of the Priory. They enlist the aid of five archaeologists and successfully enter the underground vaults. They discover a vast expanse of bones: mounds and mounds of skeletons, partial skeletons, and disparate bones—these include the victims of the de la Poer witch-cult as well as the de la Poers themselves. This discovery finally pushes Thomas over the edge; he devolves, kills Norrys, and ends up incarcerated at an asylum in Hamwell.

***

In "The Rats in the Walls," Lovecraft deploys his miscegenation narrative, cautioning his readers about the threat that intermingling between different races or cultures can pose for white Anglo-Saxons, both individually and collectively. The miscegenation in this tale is miscegenation by blood, just as it was in "Arthur Jermyn." However, there is a major difference: there is no "alien" or "foreign" blood interjected into the de la Poer clan in the past, as there was in the case of the Jermyns. Rather, there appears to be a genetic strain or perhaps, more accurately, a genetic predisposition in the de la Poers that causes some of them to make the transition from normal human being to bloodthirsty cannibal. There are two elements involved in the process of this transition: the first is reversion to type, while the second is the practice of black magic and occultism. The reason why the Delapores become hybrid, degenerative monsters is due to a combination of both of these elements, as we will see.

The first element, reversion to type, is best defined as the reappearance in a current generation of ancestral characteristics or qualities that have been absent for at least one or more previous generations. Thomas Delapore, during the latter half of "The Rats in the Walls," serves as a nearly perfect case history of how the reversion process works. Under the influence of the unwholesome environment at Exham Priority, coupled with growing delusions about rats living in the walls and increasingly horrifying dreams, he slowly reverts to an earlier, primitive state—something that would not have happened if he had remained in America. The end result is that Thomas transforms into a degenerated, cannibalistic monster. Presumably, Thomas's English ancestors—or at least, those who became cannibals—went through the same process, though Lovecraft doesn't provide any details about their individual transitions; his focus is entirely on Thomas Delapore's passage from man to monster.

Lovecraft develops an interesting theory concerning the evolutionary line between human and nonhuman organisms and this theory lays the foundation for his reversion to type theme. He refers to the theory as the "anthropological background" for his tale. This is how the theory is explained to Frank Belknap Long in a letter dated November 8, 1923:

> No line betwixt "human" and "non-human" organisms is possible, for all animate Nature is one—with differences only in degree; never in kind ... I know that the tendency is to give a separate classification to the Neanderthal—Piltdown-Heidelberg type—using the flashy word "Eoanthropus"—but in truth this creature was probably as much a man as a gorilla. Many anthropologists have detected both negroid and gorilla resemblances in these "dawn" skulls, and to my mind it's a safe bet that they were exceedingly low, hairy negroes existing perhaps 400,000 years ago and having perhaps the rudiments of a guttural language. Certainly, it is not extravagant to imagine the existence of a sort of sadistic cult amongst such beasts, which might later develop into a formal satanism.[3]

Lovecraft's argument here is that there is no firm line separating the different evolutionary stages from human to beast; thus, an individual like Thomas Delapore is able to revert to an earlier stage in humankind's evolution; the capacity to do so was always "in" him, so to speak, and only needed a little psychological prompting to be brought out. Exactly what "type" or missing link that Delapore transforms into is not specified in the tale, though judging from Lovecraft's disparaging remark about low, hairy Negroes, it is a safe bet to assume that Delapore reverted to the higher type that practiced "formal satanism" as opposed to the lower types who indulged in "sadistic" practices more suitable to beasts than to humankind. However, it is important to note that the evolutionary stages between beast and human only go one way, that is, from human to beast, not vice versa. *Thus, evolution for Lovecraft in this tale, as in all of his early tales, is in reality devolution: the Jermyn hybrids, the West menagerie, and the Martense cannibals all devolve*. And this, of course, reflects Lovecraft's careful categorization of evolution in "On the Creation of Niggers." *Homo sapiens* evolved from anthropoids sometime around 30,000 BCE and so, white Anglo-Saxons share DNA with lesser life forms such as the anthropoids. But this process ultimately led to the establishment of groups of carefully selected (and segregated) "pockets" of species with built-in genetic barriers that exclude the members of the lower species from becoming members of the higher species, except by assimilation, though, of course, the reverse is not true—members of the higher species can move between the barriers and devolve.

* * *

The second important element in "The Rats in the Walls" is the theme of black magic and occultism. From this point on, magical backstories are frequently featured in the plots of Lovecraft's minor *and* major fictional works. The magical practices that the Delapore cannibals engage in are a mixture of beliefs and rites derived from three ancient religious sects. The first is a Druid cult, which had originally established a temple on the land that ultimately became Exham Priory. Lovecraft doesn't give us any details about the actual rites that these prehistorical cultists practiced; all that he tells us is that they were "indescribable."[4] The second sect is a Roman cult that built its temple on the same site of the Druid temple (more about this cult shortly). The third sect is a Christian monastery that took over the Roman temple around 1000 CE. This was obviously not an orthodox sect—their rites blended Christian and pagan practices, though again, we are not provided any specific information about the monastery or its rituals. Lovecraft only tells us that it was a "strange and powerful monastic order"[5] and that the villagers who lived near the monastery feared the monks and avoided their extensive gardens.

The Roman cult, thus, is Lovecraft's main focus in the tale. The cult appears to have worshipped three pre-Christian deities: the goddess Cybele; the goddess known as the Magna Mater; and the god Atys. Lovecraft only describes these entities in vague, nonspecific terms and he doesn't elaborate on their natures or powers. Likewise, he doesn't provide actual ritual texts to flesh out exactly how these entities were evoked by the Roman cultists. He does, however, give us some words, phrases, and inscriptions that were supposedly part of the rites. These are etched on the walls of the subcellar beneath the Priory and on the monoliths and ruins buried deeply in the extensive grotto beneath it.

> Inscriptions still visible in the subcellar bore such unmistakable letters as "DIV ... OPS ... MAGNA. MAT ..." sign of the Magna Mater whose dark worship was once vainly forbidden to Roman citizens. ... the walls abounded with inscriptions familiar to the antiquarians who had repeatedly explored the place—things like "P. GETAE. PROP ... TEMP ... DONA ..." and "L. PRAEC ... VS ... PONTIFI ... ATYS."[6]

Later in the tale, Sir William, one of the party of antiquarians who explore the subterranean grotto, discovers remnants of a "shocking" ritual apparently etched on one of the walls. Unfortunately, he doesn't translate this for us; instead, we are told that he translates it only for his companions and Thomas Delapore notes, in passing, that it tells "of the diet of the antediluvian cult which the priests of Cybele found and mingled with their own"—a clear allusion to cannibalism.[7]

Lovecraft's supposedly "hellish" entities in this tale are, of course, nothing of the sort. They are, in fact, not even remotely appropriate target entities for a cannibalistic cult of black magical practitioners. Cybele was originally a Phrygian goddess (Phrygia was located in the area now known as Turkey around the eighth century BCE) and imported into Greece; her name translates as "Mountain Mother" and she was identified with the traditional Greek nature goddesses Gaia, Rhea, and Demeter. Cybele was a bit of a "mystery goddess," as they were called, and she is often depicted as riding on a chariot drawn by lions. Later, she was perceived as the protector of Athens, keeping its citizens safe during wars—hardly the sort of entity to be associated with black magic and cannibalism. In Rome, around 205 BCE, Cybele became known under the name "Magna Mater," which means simply the Great Mother, and she presided over an oracle patterned along the lines of the Sibyllic oracle. Like Cybele, the Magna Mater was a nurturing, nature goddess; she ultimately became the protector of Rome just as she had been for Greece and helped Rome in its continuing wars with neighboring Carthage. Finally, the god Atys (usually spelled Attis) was nothing more than a consort to Cybele—an innocuous god of vegetation. It isn't clear why Lovecraft chose these three entities for "The Rats in the Walls"; their pedigrees were well-known, even in Lovecraft's day, and he was familiar enough with Greek and Roman mythology to select more appropriate entities.

As for the fragmentary words and phrases on the walls of the ruins, these are merely parts of Latin words that Lovecraft found in his readings and then dumped, higgledy-piggledy, into his tale. Some possible meanings include: DIV—divis or divitis, riches—possibly also divinum or divine; OPS—ops or opis—help, aid; opus—work; PROP—propter—"because of"; proprius—peculiar; TEMP—tempus, time; templum—sacred; DONA—donum, gift; PRAEC—praeclarus, noble; praeceplum—precept; and PONTIFI—pontiff, priest. There is nothing particularly mysterious or magical about any of these fragments, and certainly, they provide no evidence that the Cybele worshippers were black magic practitioners. Lovecraft appears to be merely using them to spice up his tale and make it seem more sensationalistic and lurid.

**

The hybrid, degenerative monsters in "The Rats in the Walls" are the descendants of Gilbert de la Poer, the First Baron Exham, who had been granted Exham Priory and its extensive grounds by King Henry the Third just after the Norman Conquest. As we have seen, the Priory had been built on the site of at least three successive pagan cults and there were remnants of the cultists still living on in the areas that were actively practicing magic. Not surprisingly, the earliest de la Poers came into contact with them and, over time, became drawn into the cannibal cult. Before 1261, there were no "evil" reports about the de la Poer family, but afterward, that situation changed. By 1307, the cannibalistic cult is in full operation; this is confirmed by a reference in an unnamed chronicle to the de la Poer Barons as "cursed of God."[8] Local legends up the ante even more, referring to the de la Poers as a race of veritable demons.

> Village legendry had nothing but evil and frantic fear to tell of the castle that went up on the foundations of the old temple and priory. The fireside tales were of the most grisly description, all the ghastlier because of their frightened reticence and cloudy evasiveness. They represented [Delapore's] ancestors as a race of hereditary daemons beside who Gilles de Retz and the Marquis de Sade would seem the veriest tyros, and hinted whisperingly at their responsibility for the occasional disappearance of villagers through several generations. ... The worst characters, apparently, were the barons and their direct heirs.[9]

Interestingly, the cannibal cult is only an "inner cult" in the de la Poer family; it is not a foregone conclusion that individual family members must become cannibalistic, magical practitioners. The de la Poers who *do* join the cult are very aggressive in their recruitment—they weed out those who are not genetically inclined to join up and, in some cases, the evil Barons arrange for the quiet murder of the family members who have "healthier inclinations."[10]

Lovecraft provides a frightening dream-vision of a demonic swineherd, tending a herd of flabby, fungoid beasts in a twilight grotto. Thomas Delapore sees this creature in his dreams on two occasions and clearly, it prefigures the events that follow:

> I seemed to be looking down from an immense height upon a twilit grotto, knee-deep with filth, where a white-bearded daemon swineherd drove about with his staff a flock of fungous, flabby beasts whose appearance filled me with unutterable loathing. ... as I looked at these things they seemed nearer and more distinct—so distinct that I could observe their features. Then I did observe the flabby features of one of them [the face of his friend Norrys]—and awaked with such a scream.[11]

This image is every bit as horrifying and repulsive as Lovecraft's typical hybrid, degenerative monsters. But it is not meant to represent an actual, physically embodied Delapore cannibal; it is a metaphor only, a symbol of what the Delapore cannibals transform into *internally* when they revert to type.

For in fact, the individual members of the Delapore cannibal clan are not monsters at all, at least externally. Nor do they resemble any of the horrors that we have seen in the preceding tales. There is nothing stunted, hairy, deformed, simian, or subhuman about any of them. Lovecraft has a habit of describing his horrors in meticulous detail, but he tends to devote only minimal attention to the physical appearances of most of his normal human characters. In "The Rats in the Walls," Lovecraft only identifies six of the Delapores by name: Thomas, the protagonist; his grandfather Walter; Thomas's son Alfred (who dies as a result of injuries sustained during his brief career in the Royal Flying Corps); Randolph of Carfax, a cousin who became a voodoo priest and "went among the negroes" (heaven forbid!)[12]; and two de la Poer female ancestors: Lady Margaret Trevor from Cornwall, wife of Godfrey, and Lady Mary de la Poer. We must assume that all of these individuals looked like normal human beings, since if they hadn't, then Lovecraft would have told us.

With regard to the two ladies, Lovecraft gives us some additional information that tends to confirm that the de la Poer ancestors were, indeed, the "hereditary daemons" feared by the general populace.

> Lady Margaret Trevor ... became a favourite bane of children all over the countryside, and the daemon heroine of a particularly horrible old ballad not yet extinct near the Welsh border. Preserved in balladry, too, though not illustrating the same point, is the hideous tale of Lady Mary de la Poer, who shortly after her marriage to the Earl of Shrewsfield was killed by him and his mother, both of the slayers being absolved and blessed by the priest to whom they confessed what they dared not repeat to the world.[13]

In looking at these descriptions, it is important to note that neither Lady Margaret nor Mary are being singled out for their external appearances, but rather, for their deeds only. Apparently, they both did unnamed acts that caused them to be celebrated in "horrible old ballads." But that is all.

The most terrifying thing about the Delapore cannibals, then, is that they look just like us. They have no physical traits that might warn us that something is not quite right. They only reveal their true colors when they actually do something revolting, such as killing and eating human beings. Indeed, Thomas Delapore seems normal enough to his friend Captain Norrys and to the party of explorers right up to the climax of the tale, when he suddenly rushes off into the darkness. Even then, none of them realize that Thomas is in the final stages of a mental breakdown; they think that he has had only a panic attack after seeing all the bones—those "nightmare chasms choked with the pithecanthropoid, Celtic, Roman, and English bones of countless unhallowed centuries," as Lovecraft tells us.[14] But they finally realize what Thomas has become when they catch up to him.

***

Initially, Thomas Delapore is a prime example of a privileged, white Anglo-Saxon protagonist. His grandfather Walter de la Poer establishes the American branch of the family in Virginia just before the Civil War and brings his wealth with him. Before leaving Exham Priory, Walter kills off the remaining members of the English branch besides himself—this includes a father, three brothers, and two sisters—for a total of six individuals. Presumably, Walter does this because he had learned that they are cannibalistic cultists (though Thomas doesn't really know the motives behind this act). During the war, Walter is killed and the American manor house is burned to the ground. Thomas's father, however, moves the family north and manages to build up the family fortunes again. When Thomas's father and mother die, Thomas is a wealthy man and he is running a successful manufacturing business. When Thomas is past middle age, he decides to return to England and restore Exham Priory, which is a ruin by that time. His wife is dead and his son is wounded after serving in the Royal Flying Corps (the son dies before the relocation); nevertheless, Thomas is committed to restarting his life in England—he leaves his business in the hands of his partners and then completes the restoration of the Priory, moving in on July 16, 1923.

There are, however, two major red flags that Thomas Delapore ignores as he settles into his ancestral estate. First, he discovers the truth about his ancestors and this is confirmed by the fear and hatred that the local populace in Anchester have long nourished for the de la Poer family over the course of three centuries and still hold for its most recent scion. Second, Thomas learns about a myth known as the epic of the rats—which, as it turns out, is not an ancient myth, but rather, had developed just after his grandfather left the Priory. According to the account, an army of rats appeared suddenly at Exham Priory and descended into the catacombs beneath the building, attacking and killing all living things; this plague of rats, likewise, spread out from the Priory and laid waste to the surrounding countryside, killing foul, cats, dogs, hogs, sheep, and even two human beings. Then, inexplicably, the rats disappeared. This myth is very disturbing to Thomas and it becomes even more so when he starts to have a series of hallucinations about rats living in the Priory. He can hear the rats scurrying in the walls and apparently, they appear to be moving downward into the depths of the catacombs; he can also see the tapestries on the walls moving fitfully, though none of the other human inhabitants in the Priory are able to hear or see anything—this includes Norrys and all the servants. Only the cats in the house are conscious of the presence of the rats.

Clearly, Thomas Delapore's privileged lifestyle is starting to crumble all around him. In addition, Thomas horrific dreams about the demonic swineherd begin to occur around this same time and they add to his overall discomfort and a growing fear that his retirement might not be what he had expected. Thomas' reversion to type is handled brilliantly by Lovecraft in the latter half of "The Rats in the Walls." It can be interpreted solely in psychological terms, that is, Thomas is simply having a mental breakdown. And yet, it is just as likely that Thomas' experience is, indeed, supernaturally based. Barton Levi St. Armand offers just such an interpretation, arguing that Thomas's dreams are, in effect, a "conjuration" or catalyst for the events that follow in the climax of the tale.

> The fact that Delapore is the last of his race and also, *ex officio* as it were, the head of a dangerous cult devoted to gods not quite dead, makes his very dreaming into a conjuration—a black magic practiced by an unwilling, but fatally compelled, black magician. ... Delapore, the unwilling magus of a slowly reviving cult, has also seen a vision of his own secret destiny.[15]

The vision that St. Armand refers to here is, of course, the image of the swineherd. Thus, or so it can be argued, there is a kind of occult, symbiotic connection between Thomas Delapore and the unwholesome atmosphere of Exham Priory itself. Indeed, the subterranean grotto that Thomas doesn't even know about as yet is reaching out to him, seeking to ensnare him into fulfilling his fate.

Though tinged with supernatural overtones, this situation is, nevertheless, a familiar one; it represents another playing out of the pattern of loss and failure that the protagonists in the hybrid, degenerative monster tales seem predestined to follow. The crisis is Delapore's recognition that his ancestors, both ancient and recent, are cannibalistic monsters, and once he becomes fully cognizant of this fact, he falls into a state of immobility and passivity while the reversion to type progresses. As we will see, this prefigures Robert Olmstead's similar reversion to type later on in "The Shadow Over Innsmouth" when Olmstead recognizes that he is an Innsmouth mutant. Unlike Thomas Delapore, however, Olmstead eventually becomes reconciled to his impending sea change and finds the prospect of transforming into a monster as a transcendent, glorifying event and not such a horrible thing after all.

Delapore's reversion to type happens swiftly after he, Norrys, and the five archaeologists discover the entrance to the grotto in the cellar and then promptly descend. The ruins below are quite literally a graveyard of bones, the bones of the de la Poer cannibals and the bones of their victims—the latter having been kept in slave pens. There are not only human bones—some of "supremely and sensitively developed types," we are told—but also the bones of subhumans, both bipeds and quadrupeds, and animals as well. Among these bones are a vast number of rat skeletons, and the bones of other mammals that have been gnawed and damaged by rats; thus, the epic of the rats appears to have been not a myth at all, but an actual fact. The sight of this grotto proves to be too much for Thomas Delapore; he breaks down completely and rushes off into the darkness with Norrys and his cat. Later, the rest of the party discover him in the darkness, eating his friend's dead body. Lovecraft provides an interesting stream-of-consciousness account by Thomas himself as he degenerates into a cannibalistic monster.

Why shouldn't rats eat a de la Poer as a de la Poer eats forbidden things? ... The war ate my boy, damn them all ... and the Yanks ate Carfax with flames and burnt Grandsire Delapore and the secret ... No, no, I tell you, I am *not* that daemon swineherd in the twilit grotto! It was *not* Edward Norrys' fat face on that flabby, fungous thing! Who says I am a de la Poer? He lived, but my boy died! ... Shall a Norrys hold the lands of a de la Poer? ... It's voodoo, I tell you ... that spotted snake ... Curse you, Thornton, I'll teach you to faint at what my family do! ... 'Sblood, thou stinkard, I'll learn ye how to gust ... wolde ye swynke me thilke wys? ... *Magna Mater! Magna Mater! ... Atys ... Dia ad aghaidh's ad aodann ... agus bas dunach ort! Dhonas's dholas ort, agus leat-sa! ... Ungl ... ungl ... rrrlh ... chchch.*[16]

Lovecraft admits in his correspondence that the non-Latin portion of this concluding rant, starting after the reference to Atys, is actually Gaelic, which he lifted from Fiona MacLeod's short story "The Sin Eater" (1920). This doesn't mitigate the horrific effect of the passage, however. The climax of the tale is dramatic for both Thomas and the reader, and Thomas ends up incarcerated in an asylum, as so many of Lovecraft's protagonists do.

***

Lovecraft's miscegenation narrative, specifically miscegenation by blood, is central to "The Rats in the Walls," as we have seen. The de la Poers, including both the English and the American branches, transform into hybrid, degenerative monsters due to some unexplained genetic anomaly in their blood that causes them to revert to savagery. The process, also, as previously noted, involves the practice of black magic. Lovecraft's horrifying image of the demonic swineherd—seen only by Thomas Delapore in his dreams—appears to personify what the de la Poers transform into internally. This demonic swineherd, however, serves a much larger purpose in "The Rats in the Walls."

The white, bearded swineherd seems suspiciously like a traditional, almost even cliché Anglo-Saxon slave master, while his "herd" are very much like slaves—flabby, fungoid subhuman monsters, wallowing in filth and grime. The actual ruins of the de la Poer slave pens are, in fact, discovered by Thomas Delapore, Norrys, and the team of archaeologists in the grottos. But even more disturbing, as revealed in Thomas Delapore's dreams, Norrys's face is superimposed on the body of a fungoid creature. And during his final breakdown, Thomas Delapore, in a state of denial, confirms his own role as slave master and Norrys's role as slave and victim: "I am *not* that daemon swineherd. ... It was *not* Edward Norrys' fat face on that flabby, fungous thing!"[17] *The importance of this vision of the slave master/slave relationship, dream-like though it is, lies in the fact that it represents the first appearance of the slave master/slave narrative in Lovecraft's fictional works.*

Unfortunately, however, it is hardly the last, as we will see when we move on to our consideration of Lovecraft's later weird tales.

"The Rats in the Walls" has been praised by S. T. Joshi for its subtlety and its restraint when it comes to the racist images and narratives—"It is, I suppose, to Lovecraft's credit that he has eliminated any racist overtones. ... and subtilised the idea [i.e. reversion to type]."[18] But neither of these claims are true; there are, as I have shown, plenty of "racist overtones" in this tale, and as for "subtilising," Lovecraft shows himself to be the same over-the-top prose stylist that we have seen in the other early tales; the grotesque slave master swineherd and the deliriously crafted hybrid boneyard beneath Exham Priory are quintessential Lovecraft. Lovecraft's fears concerning the decline of Western civilization, likewise, are obvious, though unlike in the other tales examined in this section, the decline is not something that is openly suggested as a possible, future occurrence. Nor do the fears concerning this decline arise out of the decline of a protagonist. *Indeed, the decline is not really contemporaneous to the action of the tale at all; it is something that has happened in the distant past.* Way back in the past, in fact; as Trask, one of the "eminent authorities" who accompany Thomas Delapore and Captain Norrys into the subterranean grottos, puts it: "the events ... must have taken place there three hundred years, or a thousand, or two thousand, or ten thousand years ago. ... some of the skeleton things must have descended as quadrupeds through the last twenty or more generations."[19] Nevertheless, Lovecraft hints—*only hints*, to be sure—that this kind of chaos and carnage is possible in the Western world if hybrids and hybridism are allowed to proliferate.

10

The Horror at Red Hook (1925)

"The Horror at Red Hook" is the longest piece of fiction that Lovecraft wrote while he was living in Brooklyn Heights; it is fully 7,500 words. He wrote it over a two-day period, August 1 and 2, 1925, which for Lovecraft was lightning fast. The tale was published in the January 1927 issue of *Weird Tales* and it is, without question, Lovecraft's most racist fictional work. S. T. Joshi doesn't pull any punches when it comes to voicing his opinions about the quality of this tale. He describes it as "nothing but a shriek of rage and loathing at the 'foreigners' who have taken New York away from the white people to whom it presumably belongs."[1] In part, this claim is justified. "The Horror at Red Hook" can be read, indeed, as one large, racist rant against the growing population of the nonwhite races in New York City and the effects that this influx was having on Anglo-Saxon culture. Passages such as the following appear frequently throughout the tale:

> Red Hook is a maze of hybrid squalor. … The population is a hopeless tangle and enigma; Syrian, Spanish, Italian, and negro elements impinging upon one another, and fragments of Scandinavian and American belts lying not far distant. It is a babel of sound and filth, and sends out strange cries to answer the lapping of oily waves at its grimy piers. … From this tangle of material and spiritual putrescence the blasphemies of a hundred dialects assail the sky. Hordes of prowlers reel shouting and singing along the lanes and thoroughfares … swarthy, sin-pitted faces disappear from windows when visitors pick their way through. … Policemen despair of order or reform, and seek rather to erect barriers protecting the outside world from the contagion.[2]

This is disheartening to say the least, and after encountering these kinds of descriptions, many readers are not too eager to read much further into the tale.

There is, however, always a distinction to be made between subject matter and quality in any literary work and we must respect that distinction. For in fact, "The Horror at Red Hook" is the best of Lovecraft's early weird tales. My reasons for thinking this are threefold. First, the two principal characters, Robert Suydam and Thomas Malone, are as well-developed as any of the characters in the major tales and surely, much more so than those in the previous set of tales. Second, the plot is coherent, lucid, and well-designed, just as the plots in the major tales. And finally, the writing is superb and holds the reader's interest throughout. The quality of the tale, indeed, is reflected by the fact that it was one of the few Lovecraft stories to find its way into horror anthologies during Lovecraft's lifetime. Christine Campbell Thompson, a British anthologist, chose three of Lovecraft tales for different anthologies that appeared between 1927 and 1931 under the Selwyn & Blount Ltd imprint: "Pickman's Model," "The Rats in the Walls," and "The Horror at Red Hook" (the latter was published in *You'll Need a Nightlight*). As we have seen from the previous chapter, "The Rats in the Walls" was another one of Lovecraft's better tales, and "Pickman's Model," not studied here, is equally fine.

The plot of "The Horror at Red Hook" is centered around Robert Suydam, an elderly, corpulent man who is the leader of a cult of black magic practitioners that operates clandestinely in the Red Hook district of Brooklyn, New York. There has been a rash of child kidnappings in the area and local gossip lays the blame for this on the cult, whose members, or so it is claimed, use the children as sacrifices in their rites. Eventually, the cult draws the attention of the police, who, led by Detective Thomas Malone, begin to investigate. No hard evidence emerges, though Malone and his colleagues start to amass a lot of disturbing information about Suydam and his cult. Over time, Suydam suddenly becomes young and handsome and this is attributed to the cult's nefarious practices. Suydam reaches the point where he is good looking enough to marry a young society woman and he does so. Apparently, he also grows tired of the cult, suggesting that he was only interested in using magic to restore his youth and get himself a trophy wife. Thus, Suydam cuts ties with the cult and plans to put his lurid past behind him. But as the couple prepares to embark on their honeymoon, they are murdered mysteriously in their stateroom on an ocean liner in New York harbor. Immediately after, a party of the cultists arrive in a tramp steamer to claim Suydam's body—inexplicably, permission to do this has been granted in a mysterious letter that the leader of the cultists bears with him. Malone continues his investigations of the Red Hook cult. In the climax of the tale, Malone traces the cultists to an underground temple, complete with a stagnant lake and a pedestal in the center. Malone sees various transdimensional entities and witnesses the reanimated body of Suydam chased by cultists as he pulls down the pedestal. All of these sights drive Malone temporarily insane. Suydam's body is never recovered and Malone ends up taking a leave of absence from his duties.

***

Lovecraft associates the Red Hook cult with the Kurdish cult of the Yezidis; as we are told by Malone, the members of the Brooklyn cult are mostly "of Mongoloid stock, originating somewhere in or near Kurdistan" and Malone recalls that "Kurdistan is the land of Yezidis, last survivors of the Persian devil worshippers."[3] It is only proper, in commencing our analysis of this tale, to examine the Yezidis association and see if there is any merit to it. The Yezidis today are basically a Kurdish clan, dwelling in northern Iraq and in parts of Armenia, Azerbaijan, and Syria. They speak Kurmanji, a Kurdish dialect, and they differ as to their views about their origins; many Yezidis believe that the clan originated in India; others that the group came from Sumer; there is no evidence to support either view. In the nineteenth and early twentieth centuries, information about the Yezidis in English-speaking countries was scanty at best. Isya Joseph, Ph.D., Union Theological Seminary, Columbia and Harvard University, published an influential book *Devil Worship: The Sacred Books and Traditions of the Yezidiz* (1919) that originated the belief that the Yezidis were devil worshippers whose principal god was Satan, or Shaitan (as they spelled it). Joseph's book contains two Yezidis texts with the kinds of intriguing titles that would have captured Lovecraft's fancy: *The Book of Revelation* ("Kitêba Cilwe," transliterated as "Kitab Al Jilwah" in the English version published in 1911) and *The Black Book* ("Mishefa Reş," in the English version published in 1913). These texts also captured the attention of Lovecraft's *Weird Tales* colleague, Robert E. Howard, who, in his tale "The Black Stone," alludes to an edition of *The Black Book*, supposedly published in Germany in 1839.

Contemporary scholars, however, are in agreement that *The Black Book* and *The Book of Revelation* are not genuine Yezidis texts, but merely clever forgeries that were perpetuated by an antique dealer in the 1890s. Indeed, the ancient Yezidis did not have written texts; their tradition was basically an oral one and their religious practices did not rely on the interpretation and analysis of doctrine, as does the Christian and Jewish traditions. Rituals were passed along via word of mouth and it was more important for devotees to correctly follow the rites than debate the legitimacy of different texts. Scholars also have challenged the view that the ancient Yezidis were devil worshippers; instead, their religious practices included elements from Christian, Islamic, Judaic, Zoroastrian, Sufi, and even Gnostic theologies. As for the equating of Shaitan and Satan, this is based on no empirical evidence other than the superficial phonetic similarities between "Shaitan" and "Satan," and when we examine the characteristics of Shaitan as delineated in authentic Yezidis texts, it is revealed that Shaitan, unlike Satan, is not a particularly evil entity at all, and certainly not the grand personification of the powers of darkness that Christian mythology insists upon.

Lovecraft knew about the existence of Isya Joseph's spurious texts through his colleague Robert Howard, but there is no evidence that he acquired Joseph's book or either one of the others mentioned above. As I have noted in the previous chapter, Lovecraft was certainly not an occult scholar (very far from it, in fact) and he got virtually all of his information about the so-called Yezidis devil worshippers from articles in the *Encyclopedia Britannica*, 9th edition, which, as S. T. Joshi observes, was found in Lovecraft's personal library after his death. The reason why Lovecraft decided to bring the Yezidis into his tale isn't too hard to guess; he liked the allusions to devil worship that he found in his outside readings and thought that these would spice up his tale. As L. Sprague de Camp puts it, "Lovecraft had never seen a Kurd, and in 1925 a writer could still get mileage out of the sinister idea of 'devil worship.'"[4] Then, too, I think, Lovecraft couldn't resist laying a charge of devil-worshippers on the immigrant populations of Brooklyn—after all, in his mind, such degraded "mongrels" are surely capable of the grossest kinds of magical practices imaginable, even if they don't actually engage in them.

* * *

Robert Suydam is Lovecraft's first fully fleshed-out, black magical practitioner and serves as the prototype for even more consequential magical practitioners in the later tales. Suydam is a privileged white Anglo-Saxon man, descended from Dutch immigrants of independent means and living in the family mansion in Flatbush. Physically, he is an elderly man in his sixties, corpulent, with "unkempt" white hair and very eccentric when it comes to his choice of attire; he usually appears in public dressed in black clothes and carrying a gold-headed cane. He is also reclusive and scholarly, and has devoted his life to occult studies. Suydam has squandered much of the family fortunes on a large library of "curious" tomes; he has even authored a pamphlet on the Qabalah. Most Lovecraft critics rightly note that Suydam is the precursor for Joseph Curwen in *The Case of Charles Dexter Ward* (see Chapter 13). Curwen, as it turns out, is nearly a carbon copy of Suydam; Curwen is also scholarly and reclusive; he has questionable companions; he is associated with kidnappings and disappearances; and he regains his youth during the course of the later story and marries a younger wife, just as Suydam will do.

Suydam first attracts the attention of the authorities when his distant relatives, the Suydams, the Colears, and the Van Brunts, all scions of illustrious Dutch families, bring a court case against him, alleging that Suydam is mentally incompetent; as proof, they hire detectives to amass evidence about Suydam's magical activities in the Red Hook district and his wide acquaintance among the disreputable locals. But Suydam is able to explain everything to the judge's satisfaction during the preliminary hearing.

The authorities, however, have taken note of Suydam's proclivities and so, they assign detective Thomas Malone to the case, along with other detectives and even a few federal inspectors. Malone now has, at last, what had been lacking in his previous investigations, that is, an actual ringleader. But he is still mystified by the Red Hook cults. Lovecraft is deliberately vague when describing the actual details of the cult's magical practices. He tells us that Suydam, in his basement flat at Parker Place, frequently conducts odd, ceremonial services behind the blinds of his windows. But we never learn exactly what these ceremonies are all about. Malone identifies some of the standard elements of Western magical workings, that is, circles, pentagrams, and such, but that is all. The cultists also make use of an old, gothic church located near the waterfront, which doubles as a dance hall on Wednesday nights, and Malone learns of the existence of other flats throughout the district that Suydam leases for special guests, accessible only to those who know the secret passwords. But the details of the magical workings done in these places remain unknown.

Lovecraft does, however, provide two texts that give us some idea about the nature of the cult's practices. The first of these is an incantation that is written above the pulpit in the desecrated gothic church used by the cult. This incantation appears two more times in the tale—once it is overheard by Malone while being recited by the cultists in the hidden catacombs beneath Suydam's flat and it is repeated again at the end of the tale, when a police officer hears an old woman teaching it to a child on the streets of Red Hook. The incantation was taken from the same *Encyclopedia Britannica* mentioned before and it runs as follows:

> O friend and companion of night, thou who rejoicest in the baying of dogs and spilt blood, who wanderest in the midst of shades among the tombs, who longest for blood and bringest terror to mortals, Gorgo, Mormo, thousand-faced moon, look favourably on our sacrifices![5]

Here, the fact that the Red Hook cultists perform blood sacrifices is confirmed; the goddesses that the cult is devoted to rejoice in "spilt blood"— they long for it, in fact.

This incantation, also, identifies the cult's principal deities. The "friend and companion of night" is, as we learn later, Lilith, the Babylonian demoness. In traditional Jewish mythology, Lilith is described as a very evil, dangerous entity, possessing virtually no positive or redeeming traits whatsoever. Lilith was originally the bride of the archangel Sammael, which, in the opinion of many scholars, was merely another name for Satan. Lilith also is spoken of as being Adam's first wife, and Rabbi Eliezer, in *The Book of Adam and Eve*, writes that Lilith bore Adam one hundred children. In Qabalistic lore, Lilith is commonly depicted in the form of a beautiful, naked woman whose lower extremities terminate in the tail of a serpent, and, unlike other demonesses, she is immortal. The names Gorgo and Mormo, which are associated with the "thousand-faced" moon in the incantation, are titles assigned to Hecate, a goddess who was even more terrifying of an entity than Lilith. Hecate—who was labeled the "Queen of the Night" by the lesbian poet Sappho—represented the waning, "evil" powers of the moon (she is one of the tripartite members of the Wiccan Triple Goddess archetype—Artemis personifying the New Moon, Demeter the Full Moon, and Hecate the Dark Moon). In appearance, Hecate was frightening—she is frequently pictured with three heads, like the hell-hound Cerberus, and six arms, brandishing torches and swords. Certainly, unlike the choice of deities for the de la Poer clan in "The Rats in the Walls," Lovecraft has chosen entities for Suydam's cult that *are* appropriate for a black magic coven.

Lovecraft's second text is not written in English; Malone finds it inscribed on the wall of Suydam's Parker Place house. This is basically a string of Words of Power, which Lovecraft describes as "the most terrible daemon-evocations of the Alexandrian decadence."[6] Lovecraft lifted this text from Arthur Edward Waite's *The Book of Black Magic and of Pacts* (1898):

HEL · HELOYM · SOTHER · EMMANVEL · SABAOTH · AGLA · TETRAGRAMMATON · AGYROS · OTHEOS · ISCHYROS · ATHANATOS · IEHOVA · VA · ADONAI · SADAY · HOMOVSION · MESSIAS · ESCHEREHEYE.[7]

The incantation, however, is hardly a terrible, "daemon" evocation; it is, in reality, nothing more than a string of various divine names representing the Hebrew God and his angels, which were drawn from ancient Hebrew and Jewish documents. As such it is difficult to see exactly how any of these names would be useful to Suydam or to his Red Hook covens; thus, we have another example of Lovecraft merely dumping a bunch of formidable-looking ancient words into his fiction just as he did in "The Rats in the Walls" and suggesting that they are somehow efficacious in raising up devils.

Indeed, in *The Book of Black Magic and Pacts*, Part II, chapters VI and VII, Waite provides translations for all the words in Lovecraft's incantation and none of them would be of any interest to a black magic practitioner. For example, Soter, or Sother, is a prosecuting angel-prince who serves the throne of divine judgment; Emmanuel means "God with us"; Messias is, of course, Messiah, another name for Christ; Adonai can be translated as "God"; Tetragrammaton is the secret name of God, IHVH; Jehovah is equivalent to the name God in Hebrew and Christian texts; Agla is the name of God that Joseph invoked when he was delivered from his brothers in the Old Testament; Saday is a diminutive for El-Shaddai, which means "God"; Homosion is a corruption of the title, "Son of Man," which is an alternate name for Christ; "Heloym" is an obvious corruption of "Elohim," which means "God"; Va is likely "Via," which in Latin means "way," and thus refers to Christ as "the way, the truth and the light"; and finally, "Eschereheye" refers to "Eserchie/Oriston," the name of God invoked by Moses when he brought the plague of frogs on the Egyptians in the Old Testament.

***

The magical objectives of Robert Suydam and his cult are not disclosed to the reader in "The Horror at Red Hook." But for Suydam personally, his workings with the Red Hook cult lead to extremely beneficial results. Over the course of the first part of the tale, he miraculously grows young. Along with these changes, Suydam dresses like a much younger man and renovates his Flatbush mansion, then begins to host parties for friends as well as relatives, even the relatives who had tried to have him committed.

> One day he [Suydam] was seen near Borough Hall with clean shaved face, well-trimmed hair, and tastefully immaculate attire, and on every day thereafter some obscure improvement was noticed in him. He maintained his new fastidiousness without interruption, added to it an unwonted sparkle of eye and crispness of speech, and began little by little to shed the corpulence which had so long deformed him. Now frequently taken for less than his age, he acquired an elasticity of step and buoyancy of demeanour to match the new tradition, and shewed a curious darkening of the hair which somehow did not suggest dye. ... all were suddenly charmed by the dawning grace and urbanity of the former hermit.[8]

Suydam's transformation into an attractive, cultivated man enables him to get a young, beautiful girlfriend. Her name is Miss Cornelia Gerritsen of Bayside and she is distantly related to Suydam. The couple eventually get married. Here, once again, the parallels between Robert Suydam and Joseph Curwen in *The Case of Charles Dexter Ward* are striking. Curwen, too, grows younger due to his magical practices and he weds a much younger woman. But there is an important difference in the latter case; Curwen is attempting to "fit in" and deceive his critics and the police into thinking that he has reformed and given up black magic. But Suydam really seems to be reforming. He mentions to acquaintances, in fact, that his former work in Red Hook has now been accomplished and he plans to enjoy his remaining years "in a brighter second youth."[9] Obviously, he has no more interest in pursuing his career as leader of a cult of "mongoloid" Kurds. And apparently, he thinks that he can easily shed his former life and extricate himself from the cultists.

Following the nuptials, Suydam and his bride board a luxury ocean liner at the Cunard Pier and prepare to take a cruise for their honeymoon. But as the ship begins to move out to sea, screams are suddenly heard in the Suydam cabin. The ship's doctor and other sailors investigate and they discover that

Suydam and his wife are dead, the wife strangled to death with a claw mark on her throat. There is a suggestion of the supernatural here; the ship's doctor momentarily sees a phosphorescence near the porthole and hears a faint tittering, but nothing else. The word "Lilith" is also momentarily seen flickering on one of the walls. Almost simultaneous with the murder of the newlyweds, a steamer pulls up next to the luxury liner and a group of Red Hook cultists "swarm" aboard—here, again, is an example of Lovecraft's "swarm instinct."

Lovecraft indulges his racism in his references to the leader of the group, "an Arab with a hatefully negroid mouth."[10] The leader is bearing a note previously written by Suydam, requesting that his body be turned over to the cultists. This, of course, stretches the credibility of the reader; police regulations and methodologies might not have been quite the same in the 1920s as they are now, but surely, Suydam's body would not have been released prematurely to any outside parties without the permission of his relatives, or without a proper examination by a coroner. Nevertheless, the captain has no qualms about committing the body into the hands of the Red Hook group and they take it. Afterward, after the steamer has departed, it is revealed that Mrs. Suydam's body has been drained of blood. This nice, gruesome touch suggests that the Red Hook cultists took her blood and are likely planning to use it as a magical menstruum for some specific purpose connected with Suydam's body.

* * *

Thomas F. Malone is Lovecraft's privileged, white Anglo-Saxon protagonist in "The Horror at Red Hook" who ultimately comes to harm due to his connection with Suydam's cult. When we first meet Malone, the events of the story have already taken place and Malone is unharmed, at least physically. Yet, his experiences have left a lingering, pernicious effect on his psyche. Malone is on medical leave and living temporarily in Pascoag, Rhode Island. Malone is a forty-two-year-old Irishman, and, as Lovecraft suggests, not the standard hard-headed, hard-boiled police detective, but instead, something of a mystic, at least in temperament. As Lovecraft writes, "He [Malone] had the Celt's far vision of weird and hidden things, but the logician's quick eye for the outwardly unconvincing."[11] Undoubtedly, it is this imaginative streak that leads Malone to experience his breakdown. He walks along a street in Pascoag that contains slightly taller buildings than those in the area where he is staying and suddenly, he starts shrieking and breaks into a frantic run, stumbling finally and falling down. He is helped to his feet by onlookers and he mutters an apology and continues on his way. Apparently, the sight of tall buildings reminds Malone of the buildings in the Red Hook district and this association, in turn, leads to his reaction. Following this strange—and admittedly, rather comic—preamble, the story is then told through a series of flashbacks.

Malone has been detailed to the Butler Street station in Brooklyn and was already well-acquainted with the Red Hook district. Malone, in fact, seems to share the omniscient narrator's views concerning this area. But to Malone there is a darker element beneath all the squalor and the vice. Malone has read Margaret Murray's treatise, *The Witch Cult in Western Europe* (1921), and though he doesn't necessarily accept Miss Murray's thesis that there was a widespread cult of witches and black magic practitioners existing in Europe in pagan times, nevertheless, he is quite willing to believe that there is, in fact, just such an extensive, interconnected group of modern black magic cultists operating surreptitiously in Red Hook at the present day, though, of course, he is not yet aware that Robert Suydam is linked to these cultists or that Suydam is a pivotal figure in their practices. But he quickly becomes aware of this and his interest intensifies. As he continues his investigations, Malone has no illusions about the power and the tenacity of Red Hook to reach out and suck in its victims, and he recognizes that Red Hook will likely continue to exert a negative influence on Suydam, even if Suydam tries to leave the cult. Malone understands, in effect, that Suydam might think that he is finished with Red Hook, but Red Hook is not necessarily finished with Suydam.

When Suydam and his wife are killed on the luxury liner, Malone's worst fears are realized; Red Hook has indeed taken its revenge on Suydam. To Malone, the death of Robert Suydam seems conclusive; a fit, ironic end to a man who unwisely indulged in pernicious magical rites. But Malone also has the good sense to recognize that the death of the cult leader doesn't mean that the cult itself is going to die out and this proves to be the case. Malone, while still toiling in the cesspools of Red Hook, takes part in a final raid on the Red Hook cultists. Three children have been kidnapped (Anglo-Saxon children, of course, to add insult to injury) and a large band of police officers, detectives, and investigators descend on Red Hook. Malone is part of the group that raids Suydam's basement flat and he gets separated from the rest of the group. He ends up in a vast, underground cavern and witnesses a nightmarish scene.

The cultists are performing their rites before a golden pedestal near the shore of an oily, underground lake. An amorphous, phosphorescent entity squats on the pedestal. This entity may be linked with Lilith, or Hecate, since the devotees are paying homage to these goddesses. Or, then again, it may not. Among the hellish worshippers are the satanic entities, Moloch and Ashtaroth, and various incubi and succubae, all paying homage to Lilith and Hecate. There is organ music playing and wild, bacchanal dancing taking place. Then, a boat appears and the Red Hook group who claimed Suydam's body have now brought it to the celebration. Apparently, the effects of Suydam's magical practices have now dissipated, for Suydam's corpse appears as he had looked originally, that is, a corpulent, white-haired old man. The cultists anoint the feet of the body with Mrs. Suydam's blood and then actually pass along a bottle of the blood for the phosphorescent entity to drink.

The climax occurs when the cultists, carrying Suydam's body away from the pedestal, recite the same incantation to Lilith that we have seen before, shouting out: "Lilith, Great Lilith, behold the Bridegroom!" At this moment, Suydam's body becomes animated. Obviously, he is the bridegroom referred to by the cultists, and one could argue, on that basis, that this incident represents a neat reversal of the Lilith myth: Eve replaced Lilith as Adam's wife, and so, Lilith is now replacing Mrs. Suydam as Suydam's wife. But Suydam proves to be a reluctant bridegroom. Instead of taking charge of the cult again as the cultists, no doubt, are hoping that he will do, he decides to do the opposite and bring the cult down. He rushes back toward the golden pedestal, pursued by the phosphorescent entity and all of the cultists, and manages to pull the pedestal into the water before he dies a final death. This, of course, terminates the whole Witches Sabbat celebration.

> The corpse ... reached its goal. ... in one final spurt of strength which ripped tendon from tendon and sent its noisome bulk floundering to the floor in a state of jellyfish dissolution, the staring corpse which had been Robert Suydam achieved its object and its triumph ... the pedestal he had pushed tottered, tipped, and finally careened from its onyx base into the thick waters below, sending up a parting gleam of carven gold as it sank heavily to undreamable gulfs of lower Tartarus.[12]

These horrific events prove to be too much for Malone and he loses consciousness, as Lovecraft's protagonists sometimes do when confronted with horrifying events.

Afterward, though he comforts himself in thinking of his experience as a dream, Malone has been profoundly changed, psychologically, morally, and spiritually; in his view, what he has seen represents "a horror from the universe's very heart."[13] Thomas Malone, who formerly was a privileged member of the white race, has been damaged in this unequal contest between himself and the Other, represented here by the amorphous, slimy entity on the pedestal and the demons who join in the homage to Lilith. Malone is not as directly connected with the "Horror" as was Suydam, and so, the penalty is much less—temporary madness as opposed to actual, physical death. But as is the case with all of Lovecraft's privileged, white protagonists who consort, even indirectly, with the Other, there is always a penalty and a retribution.

***

Lovecraft's first racist narrative, the miscegenation narrative, runs like a disturbing undercurrent beneath the action in "The Horror at Red Hook." This is not miscegenation by blood, however. There are no genetic predispositions in Suydam's family tree, as there were in the case of Thomas

Delapore, nor are there any half-ape, half-human hybrids lurking about in Suydam's genealogy, as there were for Arthur Jermyn. Thus, the miscegenation in this tale is miscegenation by association. Robert Suydam, as a Teuton, and thus, a member of the superior race, is susceptible to degeneration due to his association with the alien, animalistic cultists and by the black magic practices he uses to rejuvenate himself. Consequently, he is very similar to Herbert West, whose intimate association with his menagerie proves to be his undoing.

Lovecraft dwells on each aspect of Suydam's decline as it fluctuates from simple old age and natural decrepitude to a sudden rise in youth and energy, and then, back to decrepitude again and finally, the ghastly, half-life, half-death reanimation in the underground temple. The actual dissolution of Suydam's reanimated corpse is every bit as gross and graphic as any other single passage in Lovecraft's work; Suydam dissolves into a putrid, jelly-like liquescence, much like M. Valdemar does at the end in Edgar Allan Poe's "The Facts in the Case of M. Valdemar" (1845), a tale that Lovecraft particularly admired. This horrendous death is due to Suydam's decision to use black magic, *but only in part*. What Lovecraft is also asserting not-so-subtly is that this is the kind of thing that can happen if one associates with the immigrant hordes, specifically the undocumented "Asian dregs" that comprise Suydam's inner circle of cultists. Obviously, if a decent Teuton makes the mistake of interacting intimately with the abject, non-white races, then he or she must pay the price.

"The Horror at Red Hook" is, in a sense, Lovecraft's swansong to New York City; it is also his most painstaking indictment of that city: a city that he saw as a perfect example of what can occur to a great American city if the forces of immigration, miscegenation, and hybridism are allowed to rage free and unchecked.[14] In many places in his correspondence, and particularly in the short tale "He" (1926), Lovecraft celebrates the beauty of the New York skyline at sunset—describing its buildings as though they were the towers and minarets of a fantastic, half-fabulous dream city. But this is only in the distance, for when one gets closer, "garish daylight" [shows] "only squalor and alienage," as he puts it in "He." Indeed, in the latter tale, Lovecraft states bluntly that New York "is in fact quite dead, its sprawling body imperfectly embalmed and infested with queer animate things which have nothing to do with it as it was in life."[15] This is the decline of the West taken to extreme limits, and if this can happen to the greatest city in the United States and possibly in Europe as well, then it can happen to any city and any town in the Western world.

11

Critical Commentaries

Lovecraft's hybrid, degenerative monsters have been attracting growing critical attention in recent years among academics and scholars, much more so, I think, than Lovecraft's "other" Others, that is, his cosmic slave masters. Carl H. Sederholm and Jeffrey Andrew Weinstock, in their introduction to *The Age of Lovecraft*, suggest that contemporary posthumanistic thinking lies at the roots of this interest and I tend to agree with them.

> Related to its antihumanist undoing of human exceptionalism, Lovecraft's fiction, through its persistent thematizing of evolution and, significantly, atavistic devolution, insistently calls into question the status of the "human" in general as a discrete species somehow distinguishable from other terrestrial life. ... This calling into question the status of the human indeed is what has been embraced so fully by posthumanist theorists such as Rosi Braidotti who take issue with the "humanistic arrogance of continuing to place Man at the centre of world history" ... As part of the pricking of humanist pretensions, Lovecraft's fiction undercuts human exceptionalism and realigns the human as part of a vast system of life, one that is deeply connected to other species and the planet more broadly. For Lovecraft, humans are neither distinct from other animals nor proudly sitting on top of the evolutionary ladder.[1]

I have taken issue with some of these statements in the preceding chapters, for surely, as we have learned from Lovecraft's racist poems, white, privileged humans are seen by Lovecraft as distinct from Blacks, apes, and the higher mammals, whether this is due to "divine fiat," as the poem "On the Creation of Niggers" claims, or whether this is due to natural law, that is, evolutionary processes that end up creating separate species. And surely, also, Lovecraft does view white Anglo-Saxons sitting on top of the evolutionary ladder. But let us set these concerns aside for the moment.

For in fact, there does seem to be a definite synergistic connection between Lovecraft studies and posthumanist theories and this has, I think, inspired a bevy of essays on the subject of Lovecraft's early tales, since, after all, it is in these early tales where Lovecraft's "pricking of humanist pretensions" and undercutting of "human exceptionalism" is most apparent. It is in these early tales, also, where the hybrid, degenerative monsters can be found and so, it is only natural for the scholars who are interested in Lovecraft's posthumanistic inclinations to become interested in the hybrids themselves. As should be evident from my readings in Part II, both Lovecraft and his protagonists are unanimous in their animosity toward the hybrids—they show only disgust, horror, and revulsion toward them. However, in some of the more recent studies, critics argue the exact opposite; they suggest that the protagonists, along with Lovecraft, may feel a kinship with the hybrid monsters and, perhaps, even be attracted to in addition to being repulsed by them.

In this, my first critical commentaries chapter, I want to examine the essays of two contemporary Lovecraft scholars, David Simmons and Jed Mayer, each of whom in his own way makes the argument identified above, and see if their views are defensible in terms of the Lovecraft texts. In addition, I want to examine the "Lovecraft paradox" (as it is often called)—an idea that emerges from Mayer's study—and, specifically, determine if there actually is such a paradox and if so, then what effect this may have had on either Lovecraft's philosophical or political thinking.

* * *

Intriguingly, Dr. David Simmons, in "'A Certain Resemblance': Abject Hybridity in H. P. Lovecraft's Short Fiction" (2013), approaches the hybrids in Lovecraft's early works from a slightly different perspective than I do in this book; he directs his attention on the *place* from which the hybrids originate—specifically, Africa and Egypt—rather than on hybrids and hybridity in American and European "habitats" (if that is the proper word). Simmons, also (and rightly), confines his attention to only two tales—"Arthur Jermyn" and "Imprisoned with the Pharaohs" (1924)—because, outside of these tales, Lovecraft shows no particular interest in either Africa or Egypt in any of his other weird tales. Simmons's thesis statement is interesting and reveals, as we would expect, the directions that his essay will take and the claims that he will be making.

> Lovecraft [constructs] ... the African subcontinent as a homogenous, abject *Other* in a manner that ignores the multitudinous differences between the peoples and cultures of such a diverse continent in favor of utilizing it as an aesthetic signifier. The presentation of the African subcontinent in these stories reflects a process, which I wish to propose is significant for its ability to situate Lovecraft in a Gothic tradition; its

reflection of wider American fears concerning miscegenation; and its self-reflexive expression of Lovecraft's deep-seated anxieties concerning his own American nationality and subjectivity.[2]

Simmons's first claim is, indeed, warranted; I will examine this claim and what Simmons makes of it in this section.[3] Simmons's other, "process claims" are equally defensible, though space prohibits me from analyzing them in detail.

In "Arthur Jermyn," Lovecraft does, in fact, imagine the African subcontinent—specifically, the Congolese area of the continent—as an abstract, homogeneous Other. He totally ignores the fact that Africa in the 1920s was (and still is) as diverse of a country in terms of its peoples and cultures as any other continent in the East. Indeed, Africa, along with its indigenous African populations, also played "host" to a variety of European colonizing nations—primarily British, French, German, and Portuguese; these, too, added to the diversity of the continent (whether the indigenous populaces liked it or not). Lovecraft, well-versed on world history from his extensive forays into his grandfather's library in Providence, knew just how diverse Africa was. And yet, in this tale, Africa's main importance is that it is a dark, savage, barbaric place. This fact is underscored when Arthur Jermyn visits the continent to seek out information about the mummy of the white ape in the Onga and Kaliri districts and discovers that the stone city where Sir Wade and the white ape ruled temporarily as god and goddess has been destroyed by the "warlike" N'bangus tribe, who, in turn, kill all of the people in the village, humans and hybrids alike, and carry the mummy away. The implication here, of course, is that Africa is a repository for the kinds of violence, chaos, and savagery exhibited by the N'bangus. It is, in short, a place that exudes the abject: it is inhuman; it is uncivilized; and it is dangerous to white Anglo-Saxons.

As he analyzes "Arthur Jermyn," Simmons makes two arguments about the Jermyn clan. He claims, first, that they journey to Africa to seek a more "multifaceted engagement" with the Other and possible "empowerment." He argues, also, that the members of the Jermyn clan are not only repulsed by but *attracted* to the Other, an attraction that grows over the course of their repeated journeys to and from the Congolese territory in Africa. As Simmons writes:

> [Lovecraft's] protagonists recurrently encounter non-Western peoples and their cultures. ... [and] find their sense of identity fragmented by their at least partial realization of an essential communality between all peoples. ... the abject not only signals that which is repulsive and threatens identity, but also represents a source of attraction: "a composite of judgment and affect, of condemnation and yearning" ... This multifaceted aspect of abjection implies an at least unconscious desire for

a greater understanding of non-Western peoples and cultures, perhaps as a means of empowerment.[4]

Simmons bases his ideas here on Julia Kristeva's theories on the abject, as articulated in *Powers of Horror: An Essay on Abjection* (1982). In this essay, Kristeva defines the abject generally as something opposed to the "I." It can be an aesthetic signifier, of course, or an object, such as a hybrid, degenerative monster. But the abject is not limited to these two categories. It could, in fact, be something as minor as "food loathing," or conversely, something as major as death, chaos, or nothingness.[5] As Kristeva pursues manifestations of the abject in literature, psychology, and philosophy, she does not focus specifically on the topic of race. Simmons, on the contrary, does exactly that, linking Kristeva's theories directly to his own "racially informed" views about white "Westerners" and their connection to the non-Western.

There are, however, problems with Simmons's two arguments, as identified above. First, the Jermyns who visit Africa go there for reasons that are never connected to "increased understanding" of the abject or empowerment. Second, as I have shown in Chapter 6, there is only *one* instance of a pureblood, white Anglo-Saxon showing attraction to the abject in "Arthur Jermyn"—Sir Wade's sexual liaison with the female white ape. This is, as I have noted, the original sin committed by Sir Wade and it leads to his own ruin and the ruin of his family line. In contrast, the members of the Jermyn clan *after* Sir Wade are not pureblood, white Anglo-Saxons; they are all tainted by abject DNA and are now the Jermyn hybrids. Thus, Sir Wade's son, Philip, who travels to Africa as a sailor on a merchantman and disappears into the Congo, is merely a hybrid, degenerative monster returning to his homeland. Similarly, Sir Wade's great-great grandson, Alfred Jermyn, who runs off to join the circus and develops an "attraction" to an anthropoid, is nothing more than a hybrid, degenerative monster hooking up with his savage BFF—two abjects, in effect, bonding. Significantly, in comparison with the other Jermyn hybrids, Arthur Jermyn himself is closest to being a white Anglo-Saxon, at least mentally, and he is not interested in engaging with the Other for sexual purposes, or for empowerment purposes or for any other purpose—he is simply searching for information about his past ancestry. As for his attitude toward the abject, this is the same attitude that all self-respecting white Anglo-Saxons have for the abject (at least in Lovecraft's opinion)—horror, fear, loathing, and disgust. I have made the point in Chapter 4 (and will make it again later on in this study) that when a white Anglo-Saxon transforms into an Other, then she or he must leave humankind behind—and this includes leaving behind human needs, desires, and attractions.

Turning next to "Imprisoned with the Pharaohs," Lovecraft again constructs a "homogeneous, abject Other" and it is, likewise, the African subcontinent—though now Egypt, rather than the Congo. "Imprisoned with the Pharaohs"—Lovecraft's own title is "Under the Pyramids"—was ghost-written by Lovecraft for the escape artist Harry Houdini. *Weird Tales* owner J. C. Henneberger commissioned several writers, including Lovecraft, to ghost-write tales for Houdini, intending to publish them in *Weird Tales* to boost sales—this particular tale did, in fact, appear in *Weird Tales* in 1924. Lovecraft did a substantial amount of research before writing the tale; he wanted to get the details of the plot down correctly and present an accurate picture of Egypt in the early twentieth century. This research revealed that the populace of Egypt was just as culturally and racially diverse as Africa (though mostly of Muslim and Arab descent, rather than African). Yet, Lovecraft ignored this information and went about depicting an Egypt that is pretty much like the Africa in "Arthur Jermyn"—a savage, chaotic, inhuman place. Lovecraft's protagonist is Houdini himself, who, while visiting Cairo in the company of his wife, ends up getting separated from her and kidnapped by locals, who bind and cast him down into the depths of the Temple of the Sphinx. Houdini, in his efforts to escape, encounters a group of the oddest hybrid monsters to appear in Lovecraft's early work: a living collection of "composite mummies" created in the best Herbert West style by ancient Egyptian priests who artificially attached human trunks and limbs to the heads of animals. At the end of the tale, Houdini finds himself facing an enormous creature that presumably has five heads, but which, it turns out, is merely the five-fingered paw of an even larger creature beneath it. This creature could, in fact, be the visible embodiment of the abject Other in Egypt. Luckily, however, Houdini's harrowing experience proves to be a dream and he doesn't have to deal with either this creature or the hybrids.

In his analysis of "Imprisoned with the Pharaohs," Simmons's arguments follow the same pattern that we see in his previous analysis of "Arthur Jermyn": the protagonist visits the African subcontinent to engage intimately with the Other and the protagonist is attracted to the Other. Simmons can very easily make the first claim stick in this tale. The Houdini protagonist himself in various places in the text notes that he is visiting Egypt specifically to experience an exotic, non-Western milieu—that is, seeking "curiosities." Simmons, however, cannot make the second claim, that is, that the Houdini protagonist is attracted to the abject—either to Egypt itself or to the hybrids who live in Egypt. Such a claim would, in fact, be ridiculous; Houdini finds only chaos and violence in Egypt, while the hybrids, in turn, are all thoroughly, morbidly repulsive, many of them, in fact, in advanced stages of decomposition. Lovecraft describes them as follows:

> I *would not* look at the marching things. That I desperately resolved as I heard their creaking joints and nitrous wheezing. ... It was merciful that they did not speak ... but God! *their crazy torches began to cast shadows on the surface of those stupendous columns. Hippopotami should not*

> *have human hands and carry torches ... men should not have the heads of crocodiles.* ... I tried to turn away, but the shadows and the sounds and the stench were everywhere ... I had to shut my eyes again when I realized how many of the things were assembling—and when I glimpsed a certain object walking solemnly and steadily *without any body above the waist.*[6]

These monsters are so grotesque, and *gross*, that no white Anglo-Saxon protagonist in Lovecraft's fiction would want to get near them, not even Sir Wade Jermyn. Indeed, none of the degenerative hybrids in the five tales studied in Part II—Sir Wade's offspring, the West menagerie, the Martense cannibals, the Delapore clan, or, especially, the swarthy immigrants in the Red Hook district of New York—would desire any sort of intimate contact with them.

***

Jed Mayer, in "Race, Species, and Others: H. P. Lovecraft and the Animal" (2016), approaches Lovecraft and his work in terms of early-twentieth-century speciesist theories that group humans, nonhumans, and animals into hierarchical categories and "privilege" one species—white Anglo-Saxons—over all of the others. In examining these theories, Mayer takes up Simmons's idea that white Anglo-Saxons, in confronting the Others, often harbor attraction toward them. Mayer cites the same passage from the Simmons essay that I cited above and then states his own version of the hybrids-as-objects-of attraction argument: "Biological universality may extend across species barriers as well as racial barriers, and while Lovecraft's narrators experience fragmentation of their human identities, they also encounter a sense of kinship where once they knew only difference."[7]

In order to prove this argument, Mayer uses for his examples the Innsmouth mutants rather than the Jermyn hybrids. He picks up on his "kinship" idea that he posits after the Simmons citation and claims that Lovecraft's narrator, Robert Olmstead, is only "initially repulsed" by the Deep Ones, but then recognizes that they are his kinsfolk:

> In contrast to an earlier work like "The Festival," where the narrator is initially drawn to his ancestral home to participate in an ancient family ritual only to flee in horror when he discovers the truth of his monstrous lineage, Robert Olmstead. ... is initially repulsed by the denizens of a cursed seaport town, but gradually comes to recognize his kinship with them, and ... ultimately decides to join them in their underwater city.[8]

I will be studying the Innsmouth mutants in detail in my analysis of "The Shadow Over Innsmouth" in Chapter 15 and I don't want to anticipate the arguments that I will be making in that chapter. However, I will say here that the Innsmouth mutants are similar to the Jermyn hybrids in that they, too, are the product of "tainted" DNA—that is, the "Innsmouth Look," as it is referred to in "The Shadow Over Innsmouth." Consequently, white Anglo-Saxons who transform into Deep Ones become alien entities; the Innsmouth Look burns away the humanity of the Deep Ones-in-Training, along with their human desires. And so, any attraction that fledgling Deep Ones feel toward the other Deep Ones, or to Innsmouth, or to the underwater city of Y'ha-nthlei where they all eventually reside, cannot be considered as pureblood, white Anglo-Saxons showing attraction to the Other; this is, in effect, aliens attracted to other aliens and their alien environments. This fact becomes very clear in the final pages of "Innsmouth." When Olmstead sees the first signs of the transformation in his mirror, he is still pure blooded enough to be disgusted and horrified—just as Arthur Jermyn and Lovecraft's other privileged white narrators and protagonists always are in the presence of hybrids—but as the impure, alien DNA takes charge of his body and mind, he becomes more fascinated by what he is becoming than revolted. Eventually, he accepts the hybrids as kinsfolk, but only after his transformation is nearly complete—that is, when they really *are* kin to him.

The Lovecraft paradox comes into play early on in Mayer's essay. Carl H. Sederholm and Jeffrey Andrew Weinstock describe the Lovecraft paradox in their Introduction to *The Age of Lovecraft* as follows:

> At the same time that Lovecraft's antihumanism is highlighted and celebrated by modern theorists, however, for others the realization that human beings are simply one species among many—and perhaps not even the one best adapted to survive—is a horrific realization to be resisted. And indeed, the paradox of Lovecraft is that he could on the one hand hold such noxious views concerning race and on the other assert the relative insignificance of the entire species. What good is being atop the racial totem pole, one may ask, if one's entire civilization is doomed to decline and the achievements and powers of other species far outstrip those of one's own?[9]

Mayer, in his thesis statement, identifies the same four elements of the Lovecraft paradox that Sederholm and Weinstock allude to above: (1) Lovecraft's "racial totem pole"; (2) the entities that exist *inside* the parameters of that totem pole; (3) the entities that exist *outside* the range of the totem pole—the cosmic slave masters; and finally, (4) Lovecraft's racism toward the entities on the lower rungs of the pole—the hybrids.

Mayer argues that there is a "tension" in Lovecraft's work and this, in turn, leads to a paradox when it comes to Lovecraft's view of his nonhuman entities, that is (as he argues), Lovecraft's narratives offer "imaginative accounts of the intelligence and complexity of nonhuman beings" paradoxically juxtaposed against fear and repugnance toward "the presence of the nonhuman within the supposedly sovereign human self" (see below). This is Mayer's understanding of the Lovecraft paradox and it can be equated, at least conceptually, with Sederholm's and Weinstock's contention that "Lovecraft ... could on the one hand hold such noxious views concerning race and on the other assert the relative insignificance of the entire species."

> Without seeking to escape the implications of Lovecraft's racism, I would like to propose an alternative way of contextualizing the author's racial prejudices within a broader posthumanist perspective, one that subverts constructions of human uniqueness and superiority. This subversion manifests itself in his narratives through imaginative accounts of the intelligence and complexity of nonhuman beings, and of the presence of the nonhuman within the supposedly sovereign human self. His narrators undergo journeys into the heart of the nonhuman, discovering alien intelligences that dwarf our own and traces within ourselves of a physical and mental heritage that is decidedly alien. Moreover, Lovecraft's work gives form to a tension in our relationship with nonhuman beings that remains a preoccupation among scholars in the field of animal studies: namely the complex, often conflicted relationship between interspecies kinship and difference, community and subjectivity, empathy and enmity.[10]

In support for the above arguments, Mayer directs our attention to two of the early tales: "Arthur Jermyn" and "The Rats in the Walls," stories in which, as we have seen, the main white protagonists discover their monstrous ancestry and experience racist fears of miscegenation and degeneration. Mayer links Darko Suvin's concept of "cognitive estrangement" (*Metamorphoses of Science Fiction: On the Poetics and History of a Literary Genre*—1979) to Lovecraft's concept of cosmic alienage and argues that Lovecraft's protagonists in the later weird tales often discover what it is like to occupy the body of an extraterrestrial alien entity; he cites, in particular, Nathaniel Wingate Peaslee, the protagonist of "The Shadow Out of Time," who is literally displaced from his body and forced to live inside the body of a member of the Great Race for a period of roughly five years (see Chapter 17). As a result of what both the early and later protagonists discover, Mayer concludes that they develop admiration for nonhumans and yet, they are repulsed by the nonhuman and harbor existential fears against hybrids and cosmic slave masters alike.

Lovecraft, of course, perceived no tension (and certainly, no paradox) in either his attitudes toward his Others or in his interpretations of them. What Mayer (and other critics who make these kinds of arguments) is ignoring is that *there are two sets of nonhuman entities in Lovecraft's major works and they are different from one another—radically different. And, correspondingly, Lovecraft and his protagonists exhibit different attitudes toward these entities—radically different attitudes.* As I have shown in Chapter 4, Lovecraft, in his racist poems and later, in "The Rats in the Walls," upends the theory of evolution, suggesting that there were parallel evolutionary processes at work in the remote past that led to the establishment of groups of carefully selected (and segregated) "pockets" of species with built-in genetic barriers that excluded the members of the lower species from becoming members of the higher species. *These processes, in effect, appear to have worked alongside natural selection; they may be, indeed, part of the natural selection process itself.* Therefore, since hybrid degenerative monsters, Blacks, and anthropoids are not human and are, moreover, a threat to the safety and longevity of the white race, it is only natural for Anglo-Saxons to keep them in line and at bay on the lower rungs of the racial totem pole. In contrast, when it comes to the cosmic slave masters, these entities are superior to humankind and the relations between white Anglo-Saxons and the alien races have little to do with the relations between Anglo-Saxons and the lower, subhuman life forms. Here, we see an instance of cosmic law. The cosmic slave masters are naturally superior to humankind and so, white Anglo-Saxons who admire and yet fear them are only acknowledging cosmic law. Therefore, there is no paradox—Lovecraft's racist attitudes toward the lower life forms are entirely in keeping with natural law, while his grudging admiration for the superior life forms is entirely in keeping with cosmic law.

I have made the point frequently in my analysis of the tales in Part II that Lovecraft's *central* concern in both his life and work was the continuance and preservation of Western civilization. He makes this abundantly clear in a letter to Woodburn Harris, dated February 25–March 1, 1929:

> I ... don't give a hang about the masses except so far as I think deliberate cruelty is coarse and unaesthetic—be in towards horses, oxen, undeveloped men, dogs, negroes, or poultry. All that I care about is *the civilization*—the state of development and organization which is capable of gratifying the complex mental-emotional-aesthetic needs of highly evolved and acutely sensitive men. Any *indignation* I may feel in the whole matter is not for the woes of the downtrodden, but for the threat of social unrest to the traditional institutions of the civilization. The reformer cares only for the masses, but may make concessions to the civilization. I care only for the civilization, but may make concessions to the masses.[11]

Naturally, Lovecraft considered himself among the elite—"highly evolved and acutely sensitive," even though he knew that he really didn't "fit the bill," so to speak, as I have shown in Chapters 1 and 2.

Of *secondary* concern to Lovecraft was his attitudes toward his Others; he saw his hybrid, degenerative monsters and his cosmic slave masters primarily in their relation to Western civilization and particularly, in terms of the threats that they pose toward the longevity and continuance of Western civilization. His racial hatred was intended to counteract the threat of the "alien within," as Simmons and Mayer refer to it—the subhuman, hybrid monsters that are clawing their way up the racial totem pole; these include not only the monsters in the tales that I have examined in Part II of this study but also African Americans and the nonwhites that are unable to assimilate into the American culture. *Lovecraft's racism is an attempt, therefore, to protect civilization.*

Lovecraft's admiration for (and implicit fear of) the cosmic slave masters, on the other hand, reflects Lovecraft's frank admission—the same admission that all intelligent, thinking persons must acknowledge—that humankind as a whole will eventually face an apocalypse that will ultimately destroy all human beings, whether this is the fanciful apocalypse of the cosmic slave masters returning en masse to enslave and destroy humankind or more probably one of the apocalypses envisioned by contemporary science—the Big Crunch, the Big Freeze, perhaps, or, closer to home, the sun turning supernova and burning up Earth's atmosphere and ourselves in the process, or, perhaps, global warming or one of the global pandemics that seem to be a constant worry among many of us these days. Naturally, of course, the destruction of humankind means the destruction of Western civilization, and this is, in a sense, the recognition and fear that lies at the heart of Lovecraft's cosmicism. *Lovecraft knew that there was nothing that he or humankind could do to protect Western civilization against an apocalypse.* And so, he does the only thing that all of us as human beings can do when facing an impending crisis that is unavoidable: he becomes reconciled to the fact.

PART III

Humankind against the Cosmic Slave Masters

12

Lovecraft's Later Weird Tales

In the summer of 1926, Lovecraft was entering into his mature writing phase. By all accounts, he was very happy to be back in Providence in his old familiar neighborhood near College Hill and this undoubtedly had a strong effect on the quality of his new literary compositions. Lovecraft's later weird tales are generally known as the Cthulhu Mythos stories, and they focus specifically on his pantheon of extraterrestrial, terrestrial, and trans-dimensional entities. The term "Cthulhu" refers to only one of these entities, who appears in a single tale, "The Call of Cthulhu" (1926), and yet, the entire Mythos stories are named after him. Lovecraft's colleague August Derleth is credited with coming up with the designation. Lovecraft himself never specifically distinguished these stories from his other fictional compositions—he sometimes referred to them whimsically as "Yog-Sothothery," or the "Arkham cycle," but made no efforts to link them in any other way.

The two themes that I identify in Chapter 5 reach their fruition in the mature tales. The theme of the lonely, scholarly elitists who encounter supernatural entities in isolated locales is now fully developed. Detailed fictional biographies and genealogies are provided for each of the privileged, white Anglo-Saxon protagonists, and as we will see, most of these characters are either modeled directly on Lovecraft himself or, at the very least, draw on elements from his own life. This is particularly true when it comes to Charles Dexter Ward, in *The Case of Charles Dexter Ward*, and Robert Olmstead in "The Shadow Over Innsmouth." Also, Lovecraft's protagonists, like the protagonists in the early tales, respond to their various crises in the same way that Lovecraft responded to his own personal crises; we will encounter, thus, the same pattern of loss and failure that we have been tracing throughout this study. Lovecraft's second theme, the existence of alien astronaut races living on earth in the dim past, is likewise fully developed.

In the following tales, there are three extraterrestrial races and one terrestrial alien race. Lovecraft provides complex, meticulous histories, morphologies, and backstories for all of these entities, including their cultures, technologies, and even political systems. Due to the amount of detail in the later tales, they are much lengthier than the hybrid, degenerative monster stories. Indeed, *The Case of Charles Dexter Ward*, *At the Mountains of Madness*, and "The Shadow Out of Time" are novel length and ironically, though these tales are Lovecraft's masterpieces, they were so long that he had trouble getting them into print. Farnsworth Wright, the editor at *Weird Tales*, preferred not to publish long tales since they would have to be serialized and readers didn't like to wait for the endings. *The Case of Charles Dexter Ward* was never published in Lovecraft's lifetime. *At the Mountains of Madness* was rejected by Wright when Lovecraft submitted it to *Weird Tales* in 1931—it eventually appeared in a competing magazine, *Astounding Stories*, in 1936. And "The Shadow Out of Time," again, was picked up by *Astounding Stories*, also in 1936, when Lovecraft couldn't sell it to any of his regular markets.

Lovecraft's later weird tales focus on the Other as aliens rather than monsters per se. In the first, *The Case of Charles Dexter Ward*, Joseph Curwen, necromancer and slave master, creates a collection of hybrid, degenerative monsters, which is reminiscent of Herbert West's menagerie; his practices, too, are similar in that he essentially reanimates these monsters, though they are not the main focus of his experiments. In the second tale, "The Whisperer in Darkness," the aliens are the Mi-Go, an extraterrestrial alien race of cosmic slave masters that has been on the earth since 215,000,000 CE, conducting hidden mining operations in the isolated hills of Vermont. Third, in "The Shadow Over Innsmouth," the aliens are the Deep Ones, a home-grown, terrestrial alien race that resulted from an evolutionary process that ran concurrent to human evolution. In the fourth tale, *At the Mountains of Madness*, the aliens are the Elder Things, an extraterrestrial alien race of cosmic slave masters who had colonized the earth in the polar regions around 1,000,000,000 BCE, but then disappeared (presumably) in 50,000 BCE well before *Homo sapiens* evolved. Finally, in the last tale, "The Shadow Out of Time," the alien astronauts are the Great Race, an extraterrestrial race of cosmic slave masters who occupied the earth's warmer areas from 150,000,000 BCE up to 50,000,000 BCE, when they depart into the future using their mind-transfer technology.

Unique to the mature tales is Lovecraft's second racist narrative, the slave master/slave narrative. Although the miscegenation narrative continues on into Lovecraft's mature period, as do the racist images, these are featured only in two tales: *The Case of Charles Dexter Ward* and "The Shadow Over Innsmouth." The reason for this is simply a matter of logic. As we have seen in Part II, Lovecraft uses racist images and narratives to enhance the horror in his early fiction and to increase the reader's interest. Lovecraft assumed, of course, that his readers would be horrified by monsters that looked like Blacks and other members of the hated races and that readers, likewise, would be outraged by the thought of miscegenation between Blacks and whites. But in the later tales, Lovecraft's aliens are simply too alien—physically, mentally, and in all ways—to sustain human-centric characteristics. Similarly, miscegenation, whether by blood or by association, is not possible. Lovecraft's aliens are not sexual beings in any way that we can understand and if they procreate at all, they produce younglings much as plants can do. And certainly, the aliens do not want to associate closely with humankind; they accept human beings as servitors when it suits them and are prepared to kill them if they become a nuisance, but that is all.

Most disturbingly in the mature tales, Lovecraft envisions the prehistoric earth as a vast plantation planet. The Mi-Go, still living on earth, enslave humans who get too close to their secret mining operations. This is not enslavement of the body, however, but rather, of the mind. The Elder Things come to the earth and create a race of protoplasmic slaves, the shoggoths, to assist them in building their great cities in the inhospitable northern regions of the planet. They also create multicellular life and they even go so far as to take up some primitive, ape-like humans and spark their further evolution, thinking that they might enslave these humans just as they do their shoggoths, but the humans don't pan out as viable slaves. The shoggoths, however, remain on the plantation for almost nine hundred million years until they inevitably (and predictably) stage a rebellion. The rebellion is quickly squashed and later, in 500,000 BCE, the plantation moves underground when the Elder Things retreat to a vast lake under their last Antarctic City. The Great Race, also, keep slaves on their own plantations during the late Jurassic Era, but these are another alien race known as the Flying Polyps, not a manufactured race. The Great Race use their mind-transfer technology to create a new type of slavery; they inhabit the bodies of other species and project the ousted minds back to their own bodies in the past. The Flying Polyps, however, prove to be more formidable than the shoggoths; their slave rebellion is successful and the Great Race is forced to flee into the future.

By the time human beings start to evolve on the earth—Neanderthals in 350,000 BCE; *Homo erectus* in 100,000 BCE; and *Homo sapiens* in 30,000 BCE—the cosmic slave masters and their slaves are long gone. Humankind eventually becomes the dominant species. But for Lovecraft, there is always the strong possibility that the alien races will return—indeed, by 100,000–150,000 CE, Lovecraft speculates that humankind will be entirely gone, supplanted by a race of gigantic, telepathic beetles. In "The Dunwich Horror," Lovecraft writes:

> Nor is it to be thought. ... that man is either the oldest or the last of earth's masters, or that the common bulk of life and substance walks

alone. The Old Ones were, the Old Ones are, and the Old Ones shall be. Not in the spaces we know, but *between* them, They walk serene and primal, undimensioned and to us unseen. ... Man rules now where They ruled once; They shall soon rule where Man rules now. After summer is winter, and after winter summer. They wait patient and potent, for here shall They reign again.[1]

Although this passage refers specifically to Lovecraft's trans-dimensional aliens, it applies to *all* of the alien races. *For Lovecraft, the dead and the gone never stay dead or gone*. The cosmic slave masters will return sooner or later and the plantation planet will be up and running again.

13

The Case of Charles Dexter Ward (1927)

The Case of Charles Dexter Ward (1927) is Lovecraft's longest work of fiction at approximately 51,000 words. Because of its length, some critics have referred to it as a novel rather than a story and this view is certainly justifiable; I will be considering it as a novel in this study. The book has been rightly praised for its realistic treatment of Providence, Rhode Island, not only as it was in Lovecraft's own lifetime but also, as it might have been in colonial days during the late 1600s to the mid-1700s. Lovecraft's attention to historical details is, in fact, thoroughly meticulous; he conducted research to write the novel, studying Gertrude Selwyn Kimball's *Providence in Colonial Times* (1912), which he read at the New York Public Library. Lovecraft also used the knowledge that he had already amassed about the Thomas Lloyd Halsey mansion on Prospect Street in Providence; Ward's manor house is directly modeled on the Halsey mansion (which was, incidentally, reportedly haunted). Around this same period, Lovecraft was delving into Western occultism, reading the works of Margaret Murray, Cotton Mather, Montague Summers, Arthur Edward Waite, and Eliphas Levi Zahed. This material, as we will see, is used deftly by Lovecraft to lend a certain amount of verisimilitude to the events in the tale. Oddly enough, however, almost immediately after he wrote his novel, Lovecraft inexplicably developed an antipathy toward it; he put it in a drawer and forgot about it. The novel ended up being posthumously published in *Weird Tales* in two installments, May and July 1941.

Rigorously structured as well as rigorously written and researched, *The Case of Charles Dexter Ward* has drawn praise for its tight, coherent structure; it is, in fact, one of Lovecraft's most perfectly designed tales.

There are subheadings for each of the five major sections and the divisions within each section are carefully sequenced. In the first section, Charles Dexter Ward, a young antiquarian, discovers the existence of his great-great-great grandfather Joseph Curwen, slave-master and necromancer, whose history has been deliberately purged from official records by his contemporaries. Ward unearths more and more information about Curwen and slowly finds himself becoming fascinated by Curwen's occult practices. Eventually, he feels compelled to skip college as he researches Curwen's career instead, even going so far as to travel abroad for documents that he cannot obtain in the States. In the second section of the novel, Lovecraft, in a flashback chapter that takes us back to the seventeenth and eighteenth centuries, details the life and death of Joseph Curwen. Curwen restores the bodies and minds of the dead, especially the ancient dead, to seek out knowledge and riches. Curwen's illicit activities attract the attention of a group of colonial vigilantes who eventually raid his Pawtuxet farmhouse and kill him, presumably eliminating forever the threat that Curwen poses both for the colonials and for the future of humankind. In the two following sections, Lovecraft returns to the twentieth century and narrates the further activities of Charles Dexter Ward, who raises Curwen from the dead; in repayment, Curwen kills him and takes over his identity. Finally, in the last section of the tale, Dr. Willet, the Ward family physician, realizes what Curwen has done and destroys him by using his magic against him.

***

Joseph Curwen is Lovecraft's most complex and well-developed magical practitioner. Lovecraft devotes all of Section II of his novel to a full explication of Curwen's life and death. Curwen originally lived most of his adult life in Salem, Massachusetts, but he relocates to Providence in 1692. The witch trials were underway at that time and Curwen's unnaturally youthful appearance, which seemed supernatural in origin, along with the rumors of his magical practices, had convinced him that it might be expedient to take up residence in one of the other colonies. Once in Providence, he purchases a home on Olney Street that he later replaces with a new mansion in 1761. Concurrently, he purchases a farmhouse out on Pawtuxet Road where he does the bulk of his magical and alchemical work. He continues to pursue his career as a slave trader and flesh merchant—apparently, witchcraft was problematic for New England provinces, but slave trading was still okay. Ward, in his research, uncovers information about Curwen's shipping accounts that is very revealing:

> Charles Ward examined a set of his [Curwen's] accounts and invoices in the Shepley Library [that detail] the large number of Guinea blacks he imported until 1766, and the disturbingly small number for whom

he could produce bona fide bills of sale either to slave-dealers at the Great Bridge or to the planters of the Narragansett Country. ... Prior to the change in 1766, [Curwen's] boats had for the most part contained chained negroes, who were carried down and across the bay and landed at an obscure point on the shore just north of Pawtuxet; being afterward driven up the bluff and across country to the Curwen farm, where they were locked in that enormous stone outbuilding which had only high narrow slits for windows.[1]

Curwen's slaves serve a useful purpose apart from the financial considerations; they provide food for his hybrid, degenerative monsters. Interestingly, Curwen, on occasion, feeds his own sailors to the monsters as well. The sailors are described by Lovecraft in terms that remind us of his descriptions of the immigrant "hordes" in "The Horror at Red Hook":

All his sailors were mongrel riff-raff from Martinique, St. Eustatius, Havana, or Port Royal ... A crew would be turned loose in the town on shore leave, some of its members perhaps charged with this errand or that; and when reassembled it would be almost sure to lack one or more men. That many of the errands had concerned the farm on the Pawtuxet Road, and that few of the sailors had ever been seen to return from that place, was not forgotten.[2]

Curwen specializes in a form of magic known as necromancy. The term "necromancy" derives from two Greek words—nekrós, "dead body," and manteía, "divination by means of." Basically, necromancy is used by black magicians to discover hidden information. The theory behind necromancy is that the dead, no longer bound by the limitations of the mortal, physical plane, can see the events of the future and can be compelled to reveal them. Likewise, the dead have knowledge about the location of buried treasure. The mildest types of necromancy include spiritualism, sometimes known as "channeling," and the practices of psychic "readers" who use Ouija boards, Tarot cards, I-Ching sticks, runes, and so on to contact spirits. The more intense, nasty forms of necromancy make use of corpses; these are brought back to life, much as Robert Suydam is brought back to life in the climax of "The Horror at Red Hook." In terms of intent, Joseph Curwen is clearly a necromancer whose goals are essentially equivalent to the goals of the ancient necromancers. Curwen uses corpses, or at least, the *dust* of corpses—that is, the *essential saltes*—to reanimate the dead. Dr. Willett, in fact, succinctly describes what Curwen and his two associates Simon Orne and Edward Hutchinson are up to:

They were robbing the tombs of all the ages, including those of the world's wisest and greatest men, in the hope of recovering from the bygone ashes some vestige of the consciousness and lore which had once animated and informed them ... and from what was extorted from this centuried dust there was anticipated a power and a wisdom beyond anything which the cosmos had ever seen concentrated in one man or group.[3]

Curwen's necromantic rites are performed in a special magical temple located in the catacombs beneath his Pawtuxet farmhouse and he uses many of the elements of standard magical practice. However, the process itself is largely scientific, reminiscent of alchemical rather than magical workings, and it seems clear that Lovecraft in this tale is deliberately transforming the practice of necromancy from a magical art into a science; this reflects, of course, Lovecraft's materialistic, scientific side, which, in the mature tales, now becomes a significant element in Lovecraft's work. Curwen keeps two sets of "essential saltes" on the shelves in various chambers. In tall, Grecian lekythos or oil jugs with metal stoppers are the "Custodes"; these are the saltes of the "Guards," that is, the entities that are brought back to bodily form in order to keep the resuscitated bodies of the other group of entities under control when they are interrogated by Curwen and his associates; Curwen is primarily interested in discovering hidden treasure to finance his operations, so the interrogations are largely about the possible locations of treasure, although Curwen is equally happy to acquire information that might prove useful if he needs to blackmail any of his contemporaries. The other set of saltes, the "Materia," or "Materials," are the actual entities that Curwen wishes to question; these are kept in Phaleron jugs, which are smaller than the lekythos and have a conical neck. The Materia entities are, as Lovecraft puts it, "the mortal relics of half the titan thinkers of all the ages."[4]

Although Lovecraft doesn't picture Curwen himself personally performing a necromantic rite, he provides enough hints and fragments of the rite, as enacted later by Charles Dexter Ward and Dr. Willett, making it very easy to reconstruct the actual ceremony and the process. In the magical chamber, the saltes of the target entity are siphoned out into a hollowed-out shallow cup of lead, or kylis (modelled after the kylikes vases in Grecian art), and this, in turn, is placed in one or another of the circles in the magical chamber. The ritual is then performed, using a text known as the Dragon's Head conjuration; once the entity has materialized, it can be interrogated; there are special chairs in the chamber with clamps and wheels, as well as a variety of medieval torture devices and whips if torture is necessary to constrain the entity to speak. If "custodes" or guardians are needed to assist in the interrogation process, then these must be summoned previous to the necromantic rite. After the interrogation, a second text, the Dragon's Tail conjuration, is used to reduce the materialized entity back into its saltes. The Dragon's Head and Dragon's Tail conjurations are as follows:

Y'AI' NG'NGAH,	OGTHROD AI'F
YOG—SOTHOTH	GEB'L—EE'H
H'EE—L'GEB	YOG—SOTHOTH
F'AI THRODOG	'NGAH'NG AI'Y
UAAAH	ZHRO[5]

Lovecraft provides no translation for these words; the only recognizable name is Yog Sothoth, indicating that this trans-dimensional Great Old One has an intimate connection with the rite. Extraterrestrial or transdimensional entities such as Yog Sothoth are, of course, the "engines" that run the magic in the tales that focus on the practice of the black arts; they are either created or called by the magical practitioner, and then, once the entities are present, the magic happens. Elsewhere in Lovecraft's work, "The Dunwich Horror" in particular, Lovecraft speaks of Yog Sothoth as a gatekeeper between alternate dimensions and our own world; thus, in Curwen's necromantic rite, Yog Sothoth is likely functioning in a similar capacity—allowing for the translation of the entity from the shadowy, nether world of death into the physical world again.

On occasion, resurrected entities pose an interesting problem for the necromancer, and here, I think, Lovecraft ventures into something rather unusual and original in terms of the art of necromancy. It is entirely possible that the saltes of the entity, after the passage of time, become imperfect, or incomplete in some manner. If so, then three outcomes other than the expected one might occur: (1) the necromancer is unable to resurrect the entity, the saltes remain merely a pile of dust; (2) the entity, when resurrected, is deformed or distorted physically or mentally—it is a monster, in short; and (3) the entity, for whatever reason, cannot be reduced to its saltes again; it retains its physical form. Later, Dr. Willett will discover some of the subjects of Curwen's experiments still living after a century in the catacombs beneath the Pawtuxet bungalow and they are all monsters: obviously, the victims of the second outcome due to imperfect saltes. Indeed, these creatures are reminiscent of the hybrid, degenerative monsters that we have studied in the early tales. And as we might expect, these monsters afford Lovecraft an opportunity to introduce more racist imagery into his fiction.

***

Despite Curwen's occult practices, however, and despite his unnatural youthfulness and his ability to seemingly circumvent the aging process, Curwen ends up dying anyway due to violent means. During his long residence in colonial Providence, Curwen's questionable nocturnal activities have led to his becoming a pariah in the community. Hoping to reverse this situation before his business interests suffer too greatly, Curwen reasons that a high society marriage will put him back on top. He blackmails one of his ship captains, Dutee Tillinghast, to allow him to marry Tillinghast's eighteen-year-old daughter, Eliza, and the alliance does, indeed, take place in 1763. And, as Curwen hoped, the marriage temporarily puts him on top of the social circle again. But not for long. Eventually, the citizens of Providence are no longer able or willing to allow Curwen to continue his nefarious activities. Lovecraft, obviously enjoying himself, assembles a raiding party of actual historical figures: Dr. Benjamin West, Rev. James Manning, ex-Governor Stephen Hopkins, and Captain Abraham Whipple, along with the fictional Ezra Weeden and about a hundred additional men, to carry out the attack on Curwen's Pawtuxet farm. The raiding party is divided into three divisions and the raid commences after midnight on Friday, April 12, 1771.

Lovecraft handles the details of this raid very deftly; he appears to have been influenced by the ancient Greek tragedians; he keeps the specific details offstage as it were, focusing on Eleazar Smith's diary account of his participation in the raid, which was only slight. Smith's party is stationed near the shore some distance away from the farmhouse. Thus, the reader gets only bits and pieces of the action, most of it auditory; we hear distant gunshots, the throb of thunderous words in the air, the sound of a signal whistle, and so on. Additional information is provided by the Fenners, who live in the neighborhood of the Pawtuxet farmhouse, and here, Lovecraft gives us some visual as well as olfactory details. The Fenners smell sulfur in the air; they see two "flaming" things and a red fog rising up to the sky. The raid ends up successful; Curwen is killed, though the actual details of his death are not given, and Lovecraft hints that Curwen may not have been killed in the raid but rather by an extraterrestrial entity seeking retribution. But certainly, a coffin containing Curwen's body is delivered to Curwen's widow and she is told that her husband was killed in a customs battle. Afterward, an extensive obliteration of Curwen's memory is carried out by the townspeople; Curwen's widow sells the Olney Court mansion, moving back in with her father, and the Pawtuxet farmhouse is left to decay naturally over the next century.

***

Charles Dexter Ward, Lovecraft's privileged, white Anglo-Saxon protagonist, clearly plays second fiddle to Joseph Curwen—who is the undisputed "star" of *The Case of Charles Dexter Ward*. Ward's life and career, however, as detailed in Sections I, III, and IV, is accorded more pages by Lovecraft and surely, Ward can be considered as the main character of the story. Ward, also, is Lovecraft's most autobiographical character; there are no other characters in Lovecraft's fiction that are modeled as closely as Ward is on the author himself. Both men share privileged childhoods, growing up in their respective family mansions, pampered and spoiled by doting relatives. Both are introverted, self-absorbed, and elitist. Both are fascinated by weird tales. And both are too nervous and "delicate" to attend college. But Ward's history deviates from Lovecraft's in several important ways. First, unlike Whipple Phillips, Charles Dexter Ward Sr. does not die and the son and mother do not lose their inheritance; Ward stays wealthy for the rest of his life (though it doesn't help him much). Also, Ward manages to graduate from high school, which, as we have seen, is something that Lovecraft himself was unable to do. In addition, Ward develops an intense interest in magic and the occult, in contrast to Lovecraft, whose interest in these subjects was very minimal. Ward's fascination with the occult is sparked when he discovers by chance some information about his great-great-great grandfather Joseph Curwen and learns about a portrait of his ancestor in an old house in Olney Court. Ward has the portrait restored and then both portrait and mantelpiece removed from the old house and transported to a wall in his own study. Behind the gap in the wall at Olney Court, Ward is excited to discover some hidden documents: a thick copybook "*Journall and Notes of Jos: Curwen, Gent., of Providence-Plantations, Late of Salem,*" along with six other documents, including "*To Him Who Shal Come After, & How He May Gett Beyonde Time & ye Spheres*" and a travelogue "*Joseph Curwen his Life and Travells Bet'n ye yeares 1678 and 1687: Of Whither He Voyag'd, Where He Stay'd, Whom He Sawe, and What He Learnt.*" Ward begins to study these documents and very quickly, his interests veer away from antiquarianism to magic.

Ward is resolved to resurrect Curwen. He discovers Curwen's unmarked grave, obtains Curwen's essential saltes, and then, in his attic laboratory on April 15, a Good Friday, uses the Dragon's Head conjuration to bring back Joseph Curwen from the dead. Following this, Joseph Curwen and Charles Dexter Ward end up becoming magical partners, as Ward had wanted, and they continue the magical and necromantic practices that Curwen and his former associates engaged in during colonial times. The two men are rather constrained in the Ward mansion, however, and so, for the sake of privacy, Charles decides to purchase the Pawtuxet farmhouse, which is now a bungalow. After the relocation to Pawtuxet, Curwen becomes more autonomous and begins to dominate his youthful protégé. He takes on the name Dr. Allen and wears a pair of dark glasses and a fake beard. The men resume their connection with Hutchinson and Orne as well; apparently, these men had managed to survive over the centuries, as Dr. Willett and Charles Sr. discover when they intercept some correspondence addressed to Allen.

Eventually, the partnership between Ward and Curwen begins to erode at the Pawtuxet location. Lovecraft doesn't explain exactly why, but it seems likely that Ward's own will begins to reassert itself. Perhaps, Ward is having second thoughts about the practice of necromancy. Ward ends up becoming a very unwilling magical practitioner and he actively tries to resist the influence of Curwen and to sever all connections with him. He leaves the Pawtuxet farmhouse and moves back to his paternal mansion and, in a letter to Willett, advises Willett to shoot Dr. Allen on sight and dissolve his body in acid to ensure that it cannot be reanimated again. But despite Charles's resolve for the future, he is unable to completely break free from Curwen. Here, we see the usual pattern of loss and failure that we observed in the hybrid, degenerative monster tales. Charles Sr. has hired four detectives to guard his son and they are stationed at the mansion. Thus, Charles Jr. is physically safe from Curwen's machinations—or at least, so it is thought. Nevertheless, Charles is fearful and clearly in a state of stasis. He receives a call from Curwen on the telephone, which is overheard by one of the detectives. Though the detective can hear only one side of the conversation, Ward's responses illustrate the extreme condition of passivity and pathological resignation into which he has fallen: "I am very tired and must rest a while"; "I can't receive anyone for some time"; "I am very sorry, but I must take a complete vacation from everything"; "I'll talk with you later."[6]

Despite the presence of the detectives, Curwen manages to infiltrate the mansion and kill Ward in his room on the eve of a scheduled meeting with Dr. Willett. He disposes of the body and neither Willet nor Charles Dexter Ward Sr. know that Charles Jr. is dead. Indeed, Curwen takes on the identity of Charles and returns to the Pawtuxet bungalow to continue his necromancy. Curwen gets away with this deception initially because he resembles Charles very closely, except for a small scar above his right eye; thus, he no longer needs to disguise himself as Dr. Allen. However, there are large gaps in his general knowledge about the speech, customs, and contemporary events of the early twentieth century, which Dr. Willett notices after speaking with him shortly after his return to the farm. Willett, at this juncture, still refuses to believe that Curwen is alive and that Charles is dead; Willett naturally assumes that he is talking to Charles Dexter Ward and furthermore, he assumes that Charles is now suffering from some sort of serious mental aberration. The doubts escalate slowly, and finally, in March, Dr. Willett, along with Drs. Peck, Lyman, and Waite, and accompanied, of course, by Charles Sr., pay an official visit to the farmhouse. After some conversation with Curwen, they promptly take custody of him and subsequently incarcerate him at Dr. Waite's private hospital on Conanicut Island, Providence. Immediately, Curwen is put under medical observation, and Willet has several interviews with him. But Willett doesn't learn too much useful information. And so, eventually, Willett decides that he will need to investigate the Pawtuxet farmhouse extensively, for he suspects that there are tunnels and catacombs beneath the house that will provide him with the information and explanations that he requires. On April 6, Mr.

Ward and Dr. Willett visit the farmhouse and they discover an entrance to the catacombs, but Charles Dexter Ward Sr. is struck down by the miasmic, noxious fumes rising from below and Willett is forced to send him back home. Willett then descends into the catacombs by himself.

***

Lovecraft, in the final section of the story, takes us swiftly to the conclusion. Lovecraft was very skilled in the writing of strong, action-oriented prose and he makes good use of this skill in his description of Dr. Willett's experiences in the catacombs. As he had already suspected, Willett discovers that the catacombs and tunnels beneath the Pawtuxet farmhouse are fairly extensive and undertakes a full, methodical exploration, uncovering most of Curwen's secrets. In particular, he learns that some of Curwen's experiments were failures due to imperfection in the saltes and that many of these imperfectly regenerated entities, in turn, are still alive, kept imprisoned in deep, circular wells. Lovecraft masterfully avoids giving the reader a clear view of these entities; Willett only catches a glimpse of one of them briefly in shadow, and what he sees drives him literally insane for a few moments; the actual appearance of the creature is left mostly to the reader's imagination. But the brief glimpse is frightening enough.

> But Marinus Bicknell Willett was sorry that he looked again; for surgeon and veteran of the dissecting-room though he was, he has not been the same since. It is hard to explain just how a single sight of a tangible object with measurable dimensions could so shake and change a man; and we may only say that there is about certain outlines and entities a power of symbolism and suggestion which acts frightfully on a sensitive thinker's perspective and whispers terrible hints of obscure cosmic relationships and unnamable realities behind the protective illusions of common vision. In that second look Willett saw such an outline or entity, for during the next few instants he was undoubtably as stark mad as any inmate of Dr. Waite's private hospital ... What the thing was, he would never tell ... Nature had never made it in this form, for it was too palpably *unfinished*. The deficiencies were of the most surprising sort, and the abnormalities of proportion could not be described. ... it was neither thoroughly human, nor wholly allied to any animal which Pawtuxet folk had ever seen or read about.[7]

The last part of this description is in keeping with Lovecraft's arguments in the two racist poems that we have studied in Chapter 4; Curwen's monsters are not human and also not "wholly allied" to animals. They are very much like the Blacks that he writes about as being a link between humankind and apes in the poem "On the Creation of Niggers"—"A beast they wrought, in semi-human figure, / Fill'd it with vice, and call'd the thing a NIGGER."[8]

The monsters penned up like slaves in Curwen's catacombs are truly akin to the hybrid, degenerative creatures that proliferate in the early tales.

After Willett has this disturbing experience, he eventually finds Curwen's secret magical temple and, surprisingly, a pile of essential saltes has been set up and ready for the necromantic process. Obviously, Curwen was in the process of performing yet another experiment when he was interrupted by the raiding party and forced to defend himself. Willett unwisely decides to test the Dragon's Head conjuration to see if it will work with these saltes and he inadvertently reanimates the bodily simulacrum of the saltes. Not surprisingly, however, the appearance of the resulting entity proves to be too much for Willett, particularly in light of the other horrors that he has encountered in the catacombs. Willett falls into a dead faint, waking later in the bungalow. He discovers that the entrance to the catacombs has been sealed by some supernatural agency and thus, Willett has no empirical evidence to confirm his nightmarish visit into Joseph Curwen's secret world. Nevertheless, he is, at last, aware now that Charles Dexter Ward is dead and Joseph Curwen is very much alive. He is also aware that Curwen's necromantic rites actually do work, and he reasons that he might be able to reverse Charles Dexter Ward's resurrection of Curwen by simply using the second formula of the original conjuration rite used by Ward. Willett pays a climatic visit to Curwen in the mental institution and does exactly that, dematerializing Curwen into his essential saltes and effectively destroying him.

* * *

The predominate racist narrative in *The Case of Charles Dexter Ward* is the slave master/slave narrative. Curwen is, quite literally, a slave owner; I have already cited examples of this previously: the Guinea slaves and the "mongrel" hordes associated with Joseph Curwen's slave trading days previous to 1760. Shapiro and Barnard refer to the slave master/slave theme pointedly in their book *Pentecostal Modernism*:

> In "The Case of Charles Dexter Ward" (1927), the eponymous character becomes the literal ward of a resurrected ancestor Joseph Curwen, who fled Salem to become a resident of Providence in the eighteenth century and built on a fortune from the merchant trade. While "all of his sailors were mongrel riff-raff from Martinique, St. Eustasius, Havanna, or Port Royal," Curwen had monopolized "the town's trade in saltpeter, black pepper, and cinnamon" as a means of disguising his movement of "salts" that he will use to regenerate bodies. Curwen' experiments are facilitated by "the large numbers of Guinea blacks he imported."[9]

The slavery backstory here is used deliberately by Lovecraft to enhance the evil elements of the Curwen character. As noted before, *The Case of*

Charles Dexter Ward bears a remarkable similarity to "The Horror at Red Hook," a fact that has been noticed by most Lovecraft scholars and critics. This is due primarily to the close resemblance between Joseph Curwen and Robert Suydam. Both are very evil men, black magic practitioners to the core. Indeed, they are not above human sacrifice; as we have seen, Suydam sacrifices children to Lilith, Gorgo, Mormo, and the other dark gods and goddesses that he serves, while Curwen feeds his Black slaves to the monstrous reanimated entities that he is unable to return to their essential saltes. Therefore, in *The Case of Charles Dexter Ward*, the slave narrative serves the same purpose as the human sacrifice theme in "The Horror at Red Hook"; it makes Curwen seem more detestable and more of a corrupt human being than he would be otherwise. *But that is all the slave narrative is doing in this novel, intensifying the horror.* In effect, the slave narrative is used by Lovecraft solely to serve his literary purposes. And here, Lovecraft proves himself to be as cold-hearted as his character Curwen. Both the creator and his creation use slaves and the victim races as merely fodder for their purposes—to make Curwen more of a monster, in Lovecraft's case, and to sustain reanimated corpses, in Curwen's.

Lovecraft's other racist narrative, the miscegenation narrative, also plays a part in the plot of the novel. This narrative proves to be just as important, in fact, as the slave master/slave narrative. Curwen extends the concept of "human being" beyond the limitations of time and the aging process through the use of his necromancy. Lovecraft doesn't tell us what to think about Curwen's status as a human being, not directly anyway; he develops the character as fully as he can and to the best of his abilities and then lets the reader decide if Curwen has transcended humanity to such an extent that he may be considered suprahuman, or nonhuman, or, possibly, subhuman. From beginning to end, Curwen certainly acts and looks as human as anyone else, but inwardly, he is slowly degenerating. This is mainly a mental, psychological, moral, and spiritual devolution, and it stems from miscegenation by association.

In "The Horror at Red Hook," we have seen that Robert Suydam, as a Teuton, and, thus, a member of the superior race, degenerates due to his close association with nonwhite races and alien, animalistic cults, and also, with the black magic practices that these cults deploy and that he himself deploys to rejuvenate himself. We see Suydam's physical appearance as it fluctuates from simple old age and natural decrepitude to a sudden rise in youth and energy, and then, back to decrepitude again and finally, the half-life, half-death reanimation at the end of the tale. In a similar manner, Lovecraft passes the same kind of racist judgment on Curwen and his two associates (and on Charles Dexter Ward as well, for all that). Curwen, a white Anglo-Saxon male, associates with alien races; he purchases slaves from Guinea and uses them to feed his regenerated corpses. Thus, Curwen is connected to alien races as intimately as Suydam is. The only difference between the two men is that Curwen's degeneration is not so obvious; he looks basically the same throughout the tale—his degeneration is more of the nature of an internal degeneration. But it is there nonetheless and it plays a role in Curwen's eventual fate.

Similar to Suydam, Curwen also uses black magic—the magic of alien races, and this is a major factor in his deterioration and decline as well. Indeed, Curwen's use of magic is much more extensive than Suydam's; he uses magic not merely to keep himself preternaturally young; he uses it to reanimate corpses, he uses it to ensnare Ward, and he uses it to live again centuries after his death. Moreover, Curwen never once in *The Case of Charles Dexter Ward* has second thoughts about the choices that he has made in his life. He never questions his close, intimate connection with black magic and he doesn't renounce his magical practices or try to distance himself from them, as Suydam does before he goes on his disastrous honeymoon. What Lovecraft is telling us here is that degeneration is almost always the result when a white Anglo-Saxon male or female is morally corrupt enough to use black magic—the natural magic and religious practice of alien races. Black magic is, in effect, associated with the Other and with the hybrids and degenerates who serve the Other.

14

The Whisperer in Darkness (1930)

"The Whisperer in Darkness" is nearly as well-crafted as *The Case of Charles Dexter Ward*; Lovecraft exerts the same level of care in the development of his setting—here, Vermont—as he did for Providence in the previous work. This is no accident; Lovecraft visited Vermont on two separate occasions in 1927 and 1928 and recorded his impressions in "Vermont—A First Impression" (1927), from which he lifted material to put in the tale (though Lovecraft, always a careful prose stylist, rewrote the imported passages so that this wasn't merely a word-for-word transcription). Lovecraft also modeled his white Anglo-Saxon protagonist, Henry Wentworth Akeley, on an actual Vermont rustic, even going so far as to use a variation of the man's name (which was spelled "Akley") for this purpose. At 25,000 words, "The Whisperer in Darkness" is among Lovecraft's longest tales; it took him a little more time to write it than was customary for him. He started it in February and didn't complete it until September 1930. However, the extra time that he put into it paid off in the end. The story was immediately purchased by Farnsworth Wright for *Weird Tales* when Lovecraft submitted it and Wright paid $350.00, which, as it turns out, was the largest sum that Lovecraft had ever received (or would ever receive) from a single tale. The story appeared in the August 1931 issue of the magazine.

At the start of "The Whisperer in Darkness," Albert N. Wilmarth, a Miskatonic instructor of literature and a folklore scholar, is alerted by his friends about reports of strange bodies glimpsed in the waters during a spring flood in Vermont, November 1927. The bodies are purportedly not human, though none of them have been recovered and so, there is no evidence to support this belief. The more superstitious locals believe that these corpses are the dead bodies of members of the Mi-Go alien race that, or so legend has it, live in secret conclaves in the isolated hills. A local newspaper, the *Brattleboro Reformer*, prints one of Wilmarth's skeptical articles on mythology and folklore and this article attracts the attention of Henry Wentworth Akeley, a farmer and amateur scholar living near Townshend. Wilmarth and Akeley strike up a correspondence and Akeley convinces Wilmarth that the Mi-Go are not legends but actually exist. Akeley lives in an isolated farmhouse near the hills where the Mi-Go have set up one of their bases and Akeley has gotten photographs of their footprints and a curious black rock that he discovered in the deep woods that is connected with the Mi-Go's quasi-religious practices. Akeley sends the photos to Wilmarth. The Mi-Go become aware of Akeley's interest and they try to stop him from continuing his investigations—they attempt to waylay him as he drives to and from the town and, on moonless nights, they mount occasional attacks on his home. Akeley protects himself with his shotgun and a team of fierce police dogs. Wilmarth fears for Akeley's safety and urges him to abandon his farmhouse and move in with his son, who lives in California. The situation continues for a time; Akeley manages to hold off the Mi-Go, though he is forced to continually replace dogs that are killed. But then, suddenly, Akeley sends a letter that reports that he and the Mi-Go have reached a truce and that they are now on good terms. Akeley invites Wilmarth to visit and to bring the photos and the other evidence that he had sent. Wilmarth has his reservations, but he complies. He has a disturbing interview with Akeley when he first arrives at the Akeley farmhouse; this takes place in a semi-dark room and Akeley is wearing a robe and scarf. Akeley speaks in a low whisper—he becomes, thus, "the whisperer in darkness" referred to in the title of the story. But Wilmarth soon realizes that he is speaking with a Mi-Go, who is wearing a cunning mask and gloves that duplicate Akeley's face and hands. The real Akeley is nowhere to be found and Wilmarth deduces that he has become one more victim of the Mi-Go's brain cylinder technology (this technology will be examined in full detail shortly). After the interview, Wilmarth fears that the Mi-Go might want to silence him for what he knows and escapes from the house, driving away in Akeley's car.

* * *

The Mi-Go arrive on earth around 215,000,000 BCE, just before the coming of the Great Race in the late Jurassic Period. They have several bases throughout the galaxy; the closest one to earth is on the planet Yuggoth (this is Lovecraft's name for Pluto, which was just discovered around the time he wrote "The Whisperer in Darkness"). Upon their arrival, the Mi-Go establish colonies in the Himalayan Mountains and also in the isolated hills of Vermont. Alone among Lovecraft's three great alien astronaut races, the Mi-Go prove to be the most resilient; the Great Race and the Elder Things are long gone from the earth by the time that *Homo sapiens* have reach their full development (30,000 BCE), but the Mi-Go still live to this day in their secret Himalayan and Vermont conclaves. The term "Mi-Go" is synonymous with "Abominable Snowman" in the popular mind and this might strike some readers as rather odd, since the Mi-Go are definitely not anthropoids, but the explanation is that the Mi-Go that live in the Antarctic regions cover their bodies with animal pelts to protect them from the extreme cold and thus, from a distance they resemble large apes. Lovecraft describes the Mi-Go as follows:

> They were pinkish things about five feet long; with crustaceous bodies bearing vast pairs of dorsal fins or membraneous wings and several sets of articulated limbs, and with a sort of convoluted ellipsoid, covered with multitudes of very short antennae, where a head would ordinarily be.[1]

The Mi-Go, like the rest of Lovecraft's alien extraterrestrials, are neither animal nor vegetable but a combination of both; in the case of the Mi-Go specifically, they tend more toward the vegetable; Lovecraft tells us that they have a "fungoid structure" with a preponderance of a "chlorophyll-like substance" in their bloodstream.

However, Lovecraft adds another level of complexity to their physical natures. Akeley takes a photograph of a dead Mi-Go that was killed by his dogs after one of their nightly skirmishes and finds that its body doesn't appear in the developed print. As he explains it to Wilmarth:

> And here's the worst. I tried to photograph it for you, but when I developed the film *there wasn't anything visible except the woodshed.* What can the thing have been made of? ... It was surely made of matter—but what kind of matter? ... Indeed, the type is composed of a form of matter totally alien to our part of space—with electrons having a wholly different vibration-rate. That is why the beings cannot be photographed on the *ordinary* camera films and plates of our known universe, even though our eyes can see them. With proper knowledge, however, any good chemist could make a photographic emulsion which would record their images.[2]

Lovecraft is offering a theory here about the behavior of electrons that anticipates the theories of contemporary physicists. Scientists have noted that some electrons rotate in one direction and others rotate in another—the different directions are known as "spin-up" or "spin-down." By "vibration," Lovecraft appears to be referring to these rotations. Thus, the subatomic particles that serve as the basis for the physical forms of the Mi-Go may, perhaps, "vibrate" or "spin" in a manner that is utterly alien to the behavior of electrons in our space/time continuum—hence, they are not measurable by such devices as cameras, which are designed to record only phenomenon characteristic of the known universe.

The Mi-Go are highly intelligent and ultra-civilized, as are all of Lovecraft's extraterrestrial Others. Akeley, in fact, literally gushes as he describes the superiority of these entities in comparison with all other entities in the cosmos, including the other alien astronaut races. As Akeley puts it, "The Outer Beings are perhaps the most marvelous organic things in or beyond all space and time—members of a cosmos-wide race of which all other life-forms are merely degenerate variants."[3] The Mi-Go communicate among themselves by the use of telepathy, though they do have rudimentary vocal organs that can be rendered operational via surgery—many of them opt to have this surgery to make it easier to communicate with humans. The sound of their voices, however, is disquieting to humans who hear them—it is reminiscent of the buzzing of large insects. The Mi-Go, also, are able to travel in outer space in their corporal forms; they do not need the protection of metallic vessels, artificial sources of oxygen, heat or gravity, or specialized suits and gear. They can actually fly through space as they do on earth, using their powerful wings, though only for short distances. As for travel to and from more distant locales, such as from their outpost on Pluto to the earth, they have devised a method that is more or less equivalent to jumping in and out of hyperspace—though Lovecraft doesn't reveal the nature of this technology. As for their mining operations, these, too, are technologically advanced. Indeed, the reason why the Mi-Go chose the earth to colonize in the first place was that it is ideally suited for their mining operations; the planet has minerals that can be used to grow the fungi that the Mi-Go use as a food source. They eat the fungus by passing a metal capture containing it through their bodies.

Central to their technology is the brain cylinder device. The cylinder itself is a metal container, air-tight and filled with a fluid that nourishes organic matter. The container is fitted with electrodes in the front that can be connected to other, peripheral devices that duplicate the senses of sight, hearing, and speech. Through their great surgical skills, the Mi-Go are able to extract the brain of any entity, human, animal, or alien, and place that brain in the cylinder, where it can exist alive and healthy for an indefinite period of time. As for the body, this is placed in cold storage in a laboratory under Round Mountain, Vermont, where it is, likewise, kept alive and healthy, pending the return of the brain. Each brain in its cylinder remains in a deep sleep, subject to vivid dreams. When the Mi-Go wish to communicate with one of the brains, this is done simply by hooking up the cylinder to the peripheral devices. The Mi-Go tout their brain cylinder technology as the ideal method for entities that are not as physically or mentally developed as they are to travel through space; the cylinders can simply be carried by the Mi-Go as they traverse the outer gulfs. Then, once the Mi-Go reach their destination—whether this is another planet, or an alternate dimension, or even an alternate universe—the cylinder is hooked up to the peripherals at the hosting locale and the brains can experience exactly what life is like in these thoroughly alien environments.

During his visit with Akeley, Wilmarth communicates with a human being whose brain has been extracted and placed in a cylinder. This individual (whose name is not given—Wilmarth merely sees the number B-67 pasted on the cylinder) extolls the benefits of the brain cylinder technology, using the same gushing tones that Akeley himself did in describing the superiority of the Mi-Go over human beings. In particular, B-67 frames his argument in a way that would appeal to a person who values the acquisition of pure knowledge and insight above other, more human-centric or mundane concerns:

> Mr. Wilmarth. ... I myself am here with you—my brain is in that cylinder and I see, hear, and speak through these electronic vibrators. In a week I am going across the void as I have been many times before. ... Do you realize what it means when I say I have been on thirty-seven different celestial bodies—planets, dark stars, and less definable objects—including eight outside our galaxy and two outside the curved cosmos of space and time? ... I hope most heartily that you will decide to come with Mr. Akeley and me. The visitors are eager to know men of knowledge like yourself, and to shew them the great abysses that most of us have had to dream about in fanciful ignorance.[4]

Lovecraft himself was fascinated by possible journeys "across the void" and, by all accounts, had a burning desire to know what the cosmos was like beyond our solar system. And so, it is not hard to imagine that he would have jumped at the chance to make a journey such as this, whether in a brain cylinder or otherwise, if he had been given the opportunity.

**

The Mi-Go, however, are cosmic slave masters and not interested in using their brain cylinder technology to benefit humankind or to, in fact, benefit any other race, alien or otherwise. Rather, they use it solely for the purposes of enslavement. Akeley identifies a number of the alien races whose brains are currently resting inside their cylinders on the shelves of his own study:

> You see there are four different sorts of beings presented in those cylinders up there. Three humans, six fungoid beings who can't navigate space corporeally, two beings from Neptune ... and the rest entities from the central caverns of an especially interesting dark star beyond the galaxy. In the principle outpost inside Round Hill. ... you'll ... find ... cylinders of extra-cosmic brains with different senses from any we know—allies and explorers from the uttermost Outside.[5]

Lovecraft doesn't provide any actual examples of the enslavement process in these cases, nor does he suggest any motives behind the Mi-Go's choice of these races as likely candidates for enslavement. But Lovecraft does detail both the motives and the process behind Akeley's enslavement and thus, we can assume that they are similar for the alien races as well.

Though Akeley's situation is only one example, it is sufficient to convince us that the process is the exact opposite of what the Mi-Go claim; it doesn't widen intellectual horizons or opportunities—it limits them. Early in his struggles with the Mi-Go, Akeley becomes aware of the brain cylinder technology and realizes that both the Mi-Go and their human agents want to subject him to the process. Akeley naturally resists, finding the idea repugnant. As he puts it in one of his letters to Wilmarth:

> *They don't mean to let me get to California now—they want to take me off alive, or what theoretically and mentally amounts to alive*—not only to Yuggoth, but beyond that—away outside the galaxy *and possibly beyond the last curved rim of space.* I told them I wouldn't go where they wish, *or in the terrible way they propose to take me*, but I'm afraid it will be no use.[6]

Akeley, even at the earliest stages of his knowledge of the Mi-Go, immediately recognizes the brain cylinder technology for what it really is. It is enslavement, pure and simple, and definitely not a viable method for humans or aliens to use in exploring the universe and experiencing first-hand the great wonders and beauty of the cosmos; such an interpretation is only propaganda on the part of the Others and their brain-washed allies. Later, Wilmarth suspects that Akeley has been tricked into believing (or at least half-believing) the propaganda. Near the climax of the tale, as Wilmarth listens in to the meeting downstairs at the Akeley farmhouse, he notices that one of the brains is taking part in the conversation and he is certain that this is the real Akeley, who is expressing regret that he submitted to the brain transfer: "brought it on myself ... sent back the letters and the record ... end on it.. taken in ... seeing and hearing. ... damn you ... impersonal force, after all ... fresh, shiny cylinder ... great God."[7] If this is Akeley's voice (and there is no reason to think that it isn't), then Akeley is now enslaved—he must do what the Mi-Go tell him to do, under the threat of never having his brain restored to his body again.

In "The Whisperer in Darkness," the Mi-Go's plantation is housed inside Round Hill. This is an actual place in Rutland County near Shrewsbury (this town is mentioned by Lovecraft in the tale), though nowadays, it is a popular site for hiking and exploration—hardly an isolated locale for alien mining operations. In the tale, however, the Mi-Go keep their slave pens deep under the surface of the hill. The pens include two components: (1) the rooms that contain the bodies of their victims, kept alive and preserved in cryogenic cells, and (2) the rooms where all the brain cylinders are neatly catalogued. This setup is reminiscent of Joseph Curwen's slave pens in *The Case of Charles Dexter Ward*. In the latter tale, as will be remembered, Curwen kept his hybrid, degenerative monsters in separate underground cells in a single, main room, while in adjoining rooms, the essential saltes (i.e., the "minds" of the creatures, in effect) are placed in jars on the shelves.

It can be argued, in fact, that "The Whisperer in Darkness" is an extension on a grander, cosmic scale of what we have seen in *The Case of Charles Dexter Ward*. The Mi-Go are not much different than Joseph Curwen in terms of their single-minded dedication to their own self-motivated objectives, and both aliens and necromancer alike are capable of killing or enslaving weaker beings to suit their purposes.

* * *

Henry Wentworth Akeley is Lovecraft's privileged white Anglo-Saxon protagonist. In the first part of the tale, the focus is on the conflict between Akeley and the Mi-Go; in the second part, once Wilmarth arrives in Vermont, the focus is on the conflict between Wilmarth and the Mi-Go. Initially, the Mi-Go become interested in the epistolary communications between Akeley and Wilmarth because they see it as a threat to their hidden mining operations; they fear that the existence of their colony will be publicly exposed. This leads them to make various attempts to capture Akeley, either on his own land or else on the roads that he occasionally travels in his car to and from nearby Townshend.

During the first phase of the correspondence, Akeley details his continuing conflicts with the Mi-Go and their human agents; these escalate into nightly skirmishes with gunfire exchanged between the two parties. Akeley holds his own with his big-game rifle and his team of fierce police dogs. Akeley manages to send some evidence to support his claims via the post; this includes photographs of the Mi-Go's tracks and a phonograph recording of the quasi-religious rite that he overhears in the deep woods. Akeley also attempts to send Wilmarth a black stone that he discovers in the Round Hill area that presumably came from Yuggoth, but the Mi-Go's human agents manage to intercept the package. As the conflict between Akeley and the Mi-Go becomes more intense, Akeley starts to lose ground, but he stubbornly refuses to give in and leave the area, as Wilmarth advises him to do.

Here, Akeley begins to succumb to the pattern of loss and failure that Lovecraft's protagonists invariably face when confronting crises. Akeley, in effect, finds himself in a stasis, unable to decide what to do. As he describes it to Wilmarth:

> Suppose I'll be ready for moving in a week or two, though it nearly kills me to think of it. ... I would run off without anything if I could, but something inside my mind holds me back. ... But I don't know as I care.

After what I've been through, a madhouse is as good a place as any. The doctors can help me make up my mind to get away from this house, and that is all that will save me.⁸

In his next-to-the-last letter, Akeley is so far gone that he essentially gives up the fight; he advises Wilmarth to destroy the evidence that he has sent and not get mixed up any further with the Mi-Go.

Then, in a complete about-face, Wilmarth receives a letter from Akeley that contradicts all of the letters that preceded it. Here, Akeley disavows his own dire warnings about the Mi-Go and argues that the Mi-Go are beneficent entities, friends and allies to humankind. Akeley tells Wilmarth that he is now supportive of their agendas on earth. Akeley extolls the virtues of the brain cylinder technology and even goes so far as to state that he plans to subject himself to this procedure in the future. Wilmarth is invited to visit the Akeley farmhouse immediately and, as we might guess, to bring with him all the empirical evidence that he had received so that the two of them can presumably collaborate on "piecing together the whole tremendous story."⁹ Akeley cautions Wilmarth to not tell anyone where he is going.

There are three red-flags here: the letter is typewritten, unlike Akeley's other letters; also, Akeley has reversed his position that the Mi-Go pose a threat to humankind; and, finally, the mood and the tone are all wrong—not like the Akeley that Wilmarth has come to know. Indeed, it couldn't be more clear to the reader that this letter was written by someone other than Akeley and that this fake Akeley is trying to lure Wilmarth to Vermont so that the Mi-Go can destroy the evidence and then either silence him or coerce him into becoming a brain cylinder slave. But Wilmarth, like many of Lovecraft's more obstinate (and admittedly obtuse) protagonists, proves to be peculiarly block-headed when it comes to understanding the threat that he is facing. Thus, Wilmarth accepts the invitation. He takes a train to Vermont and is picked up at the station by Noyes, one of the Mi-Go's human agents, and then driven in Akeley's car to the farmhouse. Along the way, as the two men converse, Wilmarth recognizes Noyes's voice as the voice of one of the human celebrants in the phonograph record; he also finds himself disturbed by the weird Vermont scenery and by the alien footprints that he sees near the Akeley property—two more red-flags that he stolidly ignores.

***

The rest of "The Whisperer in Darkness" is basically a first-hand account of Albert N. Wilmarth vs the Mi-Go. Unlike the situation with Akeley, however, there is no violence on the part of the Mi-Go; the struggle is conducted entirely on an intellectual and psychological level; arguments are used, rather than physical coercion. Wilmarth has a long interview with his host immediately after he arrives at the farmhouse. The interview takes place in a semi-dark room and Wilmarth cannot get a clear look at Akeley's face or hands; the face looks like Akeley, but it seems unnatural, as if it were a mask. Akeley is swathed in a robe and a hood-like scarf, concealing his body. Akeley's voice, too, is disturbing; it has an inhuman, buzzing quality to it. Akeley claims that he is suffering from an acute case of asthma, but Wilmarth, at last, is beginning to figure out what is really going on. Akeley has been captured and silenced, and this fake Akeley is attempting to trick Wilmarth into submitting to the brain cylinder process. To lend more validity to his argument, Akeley instructs Wilmarth to hook up to one of the brain cylinders and speak with a human who has actually gone through the procedure. This human, who remains unidentified, attempts to convince Wilmarth to willingly undergo the transplant by appealing to his "scientific zeal," as Lovecraft refers to it; he claims to have visited thirty-seven planets and to have been to the uttermost limits of the cosmos. As further incentive, he notes that the brain, while in its cylinder, never ages and is virtually immortal. Wilmarth pretends to be interested in what he is hearing, but he now understands the full implications of what is at stake here; his life and his autonomy are both at risk. After the brain cylinder is shut off, Akeley professes himself tired by the interview and he allows Wilmarth to go upstairs to bed.

Wilmarth doesn't retire for the night, however; he plans to get out of the Akeley farmhouse as quickly and as safely as he can. He lays down on the bed, fully clothed and gripping a revolver, which he had had the good sense to pack in his suitcase. He dozes off for a short period of time, but then wakes up when he hears voices downstairs. A meeting is taking place; the guests include both the Mi-Go and their human agents. Terrified, Wilmarth waits until the meeting is over and then he creeps downstairs. He takes a quick glance in Akeley's room, trailing his flashlight beam around it, and discovers that Akeley is not there; in his chair, however, is the robe, a mask, and gloves, confirming his suspicion that he had spoken with a Mi-Go, who had been disguised as Akeley. Wilmarth steals Akeley's car and drives to Townshend, where he rouses the sheriff and his deputies. Naturally, he doesn't tell them the full story; he merely explains that Akeley has disappeared and that he is worried about him. The police investigate the Akeley farmhouse the next day. But predictably, the cylinders are gone, the evidence is gone, and Akeley is gone. Other than a few bullet holes in the outside walls of the house, there is no evidence that Akeley has been kidnapped or killed. Thus, the reason for Akeley's disappearance remains a mystery, at least officially, though Wilmarth knows better.

* * *

Lovecraft's slave master/slave narrative dominates "The Whisperer in Darkness." The tale, in a sense, serves as the prototype for the other two cosmic slave master tales that follow: *At the Mountains of Madness* and

"The Shadow Out of Time." The similarities between the three tales are, indeed, striking. In each tale, the extraterrestrial Others are not only superior in terms of intellect, technology, and culture to humankind, but to all other alien races. Each of these races, also, establishes slave plantations on earth and two of them, in fact, have no compunctions about adding human beings to their slave rolls. Thus, the implication is strong on the part of Lovecraft that superior alien races are naturally predisposed to the practice of slavery and, perhaps, are even justified in this practice, or at the very least, should be excused for it. Indeed, the right of these alien races to hold slaves may be, in Lovecraft's view, a natural, God-given right, and as such, it should never be questioned or challenged. And, in a similar fashion, the white Anglo-Saxon race, also superior, at least in comparison with the other earthly races, has the God-given right to make slaves out of the weaker races and dominate them.

"The Whisperer in Darkness" differs from the subsequent tales in one important way, however: the Mi-Go's brain slaves are totally unique in comparison with Lovecraft's other slave races. Essentially, they are bodiless brains in jars and, thus, unable to meet the physical demands invariably imposed on slaves. The Mi-Go's slaves cannot help their masters build cities or do manual labor, as can the shoggoths or the flying polyps. Nevertheless, they are very effective servants when it comes to other important tasks. They can act as consultants, giving their masters the benefit of their knowledge and experience. They can provide useful information about the civilizations they come from. Also, they can be used for propaganda purposes; as we have seen, one of them is deployed to trick Wilmarth into submitting to the brain transplant process, just as Akeley had been tricked. But more important than all of this, the brain slaves do not pose any threat to their masters. They cannot meet in secret conclaves with fellow slaves and plot against their masters since their meetings and conversations are carefully controlled by the Mi-Go. They cannot mount any sort of resistance or stage a rebellion. In order to do these kinds of things, they would have to have bodily forms, with hands, feet, and fists—or, at least, tentacles and tendrils—to strike and kick with.

As such, brains in cylinders represent, in many ways, the ideal slave.

15

The Shadow Over Innsmouth (1931)

"The Shadow Over Innsmouth" was inspired by Lovecraft's visit to the seaport town of Newburyport, Massachusetts, in 1923. Two literary works that he had read before this visit were equally important as inspiration: Irvin S. Cobb's "Fishhead" (1913) and Robert Chamber's "The Harbor Master" (1904), though, in each of these stories, there is only a single half-human, half-fish hybrid. The notion of having a whole colony of such hybrids was Lovecraft's own idea and he used it first in "The Doom That Came to Sarnath" (1919) before perfecting it in "The Shadow Over Innsmouth." The tale is 25,000 words, approximately the same size as "The Whisperer in Darkness," but when it was submitted to *Weird Tales*, Farnsworth Wright rejected it, complaining that it was too long, even though he had previously accepted "Whisperer" without any reservations. The tale remained unpublished until 1936, when Lovecraft's colleague William L. Crawford decided to issue it in book form and commissioned *Weird Tales* illustrator Frank Utpatel to execute woodcuts for it. Crawford bound two hundred copies before he ran out of money and had to abandon the project. This first edition of the tale was riddled with errors, Crawford was either a poor proofreader or else didn't have time to devote to this task. But at least, Lovecraft had the pleasure of seeing one of his tales set up between hardcovers in his lifetime.

The narrator and main protagonist of "The Shadow Over Innsmouth" is Robert Martin Olmstead, a junior at Oberlin College, who is traveling by train, trolly, and foot, exploring Arkham and its environs. He is intrigued by some artifacts he sees in the Newburyport Public Library that came from Innsmouth, a seaport town in Massachusetts, and though he hadn't planned to visit this town, he decides to include it in his itinerary. He takes the bus to

Innsmouth and notices that many of the residents suffer from a hereditary disease known as the "Innsmouth Look," which is characterized by large, bulging eyes, scaly skin, flat noses, abnormally small ears, webbed fingers, and rudimentary gills around the neck, along with other physical deformities and alterations as the disease progresses. Olmstead converses with one of the nonafflicted residents, an old alcoholic named Zadok Allen, and he learns the truth about Innsmouth. In the mid-1800s, Captain Obed Marsh, resident of Innsmouth and a prosperous sea captain, had encountered a group of South Sea islanders who had struck up a treaty with the Deep Ones, a terrestrial alien race living in great cities under the oceans. Marsh learns how to contact the Deep Ones and he sets up *The Esoteric Order of Dagon* in Innsmouth, a quasi-religious cult whose members mate with the Deep Ones. The children of these unions—whom I refer to as the "Innsmouth mutants" in this study—eventually evolve into Deep Ones themselves. Once the process is complete, they take to the sea. Unfortunately, Olmstead's interview with Allen is observed by the mutants and he is forced to flee from his hotel room late at night when they try to capture him. Olmsted escapes from the town and alerts the authorities about his experience, this sparks a raid on the town by the Feds. The hybrids are rounded up and taken away to undisclosed locations, likely federal prisons. Everything seems to have been resolved, but when Olmstead returns back home in Toledo, his health breaks down and he becomes an invalid. Searching out his ancestry, he discovers that his great-grandmother was a Marsh and thus, he, too, suffers from the Innsmouth Look.

***

The Deep Ones are an aberrant form of intelligent life that evolved from amphibians or ichthyic sources on earth rather than from primates. Lovecraft doesn't tell us exactly when this happened, but if it was a divergent strain from humankind, then the Deep Ones might have evolved around the same time that *Homo erectus* evolved, 100,000 BCE or thereabouts. The Deep Ones have gills and live underwater; thus, they never attempted at any time in earth's history to settle on the surface of the planet. As a result, their presence on earth has been largely hidden from people who live outside Innsmouth. With regard to the mutants, these Deep Ones-in-Training are not full alien-entities until they complete their transformations; consequently, they are hybrid, degenerate entities in every sense of the term, though "degenerate" only from the standpoint of humans who have an aversion to hybrids.

Lovecraft doesn't give us a clear description of the Deep Ones in the tale; he prefers to present them in shadow or half-light or else, if out in the open, at night. Usually, they are described in large groups; we catch a glimpse of them swimming off the shore at Devil Reef, or in pursuit of Robert Olmstead in the latter half of the tale.

And yet [Olmstead] saw them in a limitless stream—flopping, hopping, croaking, bleating—surging inhumanly through the spectral moonlight in a grotesque, malignant saraband of fantastic nightmare. ... I think their predominant colour was a greyish-green, though they had white bellies. They were mostly shiny and slippery, but the ridges of their backs were scaly. Their forms vaguely suggested the anthropoid, while their heads were the heads of fishes, with prodigious bulging eyes that never closed. At the sides of their necks were palpitating gills, and their long paws were webbed. They hoped irregularly, sometimes on two legs and somethings on four. ... They were the blasphemous fish-frogs of the nameless design—living and horrible.[1]

There is only a hint of racism here—the allusion to "the anthropoid." Later in the passage, Lovecraft will refer to them as "swarming," reminiscent of the Delapore cannibals and the Red Hook immigrants who likewise swarm, though primarily on land.

Interestingly, Zadok Allen, an uneducated, illiterate, and nonmutant resident of Innsmouth, suggests that the connection between the Deep Ones and humankind might be even closer than merely divergent evolutionary strains:

When it comes to matin' with them toad-lookin' fishes, the Kanakys kind o' balked, but finally they larnt something as put a new face on the matter. Seems that human folks has got a kind o' relation to sech water-beasts—that everything alive come aout o' the water onct, an' only needs a little change to go back agin. Them things told the Kanakys that ef they mixed bloods there'd be children as ud look human at fust, but later turn more'n more like the things, till finally they'd take to the water an' jine the main lot o' things daown thar. An' this is the important part, young feller—them as turned into fish things an 'went into the water *wouldn't never die*. Them things never died excep' they was kilt violent.[2]

In this passage, we see further elaboration and clarification of Lovecraft's unique evolutionary theories. To begin with, the hybrid children are of mixed race, half-human, half-Deep One, and yet, Deep One DNA seems to dominate, edging out the human DNA. This raises questions about amphibian/fish genetic material vs human genetic material—is the former more robust because amphibians and fish represent a superior life form at the basic cellular level? Or perhaps, the human DNA is merely a small part of the Deep One DNA; it is subsumed within the latter, which lends credence to the view that there might have been only the Deep One DNA in the first place and perhaps, the fiddling that the Elder Things did with primates created impurities in the strain that were not present originally. The idea of a common, missing link for both humankind and Deep Ones is intriguing and it certainly strikes at the root of the question of what it means to be human. Of course, in "The Shadow Over Innsmouth," Lovecraft leaves no doubt in the minds of his reader that the Deep Ones are an alien race, not a human race. And yet, if humans and Deep Ones share a common ancestor, then in some sense, the Deep Ones might not be, strictly speaking, so alien of a race after all; indeed, they might be a superior, more robust species of humankind.

The connection between Innsmouth and the Deep Ones began in the mid-1800s when an Innsmouth tradesman, Obed Marsh, captain of three ships, the Columbia, the Hetty, and the Sumatra Queen, encounters a tribe of Polynesian islanders in the South Seas who have made a treaty with the aliens. In exchange for gold ornaments, jewels, and abundant fishing, the tribe must set up a temple to sacrifice young men and woman to the Deep Ones and allow their males to intermingle with female Deep Ones for the production of hybrid children. Walakea, the tribal chieftain, teaches Marsh how to summon the Deep Ones. Later, when Innsmouth is facing an economic slump (sometime after 1838), Marsh summons the Deep Ones and enters into a treaty with them under the same terms as those stipulated in the Polynesian's treaty. The increase in fishing saves Innsmouth and helps make the town a thriving seaport community for the next several years. Marsh consolidates his control over Innsmouth in 1846. Pagan rites are performed at the *Esoteric Order of Dagon* and in adjoining buildings. Periodically, young men and woman are sacrificed to the Deep Ones on the two key Wiccan sabbat days, May-Eve and Halloween. Likewise, following the practices of the South Sea islanders, Obed Marsh and other prominent Innsmouth men take female Deep Ones as brides. After Marsh's death in 1878, the town begins to decline economically and morally due to the proliferation of inferior hybrid stock, but the fishing industry still thrives.

Among Lovecraft's alien races, the Deep Ones hold their own in terms of technological advancement and cultural accomplishments. Their underwater cities include Y'ha-nthlei, located off the coast of Massachusetts; Ahu-Y'hloa, near Cornwall; and G'll-hoo, which is just north of the UK (these last two are the creation of later Mythos writers). All of these metropolises are marvels of engineering, designed with artificial lighting and beautiful terraces. The Deep Ones are immortal—and this includes the Innsmouth mutants, once they have fully transformed—they cannot die of natural causes, though they can be killed by violence or accidental mishap. The Deep Ones communicate by telepathy among themselves; their vocal cords are not designed for communication—they are limited to grunts, barking, and guttural sounds. Also, the Deep Ones are a religious race; their primary god and goddess are the Great Old One Dagon and his consort, Hydra, whom they refer to as "Father Dagon" and "Mother Hydra." It is possible that Dagon and Hydra were, in ancient times, actual Deep Ones who had been deified over the years. In addition the Deep Ones pay homage to the trans-dimensional entity Cthulhu—they even use the same chant that is used by earthly devotees of this entity—"*Ph'nglui mglw'nafh Cthulhu R'lyeh wgah'nagl fhtagn!*"—which translates roughly: "In his house at R'lyeh dead Cthulhu waits dreaming!"³

* * *

There are racist images in "The Shadow Over Innsmouth" and these come into the tale primarily when Lovecraft describes the Innsmouth residents who are in the process of transitioning from human to mutant. Early on in the tale, when Robert Olmstead boards the Innsmouth bus, Lovecraft offers a rather lengthy portrait of an Innsmouth hybrid, Joe Sargent, the thirty-five-year-old bus driver. This passage demonstrates just how repulsive hybrids were to Lovecraft, and the implication couldn't be any plainer that what Lovecraft is really worried about here is the negative effects that result from intermarriages between Blacks and whites—note how Lovecraft even works in a reference to "negroids" (which, significantly, is not capitalized).

> [Sargent] was a thin, stoop-shouldered man not much under six feet tall, dressed in shabby blue civilian clothes and wearing a frayed grey golf cap. His age was perhaps thirty-five, but the odd, deep creases in the side of his neck made him seem older when one did not study his dull, expressionless face. He had a narrow head, bulging, watery blue eyes that seemed never to wink, a flat nose, a receding forehead and chin, and singularly undeveloped ears. His long, thick lip and coarse-pored, greyish cheeks seemed almost beardless except for some sparse yellow hairs that straggled and curled in irregular patches; and in some places the surface seemed queerly irregular, as if peeling from some cutaneous disease. His hands were large and heavily veined, and had a very unusual greyish-blue tinge. The fingers were strikingly short in proportion to the rest of the structure, and seemed to have a tendency to curl closely into the huge palm. As he walked toward the bus I observed his peculiarly shambling gait. ... His oddities certainly did not look Asiatic, Polynesian, Levantine, or negroid, yet I could see why the people found him alien. I myself would have thought of biological degeneration rather than alienage.⁴

Joe Sargent is an Aqua nigga, a nightmare Mariner, a distant, coastal cousin to the landlocked, hybrid degenerative monsters that we studied in Chapters 6–9 and the squalid hordes of immigrants that Lovecraft references in "The Horror at Red Hook."

* * *

Robert Olmstead is the sole white, privileged Anglo-Saxon protagonist in "The Shadow Over Innsmouth." The half-breed mutants, joined by their alien associates from Devil Reef, marshal their resources against only this single man; the contest is vastly unequal, but Olmstead proves to be much more capable than he first appears. He had never even heard of Innsmouth before setting out on his antiquarian tour of New England. Indeed, Innsmouth doesn't appear on any of the maps that he consults and none of the locals who live in nearby towns seem inclined to talk about the place. Olmstead learns about Innsmouth from a garrulous station master at Newburyport when he inquiries about cheaper travel options than the train or trolly. Despite the man's generally negative account of the town, including a guarded report about the "big epidemic" of 1846, Olmstead becomes interested in visiting the place. He also sees an odd, tiara-like artifact from the town in a private collection that wets his curiosity. Olmstead spends the night at the YMCA in Newburyport and then takes the Innsmouth bus the next morning. The bus driver, Joe Sargent, as we have seen, suffers from the Innsmouth Look and Olmstead gets his first glance of coming attractions, so to speak; certainly, Joe Sargent is not exactly a comforting sight to white men who have a racial bias against hybrids. Once Olmstead arrives in the town, he checks his valise with the desk clerk at the decrepit Gilman House and then sets out to explore the town. There aren't too many people around; those that he sees are in various stages of degeneration and Olmstead wonders about the cause behind the Innsmouth Look.

He questions the young kid (not a local) who works in the grocery store and learns about Zadok Allen, a ninety-six-year-old alcoholic who has lived in the town since he was a child. Thinking that Allen might be able to give him some useful information, Olmstead purchases a pint of bootleg whiskey—it is 1927 and Prohibition is in full effect—and then hunts down Allen. The two men find a secluded spot to talk near the ocean and Olmstead learns about Obed Marsh and the origins of the Innsmouth mutants. The interview is cut short, however, when Allen suddenly screams out and rushes away; there is no one in sight, but Olmstead sees some ripples in the water and surmises that one of the Deep Ones had seen them talking. Olmstead returns to the Gilman House to collect his valise and get back on the bus, but is informed that the bus is out of service and he must, thus, spend the night in Innsmouth. It is clear to him that he is now a marked man.

Much like Albert Wilmarth in "The Whisperer in Darkness," Olmstead stays alert in his room; he remains fully dressed and ready for action. Late at night, the Innsmouth mutants try to break into his room, but he cleverly escapes via a quick exit through a succession of adjoining rooms and then climbs out a window. The mutants organize search parties and Olmstead plays a cat-and-mouse game with them as they chase him throughout the town. This part of the story is rather exciting; Lovecraft reveals that he has a genuine knack for generating nail-biting suspense and surprises. Olmstead eventually makes his way to the abandoned railway and hides in the bushes as one of the larger search parties passes along the road. He cannot resist sneaking a peak at the mutants and the sight proves to be too much for him; he falls into a faint. In the morning, he wakes up and is able to make it to the nearby town of Rowley; then, he catches a train to Arkham and alerts the federal authorities about Innsmouth; this starts the chain of events that lead to the Federal Raid of 1927-8.

The horror, however, is not over; it is only beginning for Lovecraft's privileged narrator. Understandably, Olmstead is too shaken to resume his antiquarian tour; he returns home to Toledo and finishes his last year at Oberlin College. Then he goes to work in an insurance office, but is forced to give up his job when he starts having disturbing dreams and flashbacks about his harrowing experience in Innsmouth. It is now 1931 and Olmstead dreams about living in one of the Deep One's underwater cities. He conducts genealogical research into his past family history and discovers that his great-grandmother had been an Innsmouth Marsh. Thus, Olmstead himself carries the tainted Innsmouth DNA and will eventually transform into one of the Deep Ones.

Olmstead, however, unlike Arthur Jermyn and Thomas Delapore, accepts his fate. And here, once again, we see one of Lovecraft's characters thrown into a state of deep, profound stasis. The pattern of loss and failure that characterizes the lives of Lovecraft's white Anglo-Saxon protagonists takes hold yet again. In his escape from the town, Olmstead had shown a great deal of courage, even aggression. He demonstrated that he could think effectively on his feet as he escapes from the Gilman House and then the town itself. Of course, when he gets a clear look at the physical appearances of the Deep Ones, he loses consciousness for a time. But after Olmstead discovers exactly what he is—and what he will soon become—he essentially gives up the game.

At the end of the tale, thus, Olmstead does little more than passively await the transformation. He keeps himself secluded in his father's house—adopting "the static, secluded life of an invalid," as he puts it.[5] He studies the mirror every day, seeing the Innsmouth syndrome slowly taking control of his face and body. One morning, he recognizes that he has now acquired the "Innsmouth Look." Yet, Olmstead has undergone a subtle mental change as well due to his transformation into an alien entity; he no longer fears the transformation but actually embraces it. In his research, he has uncovered information about a distant cousin who has been confined by his uncle in the Canton asylum and he realizes that this relative had probably been sent there because he, too, was undergoing the transition from human to mutant. Thus, Olmstead begins to plan his cousin's escape. And then, the two of them will return to Innsmouth and wait until they are fully prepared to take to the sea. They will then become citizens of the city of Y'ha-nthlei off the coast of Massachusetts and "dwell [there] amidst wonder and glory forever."[6]

***

Virtually all of Lovecraft's contemporary critics have recognized that the racist miscegenation narrative, specifically miscegenation by blood, is the driving force behind "The Shadow Over Innsmouth." Lovecraft's reason for writing the story in the first place is, in fact, to warn us about the threats that miscegenation poses for the white race. Tracy Bealer, in "'The Innsmouth Look': H. P. Lovecraft's Ambivalent Modernism" (2011), argues that the tale is a "neat encapsulation of interracial contract" and further observes that the Innsmouth mutants are "for all intents and purposes, racially marked immigrants overtaking ... polluting and degrading Innsmouth's Anglo Saxon stock."[7] Shapiro and Barnard interpret the tale in a similar fashion:

> "The Shadow Over Innsmouth" ... barely contains its anxiety about miscegenation. Innsmouth is twice described as "shadowed" as a result of its racial mixture between white sailors and captured or foreign peoples. The tale involves Innsmouth's mixed coupling between old New England stock and a fish-like race that has been brought to New England to help restore profits from a fading mercantile economy devoured by the onset of foreign capital in the shape of "large-scale corporations." That the subhuman race is made up of some kind of fish-creature is a transparent elision of African identity, as indicated by the tale's use of caricatural keywords. The narrator sees "dirty, simian-visaged children" playing on the beaches. The townsmen have "bulging, watery blue eyes ... a flat nose ... long, thick lip(s)," and one is described as moving "in a positively simian way, with long arms frequently touching the ground." These features hearken back to the more overtly racist description, in the earlier "Herbert West—Reanimator" ... of a Black boxer.[8]

Interpreting the tale in this way, "The Shadow Over Innsmouth" *can* be read as an allegory of New Englanders importing Blacks into the colonies, putting them to work to boost their profits, whether maritime or otherwise, and then paying a penalty for doing so.

However, the tale might better be read as an allegory of Lovecraft's fears about the decline of Western civilization in general due to the influx of immigrants. The details of the allegory are clear. Innsmouth was a thriving seaport town, noted for shipbuilding, industry, and commerce. The Marsh refinery was in full operation. Shipping and trading were flourishing. The residents were prospering. The rich white folks—the Marshes, the Waites, the Gilmans, and the Elliots—live in beautiful mansions along Broad, Washington, Lafayette, and Adams streets. The working classes do their jobs and keep to their places. Literally, Innsmouth represents the ideal, American city, an industrious epicenter of culture and civilization. But then, immigrants from the South Sea islands come into the city and the white

Anglo-Saxon stock is diluted and made impure by miscegenation, both by blood and association. And so, Innsmouth declines and its populace degenerates, leaving only traces of the former days of glory. And as this happens to a once thriving city in New England, so it could happen to cities all over the North American continent—New York, Boston, Chicago, and San Francisco—and perhaps, the "contagion" could even spread to Europe and the rest of the Western world.

S. T. Joshi pontificates on the conflicts between different civilizations as depicted in Lovecraft's fiction and makes some rather interesting observations on "The Shadow Over Innsmouth." As Joshi writes:

> The tales present conflicts, not of individuals, but of cultures: the Old Ones versus the shoggoths; the Great Race versus the Blind Beings; the fungi from Yuggoth versus human beings. ... the Innsmouth denizens versus human beings ... (symbolized by the narrator). The horror of the last story, of course, rests in the fact that the dichotomy proves to be illusory; it is as if Lovecraft is saying that our efforts to preserve civilization are foredoomed to failure by the sins—or blunders—of our ancestors.[9]

Here, Joshi's claim that there is a dichotomy between the Deep Ones and humankind is quite correct. But this is not a dichotomy between different cultures; *it is a dichotomy between different species.* There is a clear line between the alien and the human being (this includes any one of Lovecraft's aliens, by the way) and it can never be breached. It is as inexorable as Lovecraft's cherished "color-line" between whites and Blacks. And equally true, when humans become Innsmouth mutants, they do not retain their humanity; they become aliens and leave humanity behind.

As such, "The Shadow Over Innsmouth" is quite a bit different than the rest of the tales examined in this section. *Slavery is not really an issue in this tale at all.* Despite Shapiro and Barnard's allusion to "captured foreign people" and Joshi's allusion to "the sins—or blunders—of our ancestors," the Innsmouth mariners do not enslave the Deep Ones (assuming that they even could do this); Captain Obed Marsh—"old limb o' Satan," as Zadok Allen calls him, chuckling with delight—strikes a devil's bargain with the Deep Ones and this leads to the miscegenation that ruins the town. This is the only "sin" or "blunder" in the tale and in fact, it could be seen as a blessing, at least in the short run, since the town's maritime trade flourishes again. Likewise, the Deep Ones are not interested in enslaving humans; they merely want to pursue the perks of their treaty with Innsmouth and be left alone by the outside world. The doom that comes to Innsmouth results from three factors: miscegenation; the attitudes of the white Anglo-Saxons in nearby towns who persist in seeing alien races as lesser, monstrous races, fit only to be dominated or exterminated; and, most important of all, *the unassimilable nature of the Deep Ones.*

And here, I think, is the key to a proper understanding of "The Shadow Over Innsmouth." The Deep Ones cannot be assimilated into the Anglo-Saxon civilizations; they are, thus, like Lovecraft's African Americans, since the latter also cannot be assimilated into the Anglo-Saxon civilizations—though, of course, unlike Blacks, the Deep Ones are not subhuman; as we have seen, they are highly intelligent and they have a highly developed civilization. Thus, there is only one way to preserve the white race in this case; Anglo-Saxons must fight and conquer the Deep Ones or else, the miscegenation will continue to spread across the country until all Anglo-Saxons have transformed into Deep Ones and the white civilizations are utterly eradicated. Ultimately, this is what Lovecraft is pushing for here—the fight and conquer solution—and his sympathies obviously lie with the agents of the federal government who raid Innsmouth, dynamite Devil Reef, along with some of the houses in the town, and imprison Innsmouth mutants in concentration camps.

Clearly, Lovecraft would have liked to turn back the clock; to follow in the footsteps of our ancestors and beat down the Black races. As Daisy Buchanan, in F. Scott Fitzgerald's *The Great Gatsby* remarks, mocking her husband's seriousness about racist author Lothrop Stoddard's arguments in *The Rise of the Colored Empires* (1920), "we must beat them down."[10] But in the early twentieth century, it was a little too late for that. A proper solution required complete equality between whites and the "alien" races—full inclusion, even if assimilation is not possible. But Lovecraft, of course, could never have abided that.

16

At the Mountains of Madness (1931)

At the Mountains of Madness, at 40,000 words, is Lovecraft's second longest work of fiction (just behind *The Case of Charles Dexter Ward*) and is, as S. T. Joshi tells us, Lovecraft's most "ambitious" straight sf tale.[1] Lovecraft wrote this novel in only a month, starting in February and ending on March 22, 1931; this, in itself, is a very impressive feat, given the size of the manuscript and its quality. Lovecraft was well aware that the length of the tale might cause it to be rejected by his preferred publisher, *Weird Tales*. Thus, when he sent it out to Farnsworth Wright, he indicated that the tale could be divided naturally after Section VI—roughly about the halfway point—encouraging Wright to think of publishing the tale as a two-part serial. As it turns out, Lovecraft's fears were justified; the tale was deemed to be too long by Wright and rejected. Eventually, however, Lovecraft sold the tale to *Astounding* magazine and it appeared in the form of three serial installments, in February, March, and April 1936.

The narrator of *At the Mountains of Madness* is William Dyer, professor of geology at Miskatonic University. As the story opens, he is involved in setting up an expedition to Antarctica; the object of the expedition is to collect fossils and study land and rock formations. One of his colleagues, Pabodie, has invented a drill that is able to probe deeper underground than other drills on the market. The expedition commences and has several successful borings. However, the Pabodie Expedition (as it is officially known) faces trouble when Professor Lake, a member of the team, decides to lead a spin-off party northward. The Lake party discovers a cave, which contains the frozen remains of members of an alien astronaut race known as the Elder Things, eight of which are in a state of perfect preservation. Dyer, who is in charge of the main party, loses radio contact with the Lake party and predictably, when his group catches up with the spin-off group on the following day, they find that the members of the party, with the exception of a man named Gedney, have been killed. The bodies of the Elder Things are gone. Obviously, the Elder Things have revived. Soon after this unfortunate event, Dyer and Paul Danforth, a graduate student, conduct a reconnaissance flight in one of the expedition's airplanes. They discover the existence of a vast, extensive city of the Elder Things; the last city that the Elder Things retreated to in the Cenozoic Era, just before they vanished into the oceans. The two explorers do not encounter any of the revived Elder Things, but they study the bas-reliefs on the walls of the city and learn about how the Elder Things lived, what they did, and how their civilization was organized, both socially and economically. They also discover the missing body of Gedney, tucked away in a tarp for further study and experimentation. They learn, too, of the existence of the shoggoths, the Elder Things' slave race. In the climax of the novel, the men find themselves being hunted by one of the shoggoths; however, they are able to escape from the city.

* * *

The Elder Things (also known as the "Old Ones" in the tale) represent one of the greatest extraterrestrial civilizations in the galaxy—they share this distinction with Lovecraft's other two alien civilizations, the Mi-Go and the Great Race. The Elder Things came to earth around 1,000,000,000 BCE from their homebase on either Uranus or Neptune (it might have been as early as 2 billion BCE; the exact date is not given by Lovecraft). Earth was not the only planet that the Elder Things colonized; they had previously conquered and terraformed many planets in the galaxy. It is not clear *why* they chose the earth in the first place—there are always mysteries about the motives when it comes to Lovecraft's extraterrestrial and trans-dimensional aliens. But once they arrive on the planet, they build their first city near the South Pole and this becomes their major base as they spread out across the surface of the planet.

Lovecraft's description of the Elder Things is thoroughly in keeping with his belief that alien races—if they are truly "alien"—must necessarily be as alien in appearance as can be imagined, since they are, after all, the products of evolutionary processes that are wholly outside the natural biological laws that are common to our planet. Similar to Lovecraft's other alien astronauts, the Elder Things are neither animal nor vegetable, but a combination of both. They have puffy, yellowish starfish-shaped heads with "three-inch flexible yellowish tubes projecting from each point ... at the end of [which] ... is spherical expansion where yellowish membrane rolls back ... to reveal glassy, red-irised globe, evidently an eye."[2] The bodies are even stranger:

> Eight feet long ... [with] Six-foot five-ridged barrel torso ... Dark grey, flexible, and infinitely tough ... Seven-foot membraneous wings of same

color. ... Around equator, one at central apex of each of the five vertical, stave-like ridges, are five systems of light grey flexible arms or tentacles. ... [the arms branch]. ... into five sub-stalks, each of which branches ... into five small, tapering tentacles or tendrils ...[for] a total of 25 tentacles.[3]

And if this isn't enough for the connoisseur of the weird, as our view of these creatures descends to the lower body and the bases, we find muscular arms, paddles for swimming, pseudo feet, and even more tentacles, tubes, and orifices.

As an advanced race, the Elder Things have all of the elements that make for a superior civilization, as least in Lovecraft's estimation. They are, first of all, great artists and artisans; they create beautiful bas-reliefs to decorate the walls of their massive stone buildings; a frequent design involves a five-point pattern—perhaps to reflect their five-pointed, star-shaped heads. They have thoroughly mastered the art of architecture, as shown by the minarets, domes, and angled perfection of their great city. They are also technologically advanced. They use electrochemical lighting for their cities and artificial heating. They have weapons that attack and disable the molecules of their adversaries—mostly other alien races and their own slave race, the shoggoths. They have educational centers for their young (which are grown by means of spores), and the latter receive an education "beyond any standard that we can imagine," as Lovecraft tells us.[4] Their medical sciences are state-of-the-art as well, since very few of the Elder Things die by natural causes, only by violence. In addition, they have the type of government that Lovecraft himself was gravitating toward politically in the late thirties, a form of moderate socialism in which the government takes care of the needs of the citizens.

In reading *At the Mountains of Madness*, it is clear that Lovecraft's admiration for the Elder Things is very high, even higher than it is for the Mi-Go and the Great Race. In the latter part of the novel, Dyer and Danford explore a portion of the great city and study the murals on the walls—these provide all of the above information about the Elder Things' culture and civilization. Dyer and Danford also discover the headless bodies of the Elder Things that had killed the members of the Lake party and surmise that they had been killed by shoggoths, who are apparently still alive somewhere in the depths of the city. This sight causes Dyer to feel empathy for the Elder Things—even though they had just recently wiped out half the members of the expedition—and leads him to the following observation:

Poor devils! After all, they were not evil things of their kind. They were the men of another age and another order of being. ... They had not been even savages—for what indeed had they done? That awful awakening in the cold of an unknown epoch. ... poor Lake, poor Gedney ... and poor Old Ones! Scientists to the last—what had they done that we would not have done in their place? God, what intelligence and persistence! What a facing of the incredible, just as those carven kinsmen and forbears had faced things only a little less incredible! Radiates, vegetables, monstrosities, star-spawn—whatever they had been, they were men![5]

This passage shows just how the Elder Things were ranked in relation to the other alien races; Lovecraft does not refer to any of his other aliens as "men." It reveals, also, that as far as Lovecraft was concerned, the qualities that make an entity "human" are almost entirely related to their level of intelligence, their cultural development, and the complexity of their civilization. Physical appearance is less important.

***

Notwithstanding Lovecraft's high opinion of the Elder Things, however, they are hardly an admirable race. The Elder Things, instead, are cosmic slave masters—arguably, Lovecraft's most notorious cosmic slave masters. The slaves in question are the shoggoths—Lovecraft never capitalizes this word, just as he never capitalizes the word "negro"; he is not willing to let shoggoths or Blacks have even the minimal level of respect that he accords to other races. The shoggoths represent something unique in Lovecraft's fiction; they are not an existing alien race waiting to be enslaved, as are the flying polyps in "The Shadow Out of Time." Instead, they have been created and engineered by the Elder Things themselves for the sole purpose of helping the latter build their great cities on the Antarctic continent (at that time, Antarctica was not a cold wasteland but a relatively warm, fertile environment). City building at such a vast scale requires hard, manual labor and as the following passage indicates, the shoggoths are the perfect workers:

> [The Elder Things] had done the same thing on other planets; having manufactured ... certain multicellular protoplasmic masses capable of molding their tissues into all sorts of temporary organs under hypnotic influence and thereby forming ideal slaves to perform the heavy work of the community. These viscous masses were without doubt what Abdul Alhazred whispered about as the "shoggoths" in his frightful *Necronomicon*. ... With the aid of the shoggoths, whose expansions could be made to lift prodigious weights, the small, low cities under the sea grew to vast and imposing labyrinths of stone not unlike those which later rose on land.[6]

The *flexibility* of the shoggoths, in particular, is one of their most useful traits. Their protoplasmic bodies can be altered at will, merely by the use of hypnotic suggestion. The fact that the shoggoths are also impervious to changes in temperature and sudden cold spells is an added plus. And most important, they are docile, weak-willed, and less intelligent than their masters—indeed, they have been engineered specifically to ensure that this is the case.

However, the Elder Things do not take into account the natural evolutionary processes that all living beings are subject to, even manufactured living beings. During their long period of enslavement, the shoggoths slowly become more intelligent and independent. Lovecraft explains the stages that they go through. At first, they develop a "stubborn volition" that imitates the will of their masters; this allows them to pretend that they are actually obeying the commands of the Elder Things without actually doing so.[7] Here, Lovecraft might have been speaking about Black slaves and their subtle, mental resistance against their white Anglo-Saxon oppressors in colonial times. Secondly, the shoggoths begin to use their self-modeling abilities for their own purposes. These changes occur mostly among the sea-shoggoths and, as Lovecraft tells us, is perhaps linked to the fact that they were created by a different process than that used for the land shoggoths.

> But the shoggoths of the sea, reproducing by fission and acquiring a dangerous degree of accidental intelligence, presented for a time a formidable problem. They had always been controlled through the hypnotic suggestion of the Old Ones, and had modelled their tough plasticity into various useful temporary limbs and organs; but now their self-modelling powers were sometimes exercised independently, and in various imitative forms implanted by past suggestion.[8]

These mental and "temperamental" changes ultimately make the shoggoths "peculiarly intractable" around 150,000,000 BCE. Even more problematic for the Elder Things, the new, improved shoggoths are learning how to resist the hypnotic coercion of their masters.

Eventually, the shoggoths stage a slave rebellion—something that the highly intelligent Elder Things should have foreseen. The rebellion doesn't succeed, however. The Elder Things use their molecular disturbance weapons and the shoggoths are "re-subjugated" (as Lovecraft quaintly refers to it).[9] Again, the parallels between Black slaves and their masters are evident; the white slave masters use their rifles and guns to put down slave rebellions both in America and Europe. To ensure that future slave rebellions do not occur, the Elder Things breed an entirely new race of shoggoths, replacing the fission procedure with the use of actual shoggoth tissues. These new shoggoths, interestingly (and ominously), are bigger and more intelligent than the previous versions.

> The newly bred shoggoths grew to enormous size and singular intelligence, and were represented as taking and executing orders with marvellous quickness. They seemed to converse with the Old Ones by mimicking

their voices—a sort of musical piping over a wide range ... and to work more from spoken commands than from hypnotic suggestions as in earlier times. They were, however, kept in admirable control.[10]

Around the same time that these new shoggoths are created, 50,000,000 BCE or thereabouts, the temperatures on the earth begin to drop, making it impossible for the Elder Things to continue living in their land-based cities. Thus, they retreat for good into their cities beneath the oceans and take their newest shoggoth race along with them.

Lovecraft's depiction of the master/slave relationship between the Elder Things and the shoggoths and, especially, the slave rebellion and its aftermath, is driven, no doubt, by his very real fear that there might be similar uprisings on the part of Blacks and other members of the hated races in American cities. Of course, this fear was common among slave owners in colonial America, as it is for any small conclave of white Anglo-Saxon rulers who dominate other races in countries where they are racially a minority (such as in India, for example, in the late nineteenth to the twentieth centuries). Lovecraft could certainly identify with this fear. As we have seen, during his short stay in the Red Hook district of New York in the 1920s, he saw first-hand that Blacks and other hated races were literally pouring into the country and beginning to dwarf in sheer numbers the white Anglo-Saxon populations. To Lovecraft, the gradual displacement of white Anglo-Saxons by dark, swarthy aliens was a kind of nonviolent slave uprising directed against the dominant race and would, or so he imagined, lead to the same kinds of outcomes that actual slave uprisings invariably bring about—the destruction and extinction of the white race.

* * *

Lovecraft doesn't focus on a single privileged, white Anglo-Saxon protagonist in *At the Mountains of Madness* as he does in the other cosmic slave master tales; there are a whole slew of them in the novel. In addition to the leader, Professor William Dyer, other men occupying leadership roles in the expedition are Professor Frank H. Pabodie from the Department of Engineering, who devised the state-of-the art drill that the expedition uses for boring under the ice; Professor Lake of the Biology Department; and Professor Atwood, a physics professor and meteorologist. In addition, the expedition includes sixteen assistants, seven graduate students, and nine mechanics. The only individuals in this group identified by name besides the leaders are Paul Danforth, a graduate student who stays with Dyer's main party, and Gedney and Carroll, who are members of Lake's ill-fated spin-off group. Nearly half of these individuals suffer the ultimate fate of Lovecraft's privileged protagonists: they are killed. As for the survivors, Lovecraft only focuses on Dyer and Danford, both of whom are traumatized to some degree by their experiences.

Initially, the expedition is united; several successful borings are conducted, including one at Mt. Erebus, Ross Island, and another at the Beardmore Glacier—Lovecraft had read accounts of Admiral Byrd's expedition from 1928 to 1930, so he drew on these readings for the place names and other details in his novel. However, the expedition forks off into two separate groups when Professor Lake becomes interested in some fragments of slate that come from a western location near the Queen Alexandra Range and decides to investigate in that direction. The Lake party includes twelve men, along with dogs, sleds, and equipment. They travel deep into the foothills of a titanic mountain range near the Queen Mary and Knox Land and discover a cave, inside of which are the bodies of fourteen Elder Things, eight perfectly preserved and the other six in various states of damage and decomposition. The bodies are brought back to the Lake camp for analysis and dissection. Lake conveys news of their successful find to the main party and this is subsequently released to the outside world via the wireless. Following the report, Lake signs off for the night. A storm rages early the next morning and the main party loses communication with Lake. Later in the day, Dyer and Pabodie investigate and find that the Lake party has been wiped out, including most of the dogs. Eleven human bodies are recovered, all mutilated and partially dissected; the twelfth man, Gedney, is missing, as is one of the dogs and three sleds. In addition, and equally problematic, the six damaged bodies of the Elder Things have been buried upright in nine-foot snow graves under five-pointed mounds, clearly (but inexplicably) a ritualistic burial. The eight perfectly preserved bodies of the Elder Things are gone.

Naturally, Dyer and Pabodie officially terminate the expedition; they don't have enough manpower to continue. In their official report of the incident to the outside world via the wireless, they attribute the tragedy to wind and storm. Then, after Dyer and Danford take a brief reconnaissance flight north to see if they can find tracks of Gedney and the dog, the expedition pulls up stakes and returns to civilization. Less than two weeks later, they are back at Miskatonic University. They do not reveal the true details of what happened to the Lake party nor do Dyer and Danforth reveal what they discovered during their reconnaissance mission. Lake had sent out descriptions of the Elder Things to the outside world along with his report and Dyer heavily censors any additional details; he does not display any of the fragments of the alien bodies they bring back or the photos that Lake had taken of the bodies. Dyer does not want to encourage further Antarctic exploration near the "Mountains of Madness," as he refers to the area. But when he learns that a new expedition is forming—the Starkweather-Moore Expedition—Dyer realizes that he will have to publish all of their findings to warn humankind to stay clear—it doesn't seem to occur to him that this might *encourage*, not dissuade, further exploration.

The bulk of *At the Mountains of Madness* occurs after the Dyer-Pabodie Expedition has ended. It is told by Dyer in flashback and essentially, he is revealing what he and Danforth experienced when they discover the lost city of the Elder Things, the last city that the Elder Things inhabited before they took to the oceans in 500,000 BCE. This part of the novel is the most interesting for Lovecraft's purposes; we are given a full, detailed description of the development and then decline of the Elder Things' civilization via the extensive series of bas-reliefs and murals that adorn the walls of the city. As Dyer and Danford penetrate further into the city, they find the bodies of Gedney and the missing dog, hidden under a tarp taken from the Lake camp; they also find the three missing sleds, a gasoline stove, fuel cans, and other miscellaneous equipment. The bodies are mutilated in a similar way to the dead men and the dogs at the Lake camp. Dyer and Danforth realize that the perfectly preserved bodies of the Elder Things are not dead, but alive; it is they who experimented on the dead humans, not Gedney. Continuing on, Dyer and Danford start to become a bit apprehensive that they will encounter these creatures. Instead, however, they find four of the Elder Things lying dead on the floor of a room, their bodies decapitated. At this point, the two men realize that the other revived Elder Things are probably dead as well, killed by one or more of their former slaves, the shoggoths, who appear to be still alive.

The denouement of the story occurs when Dyer and Danforth find themselves being hunted by a shoggoth, and here, Lovecraft cannot resist allowing a little more harm to happen to his last two privileged protagonists. The shoggoth pursues them through the vast corridors of the city; it is a veritable juggernaut of destruction, crying out cryptically "Tekeli—li! Tekeli—li!," which, Lovecraft tells us, is spoken in *"the imitated accents of their bygone masters."*[11]

> It was the utter, objective embodiment of the fantastic novelist's 'thing that should not be'; and its nearest comprehensible analogue is a vast, onrushing subway train ... the great black front looming colossally out of infinite subterranean distance, constellated with strangely coloured lights and filling the prodigious burrow as a piston fills a cylinder ... It was a terrible, indescribable thing ... a shapeless congeries of protoplasmic bubbles, faintly self-luminous, and with myriads of temporary eyes forming and unforming as pustules of greenish light all over the tunnel-filling front.[12]

Dyer and Danforth manage to escape from the shoggoth; they return to their plane and rejoin their party. But Dyer, understandably, is severely shaken, though he is not exactly traumatized; he returns to his teaching duties at Miskatonic University. Danforth, however, *is* traumatized and according to Dyer's later statements, he spends some time under psychiatric care. But eventually, Danforth regains his mental equilibrium and goes on to become a psychology professor at the college.

***

The strange cry that the pursuing shoggoth makes at the climax of *At the Mountains of Madness*, "Tekeli—li," deserves some attention. This word was lifted unchanged by Lovecraft directly out of Edgar Allan Poe's novel *The Narrative of Arthur Gordon Pym* (1838); it is the sound that the gigantic and "pallidly white" birds are making in the misty air near the end of the novel, just before a large, shrouded human figure rises up in the pathway of Pym, Poe's protagonist—it's skin "the perfect whiteness of the snow."[13] "Tekeli—li," also, is the cry made by the Tsalalians, a group of "jet-black" Antarctic natives, whenever they encounter something white—such as the carcass of a dead animal, or Pym's linen handkerchief, or even Pym himself. Poe scholar Kenneth Silverman, tracing the origin of this odd word, determined that Tekeli was the surname of a Hungarian patriot, who was the subject of a play, *Tekeli; or The Siege of Montgatz* (1806), which Poe's mother Eliza acted in several times during her short theatrical career.[14] Poe was only three years old when his mother died and so, he couldn't have remembered seeing her in this or in any other play; it is likely that he found out about the play, as well as the word, in an old theatre program tucked away among his mother's memorabilia. But of course, that doesn't explain *why* Poe decided to use the word "Tekeli—li" in *The Narrative of Arthur Gordon Pym*; surely it wasn't for nostalgic reasons. Even more importantly, it doesn't explain how we should interpret Tekeli—li in the context of the Poe novel.

Shapiro and Barnard, delving further into this matter, theorize that Poe did, in fact, intend Tekeli—li to be read as more than simply the disparate cry of birds, or as an expression of a general phobia on the part of the Tsalalians against whiteness. As they suggest, the word may have been a pejorative word used by the whites who presumably oppressed the Tsalalians in the past and so, when the Tsalalians later encounter Pym and other whites in their domains, they appropriate "Tekeli—li" to reflect their fear of their former masters as well as their desire to repel any possible future oppression. Poe, of course, lived his entire life during the decades preceding the Civil War and certainly had first-hand knowledge of the Atlantic slave trade and, in particular, the possibility of slave rebellions. Taking this chain of reasoning further, Shapiro and Barnard argue that Lovecraft's shoggoths use Tekeli—li in much in the same way as the Tsalalians, that is, as the appropriation of a hated word as well as a rallying cry among them when they band together to confront an impending threat.

> The sound that ends "Madness"—the Poe-derived cry "Tekeli-li! Tekeli-li!"—is given an inverted sense here, as it seems to signify black as the reverse of white. Since the narrator of "Madness" explains that the sound comes from the shoggoths's mimicking the language of their

superiors (their language consists of "the imitated accents of their bygone masters"), this implies that the syllables may be an appropriation of terms previously used to order the shoggoths about, much like the contemporary use of hate speech terms such as "nigger" or "queer" by groups formerly subjected to them.[15]

This strikes me as an entirely correct supposition. In our own era, African Americans often refer to a close friend or colleague as "nigger" or sometimes "dog," adopting the hate speech of those whom they perceive as their former oppressors; perhaps "Tekeli—li" is likewise a call to action, if not exactly an example of nineteenth-century hate speech.

* * *

In *At the Mountains of Madness*, we see a nearly perfect expression of Lovecraft's slave master/slave narrative; indeed, among the twenty-first-century critics who concentrate on the racialistic aspects of Lovecraft's work, this novel is central to their analyses. This is true especially for Shapiro and Barnard, who seize on the obvious parallels between white Anglo-Saxon slave masters and the Elder Things in *Pentecostal Modernism*. In the following passage, they use the alternate term "Old Ones" rather than "Elder Things."

> Lovecraft's tale begins with the narrator's description of an Antarctic expedition that goes awry ... Lovecraft's Antarctic murals warn that the collapse of the Old Ones did not result from "terrific battles" with other space races, but from an internal, self-generated slave rebellion. By creating "ideal slaves." ... engineered to do their hard labor and construction of buildings, the Old Ones hoped to devote themselves instead to scientific, cultural, and artistic affairs. But the shoggoths became increasingly sentient, learned their master's language, and ultimately revolted and massacred their overlords. Described as protoplasmic slime, the shoggoths are presented as an undifferentiated "mass," like the (Visi-or Ostro-) Goths overrunning the eternal city of Rome, threatening to obliterate the legacy of an empire.[16]

But Lovecraft, also, is pushing a more subtle message in this novel than the possible obliteration of the white race by slaves—a message that moves us beyond the simple working out of one of his racist narratives in a story, and this is, as we have seen, the same message implicit in "The Whisperer in Darkness."

In effect, Lovecraft is suggesting that slavery as an institution is a cosmic thing, not just endemic to European or American culture. As I have noted previously, Lovecraft admires the Elder Things as a race—S. T. Joshi puts this memorably in the following observation: "In many ways [The Elder Things] represent a utopia toward which Lovecraft clearly hopes humanity itself will one day move."[17] The Elder Things are highly intelligent, highly cultured; and technologically superior. Yet, they also own slaves and do not show any inclination to stop this practice at any time over the course of their long period of dominance on earth. Indeed, when they finally decide to forsake their last great city in the Antarctica for the seas, they take their slaves with them. Surely, one might have expected that there were a few enlightened Elder Things who denounced slavery, just as there were white abolitionists in colonial times who did so, right up to the beginning of the Civil War. But not so. Here, Lovecraft is holding up the Elder Things' civilization, along with the institution of slavery, as ideals that human civilizations should strive to emulate. And thus, indirectly, he is validating white Anglo-Saxon civilizations and their use of slaves, the argument being that if slavery is good enough for the highest, most advanced civilization in the cosmos, then it is certainly good enough for us on earth.

Indeed, Lovecraft underscores this argument by essentially cementing the association between white Anglo-Saxon slave masters and the cosmic slave masters in his novel. He does this by directly identifying the Elder Things with humankind—specifically, as I have noted, he refers to the Elder Things as "men." At first glance, this might seem to indicate that Lovecraft was finally opening up in his attitudes toward different cultures and races, even willing to entertain a "melting pot" mentality when it came to those who could be perceived as existing outside the charmed circle of white Anglo-Saxon humankind, claiming, in effect, that all intelligent, cultured beings are essentially human beings. But it must be remembered that Lovecraft excluded some human beings from the category of humankind. In his racist poem "On the Creation of Niggers," Lovecraft makes it clear that the Black race is not a human race. African Americans are vicious beasts, ape-like beasts, in fact, that look more like human beings than the other beasts and yet are not human, but instead a separate creation, just as the animals are, created only to fill a gap between the beasts and "join" the animal kingdom and humankind. As such, when Lovecraft equates the Elder Things with humans, he is referring *only* to white Anglo-Saxon humans. In Lovecraft's estimation, then, the cosmic slave masters and the Anglo-Saxon slave masters are members of two of the most intelligent, culturally superior and supreme civilizations that have existed or will ever exist throughout the entire galaxy. These slave masters rule by divine, natural, and supranatural fiat and because of this, they are allowed to dominate and enslave the members of all of the other civilizations.

17

The Shadow Out of Time (1934)

"The Shadow Out of Time" is Lovecraft's last major tale. S. T. Joshi rightly sees it as the "capstone" of Lovecraft's career, the "culmination of ... a twenty-year attempt to capture the sense of wonder and awe he felt at the boundless reaches of space and time."[1] Lovecraft lavished a great deal of care in the composition of this tale, even more so than usual; the tale went through several drafts, at least three, and the actual writing was spread out over a three- or four-month period. Lovecraft had come up with his central theme, that is, mind-exchange, as early as 1930—he discusses this theme in two letters to Clark Ashton Smith dated November 30, 1930, and March 2, 1932, respectively—and he uses it very effectively in the tale and also in "The Thing on the Doorstep" (1933). Joshi speculates that Lovecraft likely derived his mind-exchange theme from three possible sources: H. B. Drake's *The Shadowy Thing* (1928), Henri Beraud's *Lazarus* (1925), and the film *Berkeley Square* (1933).[2] Perhaps this is so, but none of these sources quite hits the mark—they handle the theme very conventionally, in contrast to Lovecraft's deliriously grandiose use of it. Not surprisingly, when it came time to think about publishing the tale, Lovecraft showed his customary ambivalence about the quality of his work. He didn't type up the finished manuscript, but instead, sent it to August Derleth to dispose of as he saw fit. Derleth passed it on to another *Weird Tales* colleague, Robert Barlow, in July 1935. Barlow ended up preparing a typescript and this went the rounds of the Lovecraft circle for comments and criticism. It boggles the mind of the contemporary reader to think that an accomplished writer like Lovecraft cared at all about the opinions of Derleth, Barlow, or any other member of the so-called "Lovecraft circle," most of whom were basically hack writers in comparison with Lovecraft himself. But as we have seen, Lovecraft was often the victim of his own insecurities. Eventually, it took another *Weird Tales* colleague, Donald Wandrei, to finally send the typed manuscript to

F. Orlin Tremaine, the editor of *Astounding*, a pulp magazine, and the tale appeared promptly in that magazine for the month of June 1936.

"The Shadow Out of Time" is breathtakingly cosmic in scope. It ranges from the early 1900s back to the late Jurassic Period in earth's history when the Great Race, an extraterrestrial alien astronaut race, flourished on the earth, and then, back again to the twentieth century. Nathaniel Wingate Peaslee, professor of history at Miskatonic University, is the target of a forced mind-exchange with a member of the Great Race. In 1908, Peaslee's body is usurped by the mind of this alien entity and is then used by the entity over a five-year period to embark on a study of early-twentieth-century history, anthropology, mythology, and related subjects. During this same period, Peaslee's mind is thrust back in time into the body of the alien entity and forced to live in its city and write a history of his own time. The experience literally destroys Peaslee's personal life; he loses his teaching position at Miskatonic University; his wife divorces him; and two of his children refuse to see him. Finally, in 1913, the invading alien entity departs, returning Peaslee to his own body while reclaiming its original body in prehistoric times. Peaslee convinces himself that his traumatic experience was only a mental breakdown—certainly, not an actual mind-transfer. He tries to rebuild his life with the help of his second son and begins to teach again. But he is troubled by recurring dreams about his time with the Great Race—at least, he thinks that these are dreams. But he slowly comes to the realization that they are memories instead. Later Peaslee and his son (who is now a university professor himself) are invited to join an expedition to Australia to excavate a ruined city buried beneath the desert sands. One night, Peaslee wanders away from the camp and discovers an entrance into the lost city, which, as it turns out, is the very city where he had been imprisoned. Pushing deeper into the ruins, he discovers the room where he spent nearly all of his captivity. In a less-than-subtle climax, Peaslee lays his hand on the actual document that he had been working on in the Great Race's archives, written in his own handwriting. Thus, he confirms his suspicion that the mind-exchange was not a dream but a reality. However, in fleeing from the city, he accidentally drops the document into a chasm and so has nothing tangible to corroborate his claims.

***

Lovecraft's Great Race, in terms of their physical appearance, are easily the most outrageously weird alien-astronaut race in all of Lovecraft's fiction—and this is saying a lot, given the nature of Lovecraft's other fictional aliens, whether extraterrestrial, trans-dimensional, or terrestrial. The Great Race are huge, corrugated cone-shaped monstrosities, half-vegetable, half-animal. As Lovecraft describes them:

[The Great Race resembles] no life-form known to science ... They seemed to be enormous iridescent cones, about ten feet high and ten feet wide at the base, and made up of some ridgy, scaly, semi-elastic matter. From their apexes projected four flexible, cylindrical members, each a foot thick, and of a ridgy substance like that of the cones themselves ... Terminating two of them were enormous claws or nippers. At the end of a third were four red, trumpet-like appendages. The fourth terminated in an irregular yellowish globe some two feet in diameter and having three great dark eyes ranged along its central circumference. Surmounting this head were four slender grey stalks bearing flower-like appendages, whilst from its nether side dangled eight greenish antennae or tentacles. The great base of the central cone was fringed with a rubbery, grey substance which moved the whole entity through expansion and contraction.[3]

Interestingly enough, these odd bodies are not the real bodies of the Great Race; rather, they are the bodies of creatures that flourished in the late Jurassic era on earth but became extinct around fifty million years ago, well before the advent of humankind. The Great Race are time-travelers; they take over the bodies of entities that are native to the planets that they are "colonizing." This adds another level of complexity to this alien race. *For in fact, we do not ultimately know what the members of the Great Race look like, or even if they look like anything that a human being could perceive or process mentally, given our flawed, all-too-human sensory mechanisms.*

Like the Elder Things, the Great Race is ultra-civilized, at least on the surface. They come from the planet Yith, which may or may not lie on the other side of our Milky Way galaxy, but could also lie outside the galaxy and thus in a place that is not subject to the laws of our space–time continuum. Lovecraft, of course, kept the location of Yith a mystery in "Shadow," thus wisely preserving the mystery and mystique of the Great Race. The Great Race is of higher intelligence than humankind, as Lovecraft tells us, and they have very advanced technologies. The Great Race, also, has a liberal, fascist, socialist government with enlightened, autocratic rulers at the top; this is the kind of government that Lovecraft himself seemed to favor, as demonstrated by his correspondence. The Great Race build great cities on the earth, the buildings rising thousands of feet into the sky. They harness atomic power to fuel these cities and run their vehicles. Most commendable (or so it seems), they embark on a mission to compile the history of the entire galaxy. This effort is accomplished by their mind-transfer technology. Members of the Great Race send their minds out into the future, selecting the bodies of exceptional scholars and thinkers from among all of the planets to exchange minds with. The process takes five years, during which time the Yithians, in alien bodies, study the period in which they find themselves, while the minds of their hosts, wearing the Yithians bodies, are forced to write a history of their own time for inclusion in the Great Race's libraries. Once the five-year period is up, the mind-transfer is reversed and the host-minds are returned to their proper period.

The crowning glory of the Great Race's civilization is, however, not their technologies but rather, their vast, galactic library. This institution is housed in the Great Race's principle city, located in an area that, in the twentieth and twenty-first centuries, is now Australia. The library consists partly of records composed by the mind-slaves of the Great Race (such as Peaslee himself) written or printed on cellulose fabric and bound into books that open from the top and are kept in individual, metallic cases within the subterranean vaults of the central archives. As Peaslee begins to remember his five-year enslavement in that same city and his long hours composing a history of his own time and place, he cannot help but reveal a grudging admiration for this library:

> In its vast libraries were volumes of texts and pictures holding the whole of earth's annals—histories and descriptions of every species that had ever been or that ever would be, with full records of their arts, their achievements, their languages, and their psychologies. With this aeon-embracing knowledge, the Great Race chose from every era and life-form such thoughts, arts, and processes that might suit its own nature and situation ... When the captive mind's amazement and resentment had worn off ... it was permitted to study its new environment and experience a wonder and wisdom approximating that of its displacer. ... and to delve freely into the libraries ... This reconciled many captive minds to their lot; since none were other than keen, and to such minds the unveiling of hidden mysteries of earth. ... forms always, despite the abysmal horrors often unveiled, the supreme experience of life.[4]

Peaslee's reference to the "unveiling of hidden mysteries" as being the "supreme experience of life" reflects Lovecraft's own views about scholarly pursuits and the quest for knowledge. For Lovecraft, only the most highly civilized individuals are engaged in these pursuits, and therefore, nations made up of citizens who are devoted to these ends are, by definition, the most highly civilized nations. Previously, we have seen that Lovecraft cares much more about civilization—particularly in the abstract—than he does for anything else. And so, as far as Lovecraft is concerned, the Great Race, in many ways, represents the epitome of civilization—perhaps even the ultimate civilization. However, the more we learn about the Great Race, the less impressive they become. In fact, the Great Race turns out to be not so great after all.

**

The Great Race are, first of all, cosmic slave masters, much like their competitors in the northern, colder climates of the planet, with only the difference that the Great Race do not manufacture their slaves, as do the Elder Things, but rather, enslave and dominate another alien-astronaut race. These are the flying polyps (also known as the polypous race), who teleported to the earth 600 million years ago from the Ogntlach star-system—the same system that hosts the planet Yith, incidentally. The polyps build great basalt cities in the warmer climes of the earth and hold undisputed sway over these portions of the world for nearly 500 million years until the Great Race arrives. The polyps are only partly material and can fly without any visible agency (hence their name "flying" polyps); they are blind, also, but possess consciousnesses and sensorium that are totally unlike any other terrestrial organisms. Of particular importance to the Great Race, the polyps are impervious to their primary weapon, that is, their mind-exchange technology, which makes the polyps a clear and continuing threat to the Great Race's goal to dominate the earth. And so, not surprisingly, the Great Race immediately wages war against the polyps, using their second-best technology—camera-like lighting guns that can destroy the polyps. The Great Race succeeds in subduing the polyps and consigning them to the catacombs and caverns that the polyps built themselves beneath their cities. The Great Race then takes possession of the cities and seals up the entrances to the underground slave pens. Thus, for the flying polyps, planet earth becomes plantation planet earth.

Essentially, the Great Race/flying polyps scenario is more or less equivalent to the Elder Things/shoggoths scenario that we have studied in *At the Mountains of Madness*. In both cases, the cosmic slave masters live in constant fear that slave rebellions will occur someday in their future. Indeed, the Great Race have premonitions that the flying polyps will eventually rise up out of the catacombs and take revenge on their captors. As Lovecraft describes it:

> But as the aeons passed, there came vague, evil signs that the [flying polyps] were growing strong and numerous in the inner world. There were sporadic irruptions of a particularly hideous character in certain small and remote cities ... and in some of the deserted elder cities which the Great Race had not peopled—places where the paths to the gulfs below had not been properly sealed or guarded.[5]

Even more disturbing to the Great Race, the flying polyps have seemingly become more powerful; they can control great winds and deploy them as a weapon. Eventually, the Great Race's fears prove to be justified; the polyps do rebel. But the Great Race has prepared itself for this contingency in advance and they leave the earth, possessing the bodies of the gigantic beetle race that will supplant humankind around 100,000–150,000 CE. And so, when the flying polyps reclaim their cities, they find the cities abandoned and they must content themselves with wreaking havoc on the half-animal, half-vegetable cone-shaped creatures whose bodies, likewise, have been abandoned by the Great Race.

Lovecraft, of course, can identify with the Great Race's fears about a slave rebellion. As we have noted in our studies of *At the Mountains of Madness*, Lovecraft feared that the Black race might eventually attempt to rise up against the white Anglo-Saxon race; he had seen at first hand the steady influx of Blacks and other hated races into the United States via New York and he had noted a similar influx, though not as extensive, in Providence. Thus, Lovecraft and the Great Race (and, for that matter, the Elder Things) fear the possibility of a racial displacement that might not only leave their races in the minority but could, in fact, wipe each of them out entirely.

***

The Great Race's natural propensity toward enslaving competing alien races, however, is not confined to the polypous race. The Great Race, also, enslaves the members of other weaker races, whom they select from a wide range of cultural and racial groups drawn not only from earth's history, past, present, and future, but also from the galaxy as a whole. The Great Race's focus is naturally on humankind, since they did choose to migrate to a planet where humankind would eventually become the dominant species and it is more logical to enslave races that are closer in proximity to their own. One human being in particular, Nathaniel Wingate Peaslee, is the central protagonist of "The Shadow Out of Time" and we will be studying his situation in full detail shortly. But Peaslee is not the only human slave of the Great Race; he is only one of many. The minds of the "chosen ones" are constrained to work in the Great Race's central archives, preparing written documents for inclusion in the immense library that Lovecraft and Peaslee both admire so much. These slaves can be classified as the cultural and intellectual elites of their respective societies and obviously, they have been selected by the Great Race for that very reason—that is, they are more likely to provide the kind of information about the earth and its peoples that the Great Race requires. Peaslee identifies a few of his fellow slaves, those whom he has been allowed to interact with for the purpose, no doubt, of making his five-year servitude more palatable.

> I talked with the mind of Yiang-Li, a philosopher from the cruel empire of Tsan-Chan, which is to come in A.D. 5000; with that of a general of the great-headed brown people who held South Africa in B.C. 50,000; with that of a twelfth century Florentine monk named Bartolomeo Corsi; with that of a king of Lomar who had ruled that terrible polar land 100,000 years before the squat, yellow Inutos came from the west to engulf it; with that of Nug-Soth, a magician of the dark conquerors of A.D. 16,000; with that of a Roman named Titus Sempronius Blaesus, who had been a quaestor in Sulla's time; with that of Khephnes, an Egyptian

of the 14th Dynasty who told me the hideous secret of Nyarlathotep; with that of a priest of Atlantis' middle kingdom; with that of a Suffolk gentleman of Cromwell's day, James Woodville; with that of a court astronomer of pre-Inca Peru; with that of the Australian physicist Nevil Kingston-Brown, who will die in A.D. 2518 ... with that of Theodotides, a Graeco-Bactrian official of B.C. 200; with that of an aged Frenchman of Louis XIII's time named Pierre-Louis Montmagny. ... and with so many others that my brain cannot hold the shocking secrets and dizzying marvels I learned from them.[6]

However, Peaslee's acquaintances are not limited to human beings; he also talks with alien minds, including a mind from one of the outer moons of Jupiter six million years in the future; three minds from the furry, prehuman Hyperborean devotees of Tsathoggua; one from the arctic Tcho-Tcho civilization; five from the Beetle Race that follows humankind; and so on. All of these entities, human or otherwise, contribute documents to the Great Race's central archives.

The Great Race's much touted galactic library, thus, is not really much of a library at all. This is evident when we compare the Great Race's library with similar libraries envisioned by other sf writers. For example, Isaac Asimov, in his *Foundation* novels, speaks of the great Galactic Library on the planet Trantor, which was established in 34,500 CE (Year 1 in the Galactic Calendar). This library contains books, documents, articles, and other artifacts composed by the leading writers, scholars, and researchers throughout the galaxy, and the library is open to anyone who wishes to use its resources. In contrast, the resources in the Great Race's archives are restricted only to the use of the Great Race. And this leads us to naturally ask: why? If the Great Race is truly as enlightened and cultured of a race as Lovecraft claims, then why don't they share their knowledge with the rest of the cosmos? Lovecraft doesn't provide an answer to this question, but we can guess for ourselves. *It seems clear that the Great Race is interested in accumulating information solely for the purposes of power and domination, not for any higher ends.* They want to collect as much information as they can about other alien races, especially those races that might be a threat to them down the road. They need that information so they can continue to dominate and control the rest of the galaxy. For in effect, domination is what the Great Race is all about; it is the motive behind their mind-exchange technology. The Great Race's ultimate goal is to promote the continued survival and longevity of their race at the expense of all other races in the cosmos. Lovecraft, in fact, confirms this in the following passage from the tale:

The beings of a dying elder world, wise with the ultimate secrets, had looked ahead for a new world and species wherein they might have long life; and had sent their minds en masse into that future race best adapted to house them—the cone-shaped things that peopled our earth a billion years ago. Thus the Great Race came to be, while the myriad minds sent backward were left to die in the horror of strange shapes. Later the race would again face death, yet would live through another forward migration of its best minds into the bodies of others who had a longer physical span ahead of them.[7]

They sent their minds en masse into that future race best adapted to house them. This tells us all that we need to know about the Great Race and surely, it is a damning indictment of the Great Race and their motives with regard to the galaxy as a whole. They want to dominate all other races "en masse"; they don't care about the existence or longevity of any other race other than their own. And in terms of my thesis, the Great Race's activities are designed particularly to ensure that they remain cosmic slave masters in perpetuity.

***

"The Shadow Out of Time," even more so than *The Case of Charles Dexter Ward*, represents Lovecraft's most meticulous and painstakingly detailed treatment of the loss and failure of a privileged white Anglo-Saxon protagonist. Nathaniel Wingate Peaslee is the prototypical New England elitist. He has an impressive familial pedigree behind him: he is the son of Jonathan and Hannah Peaslee, both of them descended from members of the Haverhill gentry—"wholesome, old Haverhill stock," as Lovecraft tells us.[8] In 1899, Peaslee enters Miskatonic University at the age of eighteen and following his undergraduate studies, he pursues a Ph.D. in economics at Harvard University. He returns to Miskatonic as an instructor in 1895. And then, for the next thirteen years, he enjoys an uneventful but satisfying academic career. He marries another Haverhill elitist—Alice Keezar—in 1896 and the couple have three children: Robert K., Wingate, and Hannah. Two years later, Peaslee becomes an associate professor and shortly after, in 1902, a fully tenured professor, achieving the ultimate goal for the upwardly mobile academic. But as we might expect (since this is a Lovecraft tale, after all), Peaslee's privileged life comes crashing down soon enough. On May 14, 1908, Peaslee is in the middle of teaching his afternoon class on Political Economy when his mind is exchanged with the mind of a member of the Great Race; Peaslee slumps down in his chair and remains unconscious for nearly seventeen hours. When he awakens, he is no longer "he" anymore; he is living in the monstrous body of an inhabitant of the Great Race's most important city in late Jurassic era and he will not be reunited with his human body for five years, four months, and thirteen days.

The effects of the mind transfer on Peaslee's career and personal life are very minutely detailed by Lovecraft. Indeed, Lovecraft devotes more attention in "The Shadow Out of Time" to Peaslee's loss of his privileged lifestyle than he does to the Great Race's efforts to achieve cosmic domination. While the real Peaslee is beginning his stint as a slave in the Great Race's central archives, the alien Peaslee must relearn how to use his vocal organs and reeducate himself in the use of his hands, legs, and body. This is hardly surprising, since the mind that controls his body is accustomed to entirely different forms of communication and movement. The alien Peaslee initially tries to conceal his obvious alienage by pretending to be suffering from amnesia, but his efforts do not fool anyone, especially his wife, his oldest son, and his daughter, who cut him out of their lives immediately (only Peaslee's second son, Wingate, decides to stick with him). Once the alien Peaslee is able to physically function in the world, he embarks on a series of travels to remote places, studying at various unnamed foreign institutions to seek out knowledge of "certain points" in history, science, art, languages, and folklore. Exactly *what* these points are is not specified. In addition, the alien Peaslee holds mysterious meetings with occultists and magical practitioners, as did Charles Dexter Ward, and he studies the usual collection of forbidden books that invariably appear in Lovecraft tales—the *Necronomicon*, the *Cultes des Goules*, the *Unaussprechlichen Kulten*, and so on. It is not clear *why* the alien Peaslee shows an interest in magic and folklore, or why he engages in these travels and research. Perhaps, he is merely scoping out individuals who are sympathetic to the Great Race's attempts to dominate other races, particularly human beings, or possibly, he is auditioning for an assistant to help him construct a mind-transfer machine when the time is ripe for him to return. Surely, the alien Peaslee isn't planning to write a document of his own to add to the Great Race's archives; this latter activity is clearly Peaslee's job and any information that the alien Peaslee might come up with would be superfluous at best. In any case, whatever the alien Peaslee's agenda is, he eventually returns to Arkham as the term of the mind transfer winds down and does, indeed, construct a mind-transfer machine to reverse the process and return Peaslee's mind as well as his own to their proper time periods.

For Nathaniel Wingate Peaslee, picking up the pieces of his previous life is a long, difficult process. Peaslee has been profoundly traumatized. He begins to have vivid dreams about his experiences as a slave in the Great Race's city; these dreams turn out to be our only sources of information about the Great Race and their art, technology, and culture. Peaslee teams up with his son Wingate (who will become a psychology professor at Miskatonic in a few years) and they compile a series of articles for the *Journal of the American Psychological Society*, which run from 1928 to 1929 and attract widespread attention from academics and even the general public. Peaslee includes drawings to accompany the articles, showing examples of the Great Race's sculpture and hieroglyphics. He also researches the case histories of other individuals who have had experiences similar to his own. He half convinces himself that his dreams are the result of pseudo-memories and that he had merely been suffering from a very unusual form of amnesia—that, in short, his dreams are not based on anything "real." But deep down, of course, Peaslee knows that the mind-transfer had actually occurred.

Eventually, Peaslee's articles are seen by a group of archaeologists who are finishing up a dig in Western Australia and they are struck by a similarity between Peaslee's drawings and the markings on some of the blocks of stone and carvings that they have unearthed. The two leaders of the dig, Dr. E. M. Boyle of Perth and mining engineer Robert B. F. Mackenzie, get in contact with Peaslee and offer to organize a new expedition to specifically seek out the buried city that Peaslee has identified in his articles, provided that he can secure funding from Miskatonic University. Peaslee recognizes that this expedition might be just the thing that he needs to find out if his experiences are only a pseudo-memory or a real memory. Funding is easily secured—Miskatonic University, apparently, is always willing to finance odd or dodgy expeditions, especially if they have anything to do with ancient folklore, subaltern science, or occultism—and soon, Peaslee and his son are working with Boyle, MacKenzie, and their crew, along with Professor William Dyer (who had headed the Miskatonic Antarctic Expedition of 1930–1, as detailed in *At the Mountains of Madness*) and other academics from the university. The denouement of "The Shadow Out of Time" is rather predictable; the expedition uncovers over a thousand blocks of stone that are decorated with hieroglyphics that are virtually identical to the architectural blocks that Peaslee sees in his dreams. However, the group has yet to discover any actual ruins until one night, on a nocturnal walk in the desert, Peaslee stumbles on the entrance to a buried city. The reader is hardly surprised to learn that this city turns out to be the same city that Peaslee occupied during his enslavement. Peaslee makes his way to the archives and finds the document that he had been writing for the last five years; he takes it with him so that he will have empirical proof that his experience was real. On the way out, however, strange whistling sounds and unnatural winds in the corridors of the city convince him that the Flying Polyps have not died out but still live. Peaslee hurriedly flees back to the surface, but in his panic, he drops the document and so, when he returns to the campsite, he has nothing to show his companions. All that he is left with is the truth about what has happened to him.

Ultimately, Peaslee fares much better than most of Lovecraft's privileged protagonists. Certainly, his life is turned upside down; he ends up estranged from most of the members of his family; he loses his job (though he manages to secure another teaching position at Miskatonic eventually); his sanity is in doubt. And yet, Peaslee does not lose his life, as does Charles Dexter Ward and the majority of the members of the Pabodie Expedition, nor does he lose his identity, as does Robert Olmstead in "The Shadow Over Innsmouth." Nevertheless, the effects of his slavery are long-lasting and permanent. Peaslee will never be able to fully recover from them. Indeed, he feels devastatingly diminished, as is clear in the following passage. As Peaslee pursues his way deeper and deeper into the buried city, he reflects:

It was all the ultimate apex of nightmare, made worse by the blasphemous tug of pseudo-memory. One thing only was unfamiliar, and that was my own size in relation to the monstrous masonry. I felt oppressed by a sense of unwonted smallness, as if the sight of these towering walls from a mere human body was something wholly new and abnormal. Again and again I looked nervously down at myself, vaguely disturbed by the human form I possessed.[9]

This is a perfect description of the slave mentality: oppression and a sense of "unwonted" smallness. And this is what it feels like to be a slave.

* * *

Thematically, "The Shadow Out of Time" is a carbon copy of *At the Mountains of Madness*. There is the superior, alien astronaut race of cosmic slave masters. There are the slaves, also an alien race, imprisoned for long centuries on plantation planet earth. And there are the scholarly, white Anglo-Saxon protagonists, who inevitably cannot help but get themselves into proximity with the cosmic slave masters, though the latter have long relinquished their slaves to the oblivion of earth's past history and left humankind far behind. In this last great tale, Lovecraft, once again, suggests that slavery is a cosmic thing, not just a European or American anomaly. And just as we have seen in *At the Mountains of Madness*, Lovecraft demonstrates a willingness to project his racist views out into the cosmos; indeed, he seems to believe that any advanced civilization, whether human or alien, cannot help but enslave lesser civilizations.

In this particular context, I think it is important to recall again the points that Lovecraft makes in his two racist poems, "De Triumpho Naturae" and "On the Creation of Niggers." Lovecraft argues that natural law decrees that certain races, such as Blacks, are inferior to certain other superior races, such as white Anglo-Saxons. Therefore, it is morally justifiable for the master races to enslave the lesser races. Domination is, in effect, for their own good. This is the same kind of specious reasoning that we find in the work of the racist historian Houston Stewart Chamberlain, who provided "intellectual" justification for Lovecraft's political thought. It is possible, in fact, to take this chain of reasoning one step further. If we postulate the existence of some sort of cosmic law that dictates the actions of alien civilizations, then, it would only be logical for Lovecraft to assume that this cosmic law might be similar to natural law on earth, which would mean, in turn, that the members of the higher civilizations are entitled to be slave masters. And if this is the case, then both cosmic law and natural law are in opposition to the attempts of any of the lesser races to break free from the domination of their masters, whether that race is the shoggoths, the flying polyps, or African Americans.

18

Critical Commentaries (II)

In Part III, my focus is on Lovecraft's cosmic slave masters *as* slave masters—I do, after all, have a thesis to defend. But the cosmic slave masters are much more than that, at least as far as Lovecraft was concerned. Lovecraft uses the extraterrestrial aliens in his work to examine two issues that were very important to him: (1) the nature of reality, and (2) the problem of human perception. Determining the nature of reality is largely a *content* issue, while addressing the problem of human perception is a *style* issue. Graham Harman makes the dichotomy between content and style in Lovecraft's work a central concern in his book *Weird Realism* and, in the process, provides a foundation for determining exactly how we should "read" Lovecraft's extraterrestrial aliens. During the course of his analysis, however, Harman's Lovecraft increasingly becomes less and less like the real Lovecraft, especially when Harman elaborates on what he refers to as the "inherent stupidity of content" and minimizes the importance of content in Lovecraft's work.

Harman reflects a growing tendency in Lovecraft scholarship on the part of scholars and critics to interject themselves into their analyses in ways that may not be particularly "seemly." Indeed, some of the recent commentaries on Lovecraft appear to be more about the writers who pen them and the pet peeves and theories that these writers cherish rather than about Lovecraft's views and what he was trying to accomplish in his weird tales. W. Scott Poole, in his essay "Lovecraft, Witch Cults, and Philosophers," examines two of the "material conditions" (as he refers to them) that underlie Lovecraft's work—his fascination with witches and witch-cults and his racist beliefs—and then launches a critique against scholars who distort or ignore conditions such as these and end up appropriating both Lovecraft and his work into serving their own political or philosophical purposes. Poole focuses his critique on Harman, though it applies equally well to Patricia MacCormack, another one of the unseemly critics, who, in "Lovecraft's Cosmic Ethics," "rethinks"

Lovecraft in the light of speculations posited by continental philosophers and feminist scholars, then brings into existence a kinder, gentler Lovecraft that bears little resemblance to the man that we have come to know and dislike in this book. I am going to examine Harman's book at length in this second critical commentaries chapter, along with the other two essays mentioned above, and hopefully, this will further broaden and clarify my interpretations of Lovecraft's extraterrestrial aliens and also lend additional support for my analysis of Lovecraft's racist beliefs.

* * *

W. Scott Poole, in "Lovecraft, Witch Cults, and Philosophers" (2016), refers to the appearance of agenda-driven scholars (as I will be referring to them in this chapter) in the field of recent Lovecraft scholarship as a "phenomenon." In what is easily the most important passage in his essay, Poole associates these scholars with "historicists," that is, historians who try to squeeze pre-twentieth- and twenty-first-century writers and artists such as Lovecraft into contemporary discourses on race, capitalism, commodity culture, and other social justice concerns. Poole himself, on the other hand, aligns himself with the modernist, formalist historians who take a more traditional approach to Lovecraft.

> This essay seeks to make another point. I'm a historian, not a historicist. My approach is, of course, to show the material conditions (broadly conceived) that gave Lovecraft his witch fascination. But it also includes wondering why these conditions have been ignored by another historical phenomenon: the philosopher who seeks to transform Lovecraft into his guide and/or bumper sticker. Some of these theorists ignore the historical context of Lovecraft to such a degree that they miss a primary element in his fiction. Both text and context are obscured by a need to insert Lovecraft into worlds of discourse that held much less interest for him than, say, his personal fascination with an exploded historical position that depended on ideas premised on Western cultural imperialism and racism ... This essay therefore is less historicist critique than a historian's refusal to allow the material conditions that informed Lovecraft's work to dissipate amid philosophical appropriations that ignore the author's own interests.[1]

Admittedly, this point is well taken—by disregarding the primary elements in Lovecraft's work, the agenda-driven scholars, more often than not, end up fashioning a Lovecraft in their own image, creating what is essentially a fictional construct, as fictional as any of Lovecraft's own creations.

Interestingly, however, Poole does a bit more in this passage than merely chide these unseemly scholars: he provides a template or perhaps a blueprint for the agenda-driven scholar who wishes to create her own fictional

Lovecraft. The key steps include (1) ignoring the material conditions that underpin Lovecraft's work; by "material conditions," Poole is referring to all of the influences that shaped Lovecraft's worldview—these include more than just his intellectual interests, philosophical views, and beliefs, but also his deepest fears, phobias, and preoccupations; (2) amassing "worlds of discourse"—that is, an abundance of sources, mostly secondary, that support the scholar's favorite theories and concerns; and finally, (3) inserting Lovecraft into the worlds of discourse; this is, as we might expect, the tricky part, since the scholar must link Lovecraft directly to this material and make the association "stick." At the end of the process, the agenda-driven scholar presents us with a new Lovecraft, transformed into her personal "guide and/or bumper sticker."

In the first part of his essay, Poole examines two of the darkest material conditions that underlie Lovecraft's work: his fascination with witches and witch-cults and, particularly relevant in terms of this study, his racist beliefs. Lovecraft's fascination with witches was piqued by Margaret Murray's *The Witch Cult in Western Europe* (1921), which Lovecraft read soon after it had become available in the states. In her book, Murray argues that witchcraft was part of an organized, pre-Christian religion that spanned the entire continent of Europe as well as the new world, and, generally speaking, Poole's analysis of how Lovecraft uses Murray's witch-cult thesis is solid. However, we are not given any insight into exactly how extensively Lovecraft uses this thesis in his fictional works. Poole only tells us that Murray's thesis appealed to Lovecraft on a "deep" level and inspired him to write stories involving witch-cults. But Murray's thesis was much more than merely the inspiration for a few disparate tales; it inspired, in fact, one of the foundational premises upon which much of Lovecraft's later fiction is based—that is, the idea that there exists an extensive yet hidden group of black magic cultists in the Western world who worship Lovecraft's transdimensional alien entities and, on occasion, offer support or help to the extraterrestrial aliens as they pursue their secret operations on earth. This premise, indeed, became the foundation for the Cthulhu Mythos as a whole.

Poole, also, is accurate when it comes to interpreting Lovecraft's racialization of the witch cults; he argues rightly that this is connected to Lovecraft's views concerning evolutionary hierarchies in the natural world. But again, we need to take this a little further. As I argue in Chapters 9 and 10, black magic cultism first comes into Lovecraft's fiction in "The Rats in the Walls" and became entrenched as an important Lovecraft theme in "The Horror at Red Hook." Surely, this is no coincidence. Both of these tales draw energy from Lovecraft's notions of evolutionary hierarchies, which are, in effect, racial hierarchies. Lovecraft's racism, in particular, reveals itself in his portrayal of the black magic cultists themselves as either abject "white trash" or as members of the hated races—Blacks, Asians, and the "hybrid squalor" of the Red Hook district in New York. In contrast, Lovecraft portrays the leaders of the cults, Robert Suydam and Lady Margaret Trevor de la Poer, to name just two, as pureblood, white Anglo-Saxons. Furthermore, as we have seen in these tales, black magic in Lovecraft's fiction works hand-in-glove with Lovecraft's miscegenation narrative—specifically, miscegenation by association. The pureblood Anglo-Saxons, over time, are degraded by their close association with the cultists.

In the second part of his essay, Poole moves us away from witches and witch-cults and cites examples of contemporary Lovecraft scholars who, in his opinion, personify the agenda-driven scholar. He mentions Timo Airaksinen, author of *The Philosophy of Lovecraft: The Route to Horror* (1999), and Eugene Thacker, author of *In the Dust of This Planet: Horror of Philosophy Vol.1* (2011), both of whom do, indeed, seem to be more intent on advocating for their agendas than explicating Lovecraft's purposes as revealed in his work. But as I have noted, Poole's main target is Graham Harman, whom, as we will see below, ignores Lovecraft's own clearly stated philosophical views and attempts to transform Lovecraft into an object-oriented ontologist. As Poole writes:

> Harman believes that he has found in Lovecraft someone to be Hölderlin to his Heidegger. Lovecraft can be best understood, he tells us, as the "poet laureate of object-oriented philosophy" ... [Harman] seems little concerned with the fact that this makes Lovecraft's own fairly clear philosophical premises fade into the background, while also making it difficult for the historian to place the author in the context without which he truly begins to feel like only a writer of particularly scary monster stories.[2]

Here, Poole essentially lumps Harman into the same category as the agenda-driven scholars he decries and certainly, there is ample justification for doing so. Harman follows the three steps outlined by Poole above in his attempt to transform Lovecraft into an object-oriented philosopher; later, we will see Patricia MacCormack following these same steps as she creates something that could perhaps be described, whimsically, as a Woke Lovecraft.

* * *

Harman's thesis for his book, *Weird Realism: Lovecraft and Philosophy* (2012), is hyperbolic, to say the least. Harman writes:

> The major topic of object-oriented philosophy is the dual polarization that occurs in the world. ... One involves a "vertical" gap, as found in Heidegger ... The other is a subtler "horizontal" gap, as found in Husserl. ... Lovecraft's constant exploitation of these very gaps automatically makes him as great a hero to object-oriented thought as Hölderlin was to Heidegger. ... Lovecraft must be read not as a Husserlian author, but

as jointly Husserlian-Kantian (or better: Husserlian-Heideggerian). This places him closer to my own position than either Husserl or Heidegger taken singly.[3]

It is obvious here that Harman wants to bring Lovecraft into the object-oriented ontology family and has no compunctions about enlisting the aid of some of the biggest "guns" in existentialist, speculative philosophy—Martin Heidegger, Edmund Husserl, and Immanuel Kant—to help him do it. Of course, it is a simple matter to determine if Lovecraft really is an object-oriented ontologist. First, we need only compare Lovecraft's views on reality to Harman's; if the two differ substantially, then Lovecraft is not an object-oriented ontologist, at least in terms of content. Next, we must compare Lovecraft's views on the problem of perception to Harman's and again, if the two differ substantially, then Lovecraft is not an object-oriented ontologist, at least in terms of style.

Content

In his letters, Lovecraft describes himself as a mechanistic materialist. One of the basic tenets of mechanistic materialism is the belief that there is a sequence of cause and effect that is in constant operation throughout the universe. This is where the "mechanistic" part of the term comes into the picture—the universe is essentially a mechanism, or machine, that runs by the fixed laws of nature. This tenet, also, is important in that it presupposes the existence of objects. Objects make up the bulk of the content in the universe and so, objects are the logical place to start in developing a theory about reality. Lovecraft doesn't provide a formal argument anywhere in his writings to prove the reality of objects, but in a letter written to his friend Frank Belknap Long, dated February 20, 1929, Lovecraft informally argues that objects satisfy the following three criteria: (1) they are real, existing objects; (2) they are composed of matter; and (3) no distinction is to be made between their substance and their qualities.

> Matter, we learn, is a definite phenomenon instituted by certain modifications of energy; *but does this circumstance make it less distinctive in itself, or permit us to imagine the presence of another kind of modified energy in places where no sign or result of energy can be discoverer?* ... For matter, it appears, really is exactly what "spirit" was always supposed to be. Thus, it is proved *that wandering energy always has a detectable form*—that if it doesn't take the form of waves or electron-streams, *it becomes matter itself.* ... The new discovery *doesn't abolish matter.* ... If any mystic thinks that matter has lost its known properties because it's been found made of invisible energy, just let him read Einstein and try to

apply his new conception by butting his head into a stone wall. He will quickly discover that matter is still the same old stuff, and that knowing more about it doesn't have much effect on its disconcerting solidity.[4]

As this passage makes clear, matter is real (whether or not we can see it); thus, objects composed of matter are real and their qualities are real.

Harman, in contrast to Lovecraft, doesn't base his views about objects on objects per se; instead, he bases them on an abstract concept, which he refers to as the Quadruple Object. He describes the Quadruple Object as follows:

What we are here calling "content" can be identified with what we have also called the sensual realm. While real objects and qualities always withdraw from access, and are incommensurable with any form of presence, we are always pressed up against sensual objects and qualities just as the faces of children are pressed against the windows of toy stores and pet shops. ... We have spoken of the withdrawal of real objects (RO) and real qualities (RQ), and the full accessibility of sensual objects (SO) and sensual qualities (SQ) This led us to reflect on the four differing permutations in which objects exist in tension with their qualities. The names given to these four were time (SO-SQ), space (RO-SQ), essence (RO-RQ) and eidos (SO-RQ).[5]

Here, Harman essentially develops his criteria for objects—what they are and whether they are "real" or not. Harman argues that real objects and their qualities are, in effect, withdrawn from us; thus, we really can't determine if they are, in fact, real at all—we have full accessibility only to sensual objects and sensual qualities. Harman, also, argues that real objects are *not* necessarily composed of matter; this is, of course, a consequence of the fact that they are not accessible to us—how can we determine if they are material or not if we can't access them? Indeed, it is not clear exactly *what* they are composed of. Finally, Harman argues that there *are* distinctions to be made between objects and their qualities—that is, SO-SQ; RO-SQ; RO-RQ; and SO-RQ. Harman stipulates that these distinctions represent "gaps" or "tensions" between the two elements in each of the pairs.

It is clear, from a comparison of the two sets of arguments above, that Harman's Quadruple Objects bear no resemblance to Lovecraft's material objects; they are the exact opposite, in fact. And so, on that basis, we can confidently conclude that Lovecraft, in terms of content, is not an object-oriented ontologist. The Quadruple/Material Object dichotomy, however, exposes a much more fundamental difference between Harman's and Lovecraft's philosophies than merely their ideas about objects. This difference, in fact, concerns the basic fabric of reality itself. Harman postulates the idea of *weird reality* (hence the title of his book: *Weird Realism*). For Harman, weird reality, unlike just plain, ordinary reality, is not real in any sense of the term. It is incommensurable, that is, it is beyond human comprehension, and not susceptible to human measurement. Lovecraft's reality, on the other hand, is *not* weird; it is just what materialism has always said it is: it is fully accessible to our senses and can be measured as well as understood by scientific methods.

But of course, there is weirdness in the real world. According to Lovecraft, *this weirdness comes from the weird things living in reality, it is not inherent in reality itself.* The weirdest things in the universe are the extraterrestrial alien races—the Mi-Go, the Elder Things, and the Great Race—and all of these things, like the rest of the objects in the universe, are material and subject to the laws of cause and effect. Yet, because the extraterrestrial races originate from *outside* our own part of the universe (and, in the case of the trans-dimensional aliens, outside the parameters of our space–time continuum), they can't help but carry with them traces of that "outsideness" as they come inside. It is precisely this outsideness that makes them different from the other objects in the universe, and it is this, in turn, that plays tricks with our human perceptual mechanisms.

Style

Style is linked to perception and this is particularly true for Lovecraft. Harman identifies Lovecraft's two most characteristic stylistic devices, his use of allusion and literary cubism. The classic example of Lovecraft's use of allusion is shown in his description of the trans-dimensional entity Cthulhu. In "The Call of Cthulhu" (1928), a Norwegian schooner lands on the island of R'lyeh, which has suddenly risen from the ocean due to a heavy storm, and the crew members encounter Cthulhu. Most of the crew members see Cthulhu as he usually appears in our space–time continuum, that is, as an immense, scaly, dragon monster with an octopus-like head, the face a mass of feelers, claws on hind and forefeet, wings. But due to his "outsideness," two crew members see Cthulhu differently.

> The Thing cannot be described—there is no language for such abysms of shrieking and immemorial lunacy, such eldritch contradictions of all matter, force, and cosmic order. A mountain walked or stumbled. God! ... Three men were swept up by the flabby claws before anybody turned ... Parker slipped as the other three were plunging frenziedly over endless vistas of green-crusted rock to the boat, and Johansen swears he was swallowed up by an angle of masonry which shouldn't have been there; an angle which was acute, but behaved as if it were obtuse.[6]

Technically, an allusion is a reference, either explicit or otherwise, to another object—usually a person, place, event, or even a literary work. On the basis of this definition, Lovecraft is certainly using allusion here; the mountainous shape and the acute/obtuse angle are references to Cthulhu. However, Lovecraft is using this device in a slightly different way than a conventional writer might use it; he is trying to give us a sense of Cthulhu's "outsideness," that is, his weirdness.

The classic example of Lovecraft's use of literary cubism is shown by his description of the dead body of Wilbur Whateley in "The Dunwich Horror." Whateley, it will be remembered, is a half-human, half-transdimensional alien and, in the passage below, he has been killed by a watch dog at the Miskatonic library while attempting to steal a copy of the *Necronomicon*.

> It was partly human … with very man-like hands and head, and the goatish, chinless face had the stamp of the Whateleys upon it. But the torso and the lower parts of the body were teratologically fabulous. … Above the waist it was semi-anthropomorphic; though its chest … had the leathery, reticulated hide of a crocodile or alligator. The back was piebald with yellow and black, and dimly suggested the squamous covering of certain snakes. Below the waist, though, it was the worst; for here all human resemblance left off and sheer phantasy began. The skin was thickly covered with coarse black fur, and from the abdomen a score of long greenish-grey tentacles with red sucking mouths protruded limply. Their arrangement was odd, and seemed to follow the symmetries of some cosmic geometry unknown to earth or the solar system. On each of the hips, deep set in a kind of pinkish, ciliated orbit, was what seemed to be a rudimentary eye; whilst in lieu of a tail there depended a kind of trunk or feeler with purple annular markings, and with many evidences of being an undeveloped mouth.[7]

Here, again, Lovecraft uses a literary device to give the reader a sense of the weirdness of an object—Wilber Whateley, in this case. Lovecraft piles on the images, each one more outrageously grotesque than the previous one, until our sensory mechanisms are overwhelmed.

Graham Harman, committed as he is to his Quadruple Object and his ideas about gaps between objects and their qualities, interprets Lovecraft's use of allusion and literary cubism quite differently. He does not see them as merely literary devices. Harman, in fact, devises two new terms: fusion, which he associates with allusion, and fission, which he associates with cubism. Concerning allusion, Harman argues that there is a gap between real objects (RO), such as Cthulhu, and their sensual qualities (SQ)—that is, Cthulhu's qualities, and that Lovecraft, by using allusion, is fusing RO with SQ, bringing them together in a relationship, albeit an unstable, uneasy relationship. Concerning literary cubism, on the other hand, Harman argues that there is a gap between sensual objects (SO), such as Wilbur

Whateley's body, and their sensual qualities (SQ)—that is, all of Whateley's weird qualities, and that Lovecraft, by using literary cubism, is splitting or "fissioning" SO and SQ into fragments, destroying the connection between them.

Lovecraft, of course, would have been surprised, perhaps even amused, by this analysis. As we have seen, Lovecraft did not believe that there was any distinction to be made between objects and their qualities; the two were, in his estimation, indissoluble. Similarly, Lovecraft did not believe that literary devices are linked in any way to how human beings actually perceive objects in the world; they are merely devices deployed by writers (or artists) to achieve aesthetic ends, nothing more. And certainly, Lovecraft did not believe that perception in itself could have any real or tangible effects in the world. Consequently, Harman's views about the problems of perception have nothing to do with Lovecraft, and for that reason, in terms of style, Lovecraft cannot be considered as an object-oriented ontologist.

***

Patricia MacCormack's essay "Lovecraft's Cosmic Ethics" (2016) takes us even further into agenda-driven Lovecraft scholarship than Harman does. MacCormack's thesis is reminiscent of Harman's; both writers link their theses directly to their favorite philosophers, though, of course, we are now dealing with a different set of philosophers—Marxist, Post-Marxist, and Feminist theorists—for the most part, rather than existentialist and speculative realists.

> Lovecraft offers entryways into feminist, ecosophical, queer, and mystical (albeit atheist) configurations of difference. Ultimately, Lovecraft's more cosmic works rethink life in an ecological mode of multiplicity and connectivity, uncannily evocative of contemporary ecosophical and chaosmological theory seen in the work of Continental philosophers such as Félix Guattari, Michel Serres, and Gilles Deleuze, while the mucosal life of his monstrous protagonists finds a strange bedfellow in the "angels of mucous" of French feminist Luce Irigaray.[8]

This is a wondrously mystical thesis and MacCormack, an astute philosopher, understands that if she plans successfully to pull this off, she must prove that Lovecraft was wondrously mystical himself, or at the very least, sympathetic to mystical theories about the universe. In addition, she must also prove that Lovecraft was inclusive and welcoming—in short, an *ethical* man; this is necessary because her thesis clearly states that Lovecraft offers "entryways" into a greater engagement with the world and the cosmos for woman, gays, transsexuals, and perhaps, all of the rest of the LGBTQ+ folks.

MacCormack devises three major claims to argue her thesis. First, she claims that Lovecraft was not just a mystic-sympathizer; he actually *was* a mystic. She premises this claim on her readings in Deleuze and Guattari and their concept of "elastic bodies."

> "Things" in Lovecraft, be they monsters, humans, hybrids, or any other kind of emergence, are also always simultaneously parts of larger collectives and are themselves fractally formed. Deleuze (after Leibniz) calls such fractal collectives "elastic bodies;" they "are not separated into parts of parts but are rather divided to infinity in smaller and smaller folds that always retain a certain cohesion" ... This can be seen explicitly in Lovecraft's development of Randolph Carter, who is at once Carter facet, Carter fragment, and Carter indissoluble for all other molecules of the universe in Lovecraft's story with E. Hoffman Price, "Through the Gates of the Silver Key."[9]

MacCormack only offers two pieces of evidence for this claim, which she mentions in the last part of the claim itself: (1) Lovecraft's development of the character Randolph Carter, and (2) the E. Hoffman Price "collaborative" story; she quotes a long passage from this story, in fact, that does seem to present a mystical view of the universe.

MacCormack's evidence, however, turns out to be problematic. There is, first, the question of Randolph Carter. Carter is the "star" of three Lovecraft stories: "The Statement of Randolph Carter" (1920), "The Silver Key" (1928), and "The Dream-Quest of Unknown Kadath" (1927). Carter is Lovecraft's venturer into the dream-worlds; he can access these realms either by falling asleep or using a magical device, the silver key. But as it is pointed out to Carter near the end of the latter tale by Nyarlathotep, one of Lovecraft's trans-dimensional entities, the world of dreams is only an illusory realm, a fantasy realm. Thus, MacCormack cannot use the Randolph Carter character as proof for Lovecraft's mysticism; Carter is a dreamer, not a mystic. There is, next, the Price story. The problem here is that this story was not written by Lovecraft at all. *It was written by Price.* Price wrote "Through the Gates of the Silver Key" as a sequel to "The Silver Key" in 1932 and sent it to Lovecraft, who was a friend of his, hoping that Lovecraft would revise it and then allow it to be published under both their names. Lovecraft didn't care much for the story but he helped Price out by revising it—he left as much of Price's original material as he was able to fit into the finished text, including the passage quoted by MacCormack. But he didn't endorse any of Price's ideas, especially Price's views about the space–time continuum. Thus, MacCormack cannot use a passage that Lovecraft never wrote (and certainly didn't agree with) as proof for Lovecraft's mysticism.[10]

MacCormack's second claim is that Lovecraft directed his nihilistic tendencies primarily against privileged white Anglo-Saxons; he did so (or so she argues) because he recognized that white privilege prevents nonwhites and the lesser life forms from full inclusion and connectivity on earth and thus, he wanted to reverse this. MacCormack's claim here, unlike the first one, is not supported by the writings of her "worlds of discourse" crew or by any primary material (whether written by Lovecraft or not). She does bring in Houellebecq, but only for "moral" support.

> Lovecraft's stance against humanity is not necessarily one against joy, but rather, as argued above, perhaps it is premised on the annihilation of a certain kind of humanity and for those subjects that only can be perceived as such. ... While the content of his writings is often offensive against and oppressive of minorities, Lovecraft's larger vision, that which has lead him to be described by Michel Houellebecq as against life, opens up the very possibilities of ethical alterity and encounters premised on the destruction of the privileged subject of the white male that are necessary in order to lead to liberation of all lives as unique emergences.[11]

It is true that white, privileged protagonists suffer the most in Lovecraft's tales; I will offer three explanations as to why this is so in the conclusion, none of which have anything to do with recognition on the part of Lovecraft that the destruction of white people is a prerequisite to the liberation of nonwhites or other living things. In any case, however, MacCormack's claim is irrational, to put it bluntly, and it runs counter to everything that this study has conclusively demonstrated. As I have shown, particularly in Part II, Lovecraft uses racist images and narratives in his tales to warn the white race that Western civilization is in a state of decline due to unrestrained immigration, miscegenation, and hybridism; thus, he didn't want African Americans or hybrids liberated; on the contrary, he would have preferred seeing them shipped back to Africa or, failing that, dead and buried. Moreover, Lovecraft makes it clear that his extraterrestrial alien entities are fully inclusive when it comes to the slaughter of human beings. They don't discriminate on the basis of race, sexual preference, or color or any other criterion and are always ready and willing to exterminate whites, Blacks, gays, lesbians, transsexuals, and any other living creatures that interfere, deliberately or otherwise, in the working out of their purposes on earth.

Finally, McCormack argues that Lovecraft's cosmic monsters are actually ourselves, and here, she has moved out of the ecosophical into the chaosmological—thus, Lovecraft's "ethics" (such as they are) become cosmic ethics.

> The frequent revelation in much of Lovecraft's work is that the monster is the self, found most profoundly perhaps in "The Outsider." The monster is me means that Lovecraft's tales are not so much populated by monsters; rather, protagonists, and readers, become part of a new territory altogether, which is why in so many tales the very terrain itself

is integral to the hybrid, strange genealogies. ... And we are inextricable from the territory, connected as parts of a singular living infinite.[12]

MacCormack offers no evidence to support this remarkable claim and, like the previous claims, it is patently not true. With the possible exception of "The Outsider," *the monster in Lovecraft's works is never the human self*. In the first set of tales studied in this book, protagonists are pictured in opposition to the monsters—humankind vs hybrid, degenerative monsters. And though protagonists do, in some cases, become monsters themselves due to miscegenation by blood or by association, this always involves loss of self and in these cases, the protagonists end up with monster-selves, not human-selves. In the second set of tales, likewise, protagonists are pictured in opposition to the extraterrestrial aliens—humankind vs the cosmic slave masters. But human-self remains separate and inviolate from monster-self; humankind and the cosmic slave masters are, after all, separate species.

***

At the end of this chapter, I want to revisit the question that Carl H. Sederholm and Jeffrey Andrew Weinstock pose at the end of their discussion of the Lovecraft debate (cited previously in the introduction): *With the "critical controversy" over Lovecraft's racism in mind, to what extent can his fiction be used ... to advance more progressive political causes?*[13]

Since neither Harman nor MacCormack successfully defend their theses, this fact might, perhaps, be seen by the traditional, formalistic Lovecraft scholars as defining the limits of the "extent" referred to above—that is, the agenda-driven scholar should advance her cause *only* so far as she can support it with solid evidence from primary and secondary sources. Personally, however, I found both the Harman book and the MacCormack essay enjoyable to read as well as intellectually stimulating and I think that these happy effects, finally, must be the deciding criteria here—that is, if the text entertains and instructs, then the agenda-driven scholar should feel free to advance her cause as far as she can take it.

19

Conclusion

Lovecraft only wrote one more original tale after "The Shadow Out of Time," an excellent short piece, "The Haunter of the Dark," which was published in *Weird Tales* in 1936. After that, he effectively ceased being a creative fiction writer (though he kept up his revisionary work and his voluminous correspondence). Concurrent with the decline of his writing career, Lovecraft's financial situation worsened. His aunt Annie Gamwell went into the hospital to be treated for breast cancer and Lovecraft lived alone at their residence, 66 College Street, but was having trouble making the rent by himself. When his aunt returned, they managed to subsist in extremely straitened circumstances. Then Lovecraft's health broke down; he developed cancer of the small intestine and was taken to Jane Brown Memorial Hospital. He died on March 15, 1937, firmly convinced that his life was a failure and that he would be forgotten as a writer.

For a while, it looked as though Lovecraft might have been right. August Derleth, of course, kept Lovecraft alive in the public mind by publishing Lovecraft's work via his small press publishing venture, Arkham House (this began in 1939 with the publication of *The Outsider and Others*), and Lovecraft got a boost from the sales of cheap paperback editions of his work for the Armed Forces in the mid- to late 1940s. But Lovecraft's fame didn't rise substantially and certainly, it wasn't helped by Derleth publishing his Lovecraft pastiches beginning as early as 1932 and continuing right up to Derleth's death on July 4, 1972. During the 1960s and early 1970s, Lovecraft fell into what can only be described as a stasis—he was admired, but mostly by small groups of readers, many of whom cherished the fact that they were members of a select, elite circle of connoisseurs; these groups included occultists and some scholars. The stasis ended around the start of the 1980s and throughout that decade, Lovecraft's fame began to finally grow, both popularly as well as critically, and scholars were starting to take note of Lovecraft.

In the 1990s, the Lovecraft "recrudescence" (as Joshi refers to it) was in full operation. Joshi describes this memorably in *The Rise and Fall of the Cthulhu Mythos* (2008):

> In the summer of 1990 the H. P. Lovecraft Centennial Conference was held in Providence. It was, in effect, the culmination of two decades of work by leading scholars to establish Lovecraft as an unassailable literary figure, and it attracted participants and an audience from around the world. ... As the 1990s progressed, Lovecraft continued to ascend in critical esteem, as testified by my three annotated editions for Penguin classics (1999, 2001, 2004), a Modern Library edition of *At the Mountains of Madness* (2005), and, as a capstone, the Library of America edition of Lovecraft's *Tales*. ... Lovecraft's popular appeal remained vigorous, as exemplified by the continuing sales of mass-market and trade paperback editions of Lovecraft's tales by Ballantine and, preeminently, by a remarkable proliferation of Cthulhu Mythos writing.[1]

As a by-product of this recrudescence, however, Lovecraft's letters (the first three volumes of which had been published in 1954, 1948, and 1971, respectively) revealed for the first time the full extent of Lovecraft's racism not only to scholars but to mainstream readers as well, including the horror and sf fanbases.

Consequently, in the early twenty-first century, there has been a growing tendency on the part of an increasing number of sf and horror readers to dismiss Lovecraft outright due to his racism and consign both him and his works to the flames. This dismissive tendency, which still continues today, has naturally caused consternation among many of Lovecraft's critics and it isn't hard to understand why. If the object of your studies—your bread and butter, so to speak—becomes a pariah and is read by an increasingly dwindling audience, then the same thing might happen to you and your own works. And if in fact Lovecraft is a racist, then what does that tell us about the people who write about him? Fears such as these have especially proliferated among the older Lovecraft critics: the first-generation critics who grew up in less technologically driven times that were free from the inundation of apps and social media platforms. Since there was no viable way to disseminate Lovecraft's more racist writings to the general public in those early, pre-online days (and since the fans either weren't telling or else didn't know about the extent of Lovecraft's racism), the Lovecraft scholar could indulge in the luxury that he or she was guaranteed a "pass" just as Lovecraft had been granted a pass for the decades following his death, right up to the early 1980s. But now, there is no escaping the facts; all of Lovecraft's works and his most lurid passages are on display for all to see and can easily be downloaded. So, no more passes can be granted, as Lovecraft's critical standing and his legacy as a great writer have taken hits that have seriously diminished his reputation, both personally and professionally—hits that would have sunk a lesser writer into oblivion.

Foremost among the Lovecraft scholars as he has been for nearly four decades, S. T. Joshi has tried to stem the downward spiral that Lovecraft's reputation has suffered by taking a rather aggressive stance in defense of Lovecraft by arguing that we, as critics, should separate Lovecraft's racial hatred from the rest of his philosophical, intellectual, and political thought. As Joshi writes:

> The one area of Lovecraft's thought that has—justifiably—aroused the greatest outrage among later commentators is his attitude on race. My contention is, however, both that Lovecraft has been criticized for the wrong reasons and that, even though he clearly espoused views that are illiberal, intolerant, or plain wrong scientifically, his racism is at least logically separable from the rest of his philosophical and even political thought ... ugly and unfortunate as Lovecraft's racial views are, they do not materially affect the validity of the rest of his philosophical thought ... [or] his metaphysical, ethical, aesthetic, or even his late political views in any meaningful way.[2]

Unlike Lovecraft's friends and colleagues in his lifetime, Joshi, to his credit, acknowledges that we can no longer "whitewash" Lovecraft by claiming that Lovecraft, in his promotion of racism, was only following the mores of his time; this is the same tired argument that Lovecraft scholars before Joshi have made: that is, since most whites were racists in the 1920s and 1930s, Lovecraft was merely following the trend and shouldn't be singled out as being any different than anyone else, or as a particular object of scorn. Joshi also acknowledges that we cannot minimize Lovecraft's racism by claiming that he hated Blacks, Jews, and other races only in the abstract but not when he actually met them face-to-face, for, as the biographical record makes clear, Lovecraft especially hated members of these races when he encountered them in the flesh and he wasn't too shy about letting those around him know it. Nor even, as Joshi states in his 1995 edition of Lovecraft's miscellaneous writings, should we attempt in any way to "be lenient" on this issue. But surely, Lovecraft's racism and white fragility *do* affect the validity of his thought on all levels, despite Joshi's claim that they do not. It is important to note also, in this context, that the separatist approach that Joshi is arguing for here *is* leniency of a sort, and it *is* something of a free pass, in spite of Joshi's dismissal of these two approaches to Lovecraft's hateful beliefs.

China Miéville, well-known author of several award-winning works (Hugo, World Fantasy, and Arthur C. Clarke awards), offers a different view as to how we might approach Lovecraft's racism and to me, this seems to be more sensible:

> So, in other words, the antihumanism one finds so bracing in [Lovecraft] is an antihumanism predicated on murderous race hatred. And this is why you don't get to escape it by saying "well, we're not really talking about humans." I don't think the racism can be divorced from the writing at all, nor should it be. What one can try to do in the case of Lovecraft—and in the case of many other writers ... of toxic opinions—is to try to metabolize it and understand and even appreciate the power of the text. You can only do so by unflinchingly taking on the extent to which that power is predicated on something which is brutal and oppressive.[3]

This is exactly what I have attempted to do in this book; I have metabolized Lovecraft's white fragility and racism as completely and as "unflinchingly" as I can, as I reexamine his works and discover anew how powerful Lovecraft's texts really are, thematically as well as stylistically. And I still feel, as I did before writing this book, that Lovecraft is (and should remain) a central figure in American and European thought in the twenty-first century. I think, also, that there is no indication that Lovecraft has "peaked" in terms of the very real and powerful appeal—creatively, intellectually, and culturally—that he continues to have on scholars, general readers, and fans alike. The reason for this can only be attributed to the dark, persistent, inexorable "rightness" of his highest insights and, equally powerful, the "resistance of his work to our full understanding or comprehension" (as Carl H. Sederholm and Jeffrey Andrew Weinstock put it).[4] Yet, admittedly, much of Lovecraft's dark, inexorable "rightness" is based on an even darker, inexorable *wrongness*—racism, racial hatred, and an infuriating sense of white privilege.

* * *

So, What Was Lovecraft All About?

Lovecraft was, as I note in the introduction, the very personification of the fragile, white male, though his fragility was only latent in his childhood and early youth. If his grandfather had lived longer and if his privileged lifestyle had continued, then this latent fragility might never have been activated. But the loss of his family home and the necessity for his mother and himself to take up residence in rented quarters with another family triggered the manifestation of his fragility and this, in only a short amount of time, transformed Lovecraft from a mildly, paternalistic racist into an extreme racist. In his use of racist images and the two racist narratives in the early and later fiction, Lovecraft's motives are, I think, clear enough. He uses his racist images, extensively in his hybrid, degenerative monster tales and in major tales such as *The Case of Charles Dexter Ward* and "The

Shadow Over Innsmouth," to increase the horror and the disgust that the Other inspires in the minds of the humans who are unfortunate enough to interact with them. The disgust, especially, is shown by Lovecraft's use of such adjectives as "horrible," "blasphemous," "loathsome," "hellish," "damnable," and so on when he describes the Others and their servitors. These are the same adjectives that Lovecraft uses when he describes Blacks, Jews, Asians, and the other members of the hated races. Lovecraft, as a good, upstanding Anglo-Saxon white man, expected his readers, also good, upstanding members of the white race, to share his disgust and horror for both the hated races and the dangerous, malefic Other. As for his use of the two racist narratives, the miscegenation and the slave master/slave narratives, Lovecraft had a more subtle, insidious purpose than simply inspiring horror. The miscegenation narrative is used to argue that hybrids— which are, in effect, an abomination against natural law—are a clear and present threat to the continued longevity and existence of the white race and thus, to the survival of Western civilization in general. Similarly, the slave master/slave narrative is used to argue for another so-called natural law. Lovecraft presents to us in "The Whisperer in Darkness," *At the Mountains of Madness*, and "The Shadow Out of Time" three brilliant and fully fleshed descriptions of highly advanced civilizations: the Mi-Go, the Elder Things, and the Great Race. These civilizations are clearly superior to any human civilization that has developed on earth (or *will* develop on earth), including the white Anglo-Saxon civilization, as manifested by the European and the American nations. The Mi-Go, the Elder Things, and the Great Race are cosmic slave masters, and indeed, as far as these races are concerned, slavery is a perfectly valid institution, endorsed not only by natural law but by cosmic law as well. Therefore, by implication, slavery is likewise a viable institution on earth.

For those who might wonder how Lovecraft could so cold-bloodedly use racist images and narratives as he does in his fiction, as if they were merely tools in his literary arsenal rather than deep-seated beliefs or phobias that needed to be addressed by intervention or professional treatment, it must be recognized that everything in Lovecraft's life and in his mind became tools for him to use and exploit. Lovecraft was the kind of writer who wasted nothing that came to him in either his waking life or in his dreams and his deeper psyche, especially the fears, the frustrations, and the dark imaginings. For example, Lovecraft uses his phobia about cold weather when crafting *At the Mountains of Madness* and in his short tale, "Cool Air" (1928), associating the cold with fear and horror. As he describes it: "As for *cold* as an element of horror—to be sure, I *personally* would be past all conscious emotion, phobic or otherwise, at the temperatures of the Antarctic continent. It is the *idea*, based on less extreme doses, which is hideous and sinister to me. ... frigidity and evil are inextricably intermixed in my emotional makeup."[5] Similarly, Lovecraft uses his phobia about seafood to fuel the visceral horror engendered by the Innsmouth Mutants in "The Shadow Over Innsmouth"—"As for sea-food—it is simply *intensely repulsive* to me ... the taste or smell of it revolts me to the point of nausea and (if too intense or prolonged) actual regurgitation."[6] Lovecraft was the supreme artist and everything that was part of him, internally as well as externally, including things that were good, bad, ugly, or even gross, ended up becoming integral parts of his fictional worlds.

* * *

Lovecraft's tendency to choose academics and scholars as the primary white, privileged protagonists in his weird tales, however, is less easily explainable.

There are, I think, three possible reasons for this. First, either consciously or unconsciously, Lovecraft, by subjecting these characters to the rigors of his pattern of loss and failure, is taking revenge against privileged Anglo-Saxon elites for being more successful adults than he was. As I have shown, Lovecraft was unable to graduate from high school and so, he couldn't attend college—at best, the only route available to him was to become an unorthodox, eccentric scholar. Barred from the more obvious routes, he strikes back by using the only weapon that he can, that is, his fiction, and he does this in a succession of tales in which academics are either killed or driven insane by the Others.[7] Second, Lovecraft, on the contrary, may have felt no jealousy or resentment toward academics at all; he merely selected them as his protagonists because he felt an affinity toward them. In fact, Lovecraft may have believed that he was, in his own way, on the same level as the academics in terms of scholarship and intellectual acumen. Thus, the struggle between the privileged protagonists and the Others is essentially the same struggle that *all* highly intelligent human beings must face if they get too close to the Others due to either curiosity or accident. Finally, the presence of academics in so many of Lovecraft's weird tales might have been merely part of Lovecraft's plan to allegorize his conviction that Western civilization is in a state of decline, with the academics representing the epitome of that civilization; the actual decline itself, of course, is pictured *incrementally*—except in *At the Mountains of Madness*, where an entire group of privileged protagonists is summarily wiped out of existence within only a twenty-four-hour period.

The problem with each of these interpretations, however, is that none of them is supported by any textual evidence—not in the tales, or in the essays, or in the correspondence. In fact, Lovecraft never tells us specifically why privileged white academics occupy such a central place in his works and why they must suffer as they do. So we are forced to speculate. My personal view (and I am offering this as a speculation only) is that *all of the above interpretations may be true*. Lovecraft was a complex person, mentally, emotionally, and psychically. And he was capable of holding two, three, or even more ideas in his head at the same time, even if those ideas were contradictory. As a case in point, consider Lovecraft's view toward his Others in his mature fiction. In some stories, the Others are pictured as trans-dimensional, supernatural entities, while in other tales, they are demythologized, extraterrestrial alien entities—contradictory views of the same kinds of entities.

Thus, as Lovecraft worked out the plots for his tales and devised protagonists that would be a perfect fit for each tale, his attitude toward his protagonists may have been just as contradictory. It may have amused him to think that the high and mighty academics that he was writing about were being fictionalized to their deaths and that he, the nonacademic, was behind the scenes, pulling the strings. Similarly, he may have seen a commonality between himself and scholarly characters such as Charles Dexter Ward and Edward Pickman Derby, who were modeled on details drawn from his own life, and imagined what it might be like for himself and other individuals in the so-called "real" world of academia—or pseudo-academia—to experience first-hand the effects of cosmic indifferentism and malevolence. And lastly, it might have occurred to Lovecraft that he was, indeed, allegorizing his theory about the decline of the West, one privileged protagonist at a time.

Shapiro and Barnard seem to be getting at the same concept that I am articulating here in their identification of what they call Lovecraft's "elliptic theorizing" in relation to his racial hatred.

> Recent commentary on Lovecraft has rightly been concerned with establishing how racializing and racist perspectives inform his writing. Beyond this basic observation, however, we want to observe how Lovecraft's fiction both thematizes a right-wing panic about racial mixture, while also elliptically theorizing and suggesting the motivation behind this experience-system ... The heart of Lovecraft's fictional racism, that is, rarely beats without some degree of awareness, no matter how tortured, of the (self-inflicted) damage entailed by compensatory bigotry, fear, and hatred. As Michel Houellebecq noted. ... this writer's apparent sadism is better understood as a form of masochism and self-loathing.[8]

There is absolutely no evidence that Lovecraft felt conflicted about his "compensatory bigoty, fear and hatred"—as I note in the introduction, he cherished these dark elements of his psyche. Also, Lovecraft wasn't "tortured" by his racism and he didn't experience any "self-loathing"—he felt that Blacks were essentially nonhuman and deserved to be hated and feared by civilized men and women *if* they become violent, much as animals deserve to be hated and feared by civilized men and women if *they* become violent. As for "right-wing panic," *there is no such thing in Lovecraft*. His characters often experience anxiety and panic, particularly in response to the crises that they are forced to undergo, but this is hardly "right-wing" panic. In the case of Lovecraft himself, his attitude was one of passive resignation, not panic, toward an indifferent cosmos and the malefic entities that inhabit it. Lovecraft's claims are twofold: (1) Western civilization is in a state of decline due to unrestrained immigration, miscegenation, and hybridism; and (2) slavery is not only endemic but justifiable among superior civilizations. As such, the possibility that the white Anglo-Saxon race (which is, after all, much weaker than the extraterrestrial races) may become enslaved in the future if and when the cosmic slave masters return is as inevitable as any other inevitable event in an indifferent cosmos. Nevertheless, and in all fairness to Houellebecq, there *does* seem to be some type of marginal, elliptical theorizing at work here in Lovecraft's attitude toward his privileged academics, which Houellebecq identifies as both sadism and masochism at the same time. Lovecraft is sadistically delighting in the violent destruction of his privileged protagonists at the hands of the malefic Others, and yet, masochistically envisions his own violent demise by the same sets of entities.[9]

Nowadays, a number of readers—especially the more socially conscious, progressive readers—often carelessly put forth the argument that Lovecraft's Others are nothing more than metaphors for Black violence directed against the white race, an argument that willfully ignores the fact that Lovecraft intended all the different types of Others that appear in his work to be interpreted as actual ontologically existing entities, not as metaphors for something else. Furthermore, the above readers often suggest that Black violence of this nature is justifiable—a restoration of equity, so to speak. Such a chain of reasoning is all well and good, as long as it recognizes that Lovecraft himself did not think that racial violence of any kind—especially when directed against whites—is justifiable in any sense of the term. Indeed, for Lovecraft, the destruction of a superior race—any superior race—is never a cause for celebration but for sadness—or at the very least, sober reflection. Shapiro and Barnard go on to make the point that Edgar Allan Poe's works, such as *The Narrative of Arthur Gordon Pym* and "MS Found in a Bottle"(1833), show an elliptical theorizing similar to Lovecraft's, conveying a sense of Black violence in response to slavery while also suggesting that this violence is righteous, even liberating. Admittedly, Poe *was* a racist—as J. Gerald Kennedy and Liliane Weissberg, in *Romancing the Shadow: Poe and Race* (2004), observe: "Poe has long personified benighted attitudes about race and slavery."[10] But just as in the case of Lovecraft, there is no evidence that Poe felt Black violence was "righteous" or "liberating." No matter how intent readers may be to create an image of Lovecraft (or of Poe) that fits their conceptions of what it means to be socially conscious—even at an unconscious, minimal level—it just isn't defensible.

***

White fragility and racism will always be the two elephants in the room wherever Lovecraft is discussed today, either in informal settings or in classrooms and seminars. When it comes to the latter, in particular, academia has been more than willing to confront these elephants directly. Likewise, university and college professors have taught their graduate and undergraduate students to do the same. But as I have noted in the introduction, there is no consensus on the issue of whether or not Lovecraft should, indeed, be canceled (or at least muzzled somewhat) and this applies to individuals both in and outside of academia. As such, as readers and students of Lovecraft, it is up to each of us to determine how much of a role Lovecraft's racism and white fragility should play in our appreciation and understanding of his work. The issues that I have raised in this book are personal to all of us and demand only personal responses. We must, therefore, decide for ourselves: metabolize, ignore, or consign to the flames. But I would urge each of us to ponder long and hard before deciding, particularly if our inclination leans toward the flames. For I think that Lovecraft still has important things to tell us, even if it isn't exactly what we want to hear or what we thought we might be getting ourselves into when we first signed up for an extended tour in Lovecraft country—the *real* Lovecraft country—a place that, as I have shown, is much richer, complex, and more fundamentally disturbing than anything that popular culture, to date, has been able to imagine.

Appendix

Lovecraft, *Lovecraft Country*, and Afrofuturism

In this appendix, I want to examine Lovecraft's connections to Matt Ruff's novel *Lovecraft Country* (2016) and to Afrofuturism in general. Arguably, *Lovecraft Country* is one of the most well-known Afrofuturist texts and it linked Lovecraft directly to the Afrofuturism movement almost immediately upon its release. In chapter 1, "Lovecraft Country," Ruff develops his main narrative. The place is Chicago, Illinois. The year is 1954. Twenty-two-year-old army vet Atticus Turner, along with his childhood friend Letitia Dandridge and his uncle George Berry, are taking a road trip to Ardham, Massachusetts—into the heart of "Lovecraft Country." They are seeking Atticus's father Montrose, who has been missing for over a week. They have reason to believe that Montrose was taken to Ardham against his will by a mysterious white man driving a silver Daimler sedan. Along the way, they are constantly harassed and disrespected by white racists whenever they are forced to stop for food or to get gas. Sometimes, the bigotry goes even further. Racist firefighters try to run them off the road in Utica, but they are magically protected by the man in the Daimler, who is following them; the firetruck is jolted off the road. Similarly, just outside Devon County, a corrupt sheriff and his deputies pull them over on the highway and march them into the woods at gunpoint. It looks as if they are about to be murdered, but the sheriff and his cohorts are attacked and devoured by invisible demons, conjured up, no doubt, by the man in the Daimler.

Eventually, Atticus and his group reach the town of Ardham and make a stop at the Ardham Lodge, a sumptuous mansion owned by Samuel Braithwhite and his son, Caleb. To their surprise, the group finds that the Braithwhites are expecting them and they are welcomed into the house as respected guests. However, Samuel's intentions toward the group are anything but benign. Samuel had used Montrose as a decoy to lure them all to Ardham and Montrose is currently chained up in a dungeon in the nearby town. Samuel is the lodge master of the Massachusetts branch of the Adamite Order of the Ancient Dawn (AOAD), a quasi-religious/magical organization that was established by his ancestor Titus Braithwhite in 1765. Specifically, Samuel is interested in Atticus and wants to use him as a sacrifice in one of the AOAD's rituals. According to AOAD doctrine, entropy came into the world after Adam and Eve were exiled from the Garden of Eden. This entropy, in particular, is embodied in the Black race—Blacks, in effect, personify entropy, chaos, and violence. To purge the entropy and return the world to its natural, Edenic state, a Black man must be bathed in the purifying "light of creation." But not just any Black man will do. It must be a Black man who is also of the same bloodline as the Braithwhites. Atticus's mother is descended from Hannah, a slave woman, who had a child with Titus Braithwhite; thus, Atticus is the perfect choice.

Naturally, Atticus and the group are suspicious about Samuel and the members of the AOAD; they occasionally meet these individuals at dinner or in the halls of the lodge and neither their host nor the lodge members seem to really want them in the house; only Caleb shows them attention and kindness. As their stay at Ardham Lodge continues, Atticus and the group learn all about Samuel's intentions and what he has planned for Atticus. They also discover Montrose imprisoned in the town and promptly set him free. Atticus and his companions make their plans to escape from the mansion, but Samuel prevents this from happening and has them locked up securely in the east wing of the building. At noon on the next day, Atticus is taken to the AOAD's magical temple, a large rectangular room located on the third floor of the mansion. Atticus has been partially immobilized by a spell and he is unable to resist the members of the order as they prop him up inside the circle. Samuel slashes Atticus's hands with a knife and the blood drips down, staining the magical pentacles on the floor. At this point, Samuel and the members of the lodge, robed in their ceremonial vestments, begin their incantations. Shortly after, light appears around the edges of the door—the light of creation, presumably—and Atticus is certain that he will be annihilated. However, Caleb Braithwhite has sabotaged the ritual, using a powerful spell that breaks apart the light of creation and floods the temple in darkness. Atticus can hear Samuel and the lodge members screaming. When the darkness lifts, the floorboards outside the circle, along with the walls and ceiling, are scorched. Samuel and the AOAD members are burnt to a crisp and crumbled up into piles of dust on the floor. Atticus rejoins his companions, who have been freed from the east wing. Under instructions from Caleb, a servant has packed up all of the group's belongings. The servant escorts them out of Ardham manor and they drive back to Chicago, glad to put Lovecraft Country behind them.

The saga of Caleb Braithwhite continues in the next six chapters of *Lovecraft Country*. Caleb relocates to Chicago and affiliates himself with the Chicago Branch of the AOAD. This lodge is run by John Lancaster, a brutish man, who is protected by bodyguards and corrupt detectives. Both Caleb and Lancaster attend a conclave of lodge masters who have come to Chicago from various lodges around the country. At this event, Caleb gives a speech that makes it clear that he wants to be the Grand Master of all the AOAD lodges in the United States. The motives behind Caleb's coup against his father and the Massachusetts lodge are finally revealed; Caleb felt that his father and the Massachusetts lodge would be impediments to his goal. As for Atticus and his group, Caleb helps them so that they will reciprocate when it comes time to overthrow the leadership of the Chicago lodge and take control of the remaining lodges. In the last chapter of the novel, Caleb, allied with Atticus and all of the other Black protagonists in the book, carries out an assault on the Chicago lodge's headquarters. They penetrate to the ballroom of the clubhouse, where the safe is kept. Caleb, who is a much more powerful magician than his adversaries, performs a spell that evokes a dark creature, which promptly swallows up Lancaster, his thugs, and the rest of the AOAD Chicago Lodge. Caleb then proceeds to open the safe—he is seeking rare occult texts that will bolster his campaign to take over the other AOAD lodges. However, Atticus turns the tables on Caleb with a spell of his own, which immediately strips Caleb of all of his magical powers and prevents him from any future association with the AOAD lodges. Caleb is likewise banned from entering Chicago, Detroit, or any other state where friends and family members of the Turner and Berry clan reside. Atticus and his group leave Caleb stranded on the state line between Chicago and Indiana, confused and baffled over what has happened to him.

Lovecraft Country is fun to read—it is fast paced, well-crafted in terms of plot, and filled with personable, interesting characters. The harrowing descriptions of bigotry and racial hatred directed against Atticus and his crew, likewise, are managed deftly by Ruff, and his treatment of Jim Crow America is largely accurate, though a bit overexaggerated. However, *Ruff's novel is not Lovecraftian—not even a little bit*—which, no doubt, disappointed the Lovecraft fans and sf readers who bought the book because of its title. To begin with, there is none of the unearthly, bracing cosmicism that permeates Lovecraft's work. In *At the Mountains of Madness*, for example, William Dyer and graduate student Danford are forced to confront their insignificance when compared to the Elder Things and to the great immensities of space and time that separate the latter from humankind. Similarly, Nathaniel Wingate Peaslee, in "The Shadow Out of Time," acutely feels his "littleness" as measured against the enormous cities of the Great Race and, likewise, is made conscious of the fact that the portion of time allotted to humans on earth is infinitesimally tiny when contrasted with that of the extraterrestrial alien races. But in *Lovecraft Country*, none of the major characters, with the possible exception of Hippolyta, George's wife, give even a passing thought to the cosmos or to their relationship with it; they are earth-gazers, wrapped up in their human-centric concerns.

Another problem with Ruff's novel is that there is none of the psychological or spiritual angst that is a common feature of both Lovecraft's early and later weird tales. Arthur Jermyn, Thomas Delapore, and Robert Olmstead all face severe identity crises and experience equally severe anxiety and dread; Lovecraft carefully and meticulously tracks every nuance of the angst in each of these characters and invites us to emphasize with it. In contrast, Atticus, Leticia, George, and the others find themselves in challenging situations, but they never question their identities or feel any deep anxiety whatsoever about what is happening around them. They always know who they are even if they don't always know where they are going or why they are going there in the first place. Atticus, for example, tells us that he "liked who and what he was. He always had. It was God's other creatures he occasionally had problems with."[1] His companions apparently feel the same way; they all have rock-solid conceptions of themselves and this serves as a bulwark shielding them from deeper, more complex engagements with the subtler aspects of their world.

In addition, Ruff's handling of the magical and supernatural elements that occur alongside the racist elements in the novel is trite, superficial, and cliché-ridden. There is the conventional good vs evil scenario: Atticus and his crew represent the forces of good, while the Braithwhites and the AOAD represent the forces of evil. There are the hokey rituals involving Atticus—Caleb's "magic Negro," as Atticus puts it. There are the equally hokey spells, such as the enchantment that Caleb puts on George Berry's car to protect him from racist highway cops in the first chapter; the magic elixir which transforms Black persons into white persons, or vice versa, in the fifth chapter; and the Mark of Cain that magicians can place on enemies to diminish their power, in the eighth chapter. These are the kinds of juvenile plot-elements that Lovecraft criticized in the work that was appearing beside his own in the pulp magazines of his day. Indeed, as I read *Lovecraft Country*, I was reminded of August Derleth's poorly conceived pastiches of Lovecraft's work, which Derleth began to churn out in the 1930s immediately after the death of his mentor. The continuing storyline of Caleb Braithwhite and the AOAD vs the African American protagonists, in particular, is very similar to Derleth's *The Trail of Cthulhu* (1944–52), a linked series of five tales centered around the battles between Dr. Labian Shrewsbury and the good magicians vs the black magicians who serve the Cthulhu Cult.

Ruff's novel has been praised extensively by the major media outlets, including *Booklist* and *The New York Times Book Review*, and the consensus seems to be that, for most critics and reviewers, the Lovecraftian horror in the book is less "horrifying" than the racism and the bigotry. This is certainly true, but only because Ruff gives us a diluted, watered-down version of

Lovecraftian horror—eliminating the cosmicism, the psychological angst, and the profundity of the magical and supernatural components—all of which are the most crucial and vital parts of the Lovecraft mythos. Ruff, in effect, stacks the deck against Lovecraft and the disturbing series of racist events that occur throughout his novel loom the larger because of it. This would not have been the case if Lovecraft's themes and tropes had been presented accurately and honestly.

Lovecraft, in a letter to Farnsworth Wright, the editor of *Weird Tales*, dated July 5, 1927, describes the "fundamental premise" upon which all of his weird tales are based, that is,

> that common human laws and interests and emotions have no validity or significance in the vast cosmos-at-large. To me there is nothing but puerility in a tale in which the human form—and the local human passions and conditions and standards—are depicted as native to other worlds or other universes. To achieve the essence of real externality, whether of time or space or dimension, one must forget that such things as organic life, good and evil, love and hate, and all such local attributes of a negligible and temporary race called mankind, have any existence at all ... when we cross the line to the boundless and hideous unknown—the shadow-haunted *Outside*—we must remember to leave our humanity—and terrestrialism at the threshold.[2]

If Ruff had made an effort to provide even an iota of the "real externality" that Lovecraft is describing here, the bigotry and racism that are a central part of *Lovecraft Country* would have paled by comparison.

* * *

Lovecraft's connection to Afrofuturism is less tenuous and far more interesting than the connection to *Lovecraft Country*.

Mark Dery, in his essay "Black to the Future" (1994), formally defines Afrofuturism as "Speculative fiction that treats African American themes and addresses African American concerns in the context of twentieth century techno culture—and, more generally, African American signification that appropriates images of technology and a prosthetically enhanced future."[3] At the most basic level, Afrofuturists place their characters in either past or future environments where, initially, they must learn to survive and adapt to their surroundings, just as space or time travelers in the traditional sf genres must do when they first step from their spaceships or out of the space–time continuum. In Afrofuturist narratives, however, there is the added element of the racial traumas that the Black protagonists have brought with them—traumas which, in turn, are often augmented and perhaps, even magnified by their new environments. As they find their way in their new worlds, the Black protagonists discover ways to liberate themselves from their traumas and proactively reclaim the future for themselves and for those who might follow. Lovecraft, of course, couldn't have cared less about Blacks, or their racial traumas or attempts at liberation. As we have seen, for Lovecraft, Blacks and people of color were a major factor in the decline of Western civilization and that was essentially all they were. Thus, if we intend on seeing any points of commonality between Lovecraft and Afrofuturism, we must remove Lovecraft himself from the equation and consider *only* his work and its inherent themes.

Kodwo Eshun, a British-Ghanaian writer and filmmaker, in his essay "Further Considerations on Afrofuturism" (2003), identifies three of the major themes in Afrofuturist texts, one of which is "extraterrestriality," which involves the juxtaposition of the extraterrestrial against the terrestrial for the purpose of exploring the subjectivity inherent in the latter condition. As Eshun describes this:

> Afrofuturism uses extraterrestriality as a hyperbolic trope to explore the historical terms, the everyday implications of forcibly imposed dislocation, and the constitution of Black Atlantic subjectivities: from slave to negro to coloured to evolué to black to African to African American. Extraterrestriality thereby becomes a point of transvaluation through which this variation over time, understood as forcible mutation, can become a resource for speculation. It should be understood not so much as escapism, but rather as an identification with the potentiality of space and distance within the high-pressure zone of perpetual racial hostility.[4]

This is similar to Lovecraft's use of extraterrestrial civilizations in his two greatest tales—*At the Mountains of Madness* and "The Shadow Out of Time" (see the previous discussion)—though, as noted before, the Elder Things and the Great Race are not intended to be read as tropes. In the first tale, William Dyer and Danford explore the (presumably) empty city of the Elder Things and confront their "subjectivities" in the most profound sense; they become aware of their own insignificance as human beings in comparison to the immensities of space and time—especially time, as represented by the vast stretches of time that separate humankind from the extraterrestrial alien races in the past and the equally vast stretches of time that separate humankind from the extraterrestrial alien races in the present and into the future. In the second tale, Nathaniel Wingate Peaslee also confronts his subjectivities in a similar fashion and he, too, becomes aware of his insignificance in the cosmos; previously, I have spoken of his feelings of "littleness" in the city of the Great Race. But in this case, "forcibly imposed dislocation" (as Eshun puts it) is, indeed, an issue, for Peaslee is a former slave as well as an explorer.

Eshun, also, identifies a mythos of sorts in Afrofuturism—the Black Atlantic Mythos—which can be understood as rivaling Lovecraft's own

Mythos or, at least, that portion of the Lovecraftian Mythos articulated in "The Shadow Over Innsmouth." And here, we enter a fascinating area of Afrofuturism that is overtly Lovecraftian (though Afrofuturists would likely deny this). Using Drexciya's written text accompanying their CD *The Quest*, Eshun speculates about the possible evolution of a race of terrestrial aliens that develops alongside—or in spite of—the evolution of humankind from primates.

> This aesthetic of estrangement was pursued to its limit-point by Drexciya, the group of enigmatic producers, synthesists, and designers operating from Detroit. In the liner notes to their CD *The Quest*, Drexciya proposed a science-fictional retelling of the Middle Passage. The "Drexciyans" are water-breathing, aquatically mutated descendants of "pregnant America-bound African slaves thrown overboard by the thousands during labour for being sick and disruptive cargo.
>
> Could it be possible for humans to breathe underwater? A foetus in its mother's womb is certainly alive in an aquatic environment. Is it possible that they could have given birth at sea to babies that never needed air? Recent experiments have shown mice able to breathe liquid oxygen, a premature human infant saved from certain death by breathing liquid oxygen through its underdeveloped lungs. These facts combined with reported sightings of Gillmen and Swamp Monsters in the coastal swamps of the Southeastern United States make the slave trade theory startlingly feasible.
>
> In treating Gilroy's *The Black Atlantic* as a science fiction which is then developed through four-stage analysis of migration and mutation from Africa to America, Drexciya have constructed a Black-Atlantean mythology that successfully speculates on the evolutionary code of black subjectivity.[5]

In "The Shadow Over Innsmouth," Lovecraft postulates an alternative evolutionary chain in earth's past—entities evolved from aquatic progenitors rather than the anthropoid. The idea of adding the water babies born from drowned female slaves into the mix is intriguing and one, I think, that Lovecraft might not have objected to. He would likely have considered this plot element as a further enhancement of the horror and revulsion that he was trying to create in the minds of his readers when he crafted the Innsmouth mutants. A strain of "hateful, negroid blood" (as Lovecraft would have phrased it) would have spiced up the predominately ichthyic DNA that gave rise to these horrors and made them much more deliciously alien.

Eshun, lastly, examines the uses of alienation in Afrofuturist texts and artifacts, amalgamating Greg Tate's and W. E. B. Dubois's views of alienation. Eshun argues that Afrofuturists introduce alienation into the future environments or "contexts" that they create for their African American protagonists in order to ultimately start a process of disalienation.

> In *The Last Angel of History*, Tate argued that "The form itself, the conventions of the narrative in terms of the way it deals with subjectivity, focuses on someone who is at odds with the apparatus of power in society and whose profound experience is one of cultural dislocation, alienation and estrangement. Most science fiction tales dramatically deal with how the individual is going to contend with these alienating, dislocating societies. ..." At the century's start, Dubois termed the condition of structural and psychological alienation as double consciousness. The condition of alienation, understood in its most general sense, is a psychosocial inevitability that all Afrodiasporic art uses to its own advantage by creating contexts that encourage a process of disalienation.[6]

One can see alienation in Lovecraft's work in terms of a similar alienation/disalienation process. But it must be understood that, for Lovecraft, when a human character undergoes the alienation process—which is to be interpreted literally as the transformation of a human into an alien entity—the human remains an alien forever and cannot go back to being a human being. *There is always in Lovecraft a clear line between human and alien—much like the color line in the Jim Crow era between Blacks and whites—and this line cannot be breached.* Consequently, the fledgling alien must learn to live with its new situation. Out of all of Lovecraft's tales, only Robert Olmstead in "The Shadow Over Innsmouth" is able to successfully do this—at the end of the tale, he accepts his transformation into one of the Deep Ones and thus, he disalienates himself. This kind of acceptance, however, is not the norm in the majority of Lovecraft's tales. The human characters who transform into alien entities—even temporarily, as in the case of Nathaniel Wingate Peaslee—usually end up either committing suicide (Arthur Jermyn) or retreating into insanity (Thomas Delapore).

Postscript

Lovecraft Country is not the only contemporary Lovecraft-inspired literary work that explores the bigotry and racism that characterized the era of segregation in America in the first part of the twentieth century. Victor LaValle's novel *The Ballad of Black Tom* (2016), published the same year as the Ruff novel, essentially does the same thing. *Black Tom* is a "revision" of Lovecraft's "The Horror at Red Hook" and it takes place in the same city and year as the Lovecraft story. The plot centers around Tommy Tester, a small-time black hustler who is recruited by a reclusive millionaire Robert Suydam to assist him and his cult in reawakening the Great Old One Cthulhu from his deathlike trance in the underwater city of R'lyeh. In addition to Suydam, Lovecraft's police detective, Thomas F. Malone, also plays a major role in the novel; the second series of chapters (Chapters 10–17) are narrated from his point of view. Like the Ruff novel, LaValle's book is crammed with magic and supernatural happenings, but the main focus is on Tester's encounters with racist police officers and with racism in general.

Black Tom didn't attract the same level of media attention as the Ruff novel—probably due to the fact that Lovecraft's name is not mentioned in the title. But the novel drew positive reviews just the same; a few of the critics, in fact, argued that LaValle's simple, rather pedestrian writing style was an improvement over Lovecraft's frenzied prose in "Red Hook." Nevertheless, *Black Tom* can be legitimately challenged on the same basis as *Lovecraft Country*. As was the case with Ruff, LaValle provides his readers with a diluted version of the cosmic fear, psychological angst, and magical plot-elements that are the most characteristic elements in Lovecraft's fictional works. Similarly, LaValle, like Ruff, stacks the deck against Lovecraft by overemphasizing the racist events at the expense of the horror. This is made blatantly clear by the main protagonist himself, Tommy Tester, who, near the end of the first series of chapters, weighs a frightening experience with a space–time portal against a particularly disturbing example of violent racism and remarks: "[The] fear of cosmic indifference suddenly seemed comical, or downright naïve … What was indifference compared to malice?"[7]

Given the popularity of the Ruff novel, it was only a matter of time before one of the major media outlets would bring out a Netflix series based on it. On August 16, 2020, HBO premiered just such a series, also named *Lovecraft Country*, created by Misha Green and produced by Warner Brothers television studios. This event gave a further pop-cultural boost to both the Ruff novel and Afrofuturism, as well as to Lovecraft (who, admittedly, hardly needed it). The first season follows the book fairly accurately and most of Ruff's storylines are used, though there are some significant changes, that is, Christina Braithwhite and the Sons of Adam, rather than Caleb Braithwhite and the AOAD, for example, are the adversaries of Atticus and his crew, and Atticus ends up killed off in the finale. On the whole, the episodes are entertaining and the cast is particularly good. But the series was short-lived; Warner Brothers canceled it before the second season could get underway. The studio's reason for the cancellation was purportedly due to the expenses incurred in producing the first season. However, I think that the real reason was that the series didn't attract a large enough audience. Projects of this kind—based as they are on the celebrity of the Lovecraft brand—must attract interest from the Lovecraft fan base, who naturally comprise the dominant audience. But the Lovecraft fan base stayed away and it isn't too hard to understand why. The series turned out to be, in fact, even less Lovecraftian than the book—it was "Derlethian" through and through.

NOTES

Introduction

1. Robin DiAngelo, *White Fragility: Why It's So Hard for White People to Talk about Racism* (Boston, MA: Beacon Press, 2018), 2.
2. H. P. Lovecraft, *Selected Letters IV: 1932–1934*, ed. August Derleth and James Turner (Sauk City, WI: Arkham House, 1976), 357.
3. Michel Houellebecq argues that Lovecraft's "well-bred" racism didn't become extreme until he lived in the Red Hook district of New York from 1925 to 1926 and was forced to confront at close quarters immigrants from other races [Michel Houellebecq, *H. P. Lovecraft: Against the World, against Life*, trans. Dorna Khazeni (Great Britain: Gollancz, 2008), 105–6]. But this interpretation is simplistic and ignores the severe trauma that followed from Lovecraft's loss of privilege in his teen years. It is this trauma, in fact, that laid the foundation for what occurs later in New York. Houellebecq, also, ignores Lovecraft's early "apprenticeship" among the writings of the racist historians of his day. As I will show in Part I, the intensification of Lovecraft's racism was not merely a sudden, swift "racist neurosis," as Houellebecq would have us believe, but rather (and more logically) the result of a process that took place over a much longer period of time before he had even considered moving to New York.
4. Robert Block, "Heritage of Horror," in *The Best of Lovecraft: Bloodcurdling Tales of Horror and the Macabre* (New York: Del Rey Books, 1982), xxi–xxii.
5. In Lovecraft's childhood, Blacks were originally confined to an area north of Olney Street in Providence—the so-called Negro district—though this area expanded considerably during the course of his continuing residence in the city.
6. Carl H. Sederholm and Jeffrey Andrew Weinstock, eds., "Introduction: Lovecraft Rising," in *The Age of Lovecraft*, ed. Sederholm and Weinstock (Minneapolis: University of Minnesota Press, 2016), 4.
7. David Simmons, "'A Certain Resemblance': Abject Hybridity in H. P. Lovecraft's Short Fiction," in *New Critical Essays on H. P. Lovecraft*, ed. David Simmons (New York: Palgrave Macmillan, 2013), 18.
8. Jed Mayer, "Race, Species, and Others: H. P. Lovecraft and the Animal," in *The Age of Lovecraft*, ed. Sederholm and Weinstock, 120.
9. Patricia MacCormack, "Lovecraft's Cosmic Ethics," in *The Age of Lovecraft*, ed. Sederholm and Weinstock, 199.

10 Stephen Shapiro and Philip Barnard, *Pentecostal Modernism: Lovecraft, Los Angeles, and World-Systems Culture* (New York: Bloomsbury Academic, 2017), 129, 131.
11 Sederholm and Weinstock, *The Age of Lovecraft*, 32–3.
12 Shapiro and Barnard, *Pentecostal Modernism*, 121.

1 Privilege Lost

1 H. P. Lovecraft, *Selected Letters I: 1911–1924*, ed. August Derleth and Donald Wandrei (Sauk City, WI: Arkham House, 1965), 32.
2 Ibid., 31, 297.
3 Ibid., 34, 297, 299.
4 Ibid., 74.
5 S. T. Joshi, *Lovecraft: A Life* (West Warwick, RI: Necronomicon Press, 1996), 44–5.
6 L. Sprague De Camp, *Lovecraft: A Biography* (New York: Doubleday, 1975), 36.
7 Lovecraft, *Selected Letters IV*, 357–8.
8 Joshi, *Lovecraft: A Life*, 59.
9 Lovecraft, *Selected Letters IV*, 358.

2 The Pattern of Loss and Failure

1 The "night-gaunts" that Joshi refers to here are leathery, black-winged, faceless creatures that Lovecraft often saw in his childhood dreams; they would suddenly appear and then whisk him off on terrifying, aerial journeys, moving at tremendous speeds and, on occasion, dropping him from vast heights.
2 Joshi, *Lovecraft: A Life*, 192.
3 Lovecraft, *Selected Letters I*, 40.
4 Ibid., 30.
5 Joshi, *Lovecraft: A Life*, 82.
6 Lovecraft, *Selected Letters IV*, 172.
7 Joshi, *Lovecraft: A Life*, 81.
8 Lovecraft, *Selected Letters I*, 41.
9 Joshi, *Lovecraft: A Life*, 85.
10 Ibid., 191–2.
11 Ibid., 195.
12 Lovecraft, *Selected Letters I*, 133–4.

13 Joshi, *Lovecraft: A Life*, 196.
14 Sonia H. Davis, "Lovecraft as I Knew Him," in *Something About Cats and Other Pieces*, ed. August Derleth (Sauk City, WI: Arkham House, 1949), 234.
15 Ibid., 243.
16 De Camp, *Lovecraft: A Biography*, 256–7.
17 H. P. Lovecraft, *Selected Letters II: 1925–1929*, ed. August Derleth and Donald Wandrei (Sauk City, WI: Arkham House, 1968), 45–7.
18 Davis, "Lovecraft as I Knew Him," 243–4.
19 De Camp, *Lovecraft: A Biography*, 262.

3 Racist Influences

1 DeCamp, *Lovecraft: A Biography*, 253–5.
2 Joshi, *Lovecraft: A Life*, 134.
3 Houston Stewart Chamberlain, *The Foundations of the 19th Century*, 2nd ed., trans. John Lees (Great Britain: Bodley Head, 1912), 187–8, 206, 229.
4 Lovecraft, *Selected Letters II*, 120.
5 Oswald Spengler, *The Decline of the West: Perspectives of World History*, Vol. II, trans. Charles Francis Atkinson (2007): 119, 125, 126, 127. http://archive.org/details/declineofwest02spenuof/page/n5/mode/2up (accessed April 20, 2023).
6 Lovecraft, *Selected Letters IV*, 230.

4 Racist Writings

1 De Camp, *Lovecraft: A Biography*, 256.
2 Ibid., 94.
3 Paul Rolland, *The Curious Case of H. P. Lovecraft* (London: Plexis, 2014), 37.
4 H. P. Lovecraft, "The Crime of the Century," in *Miscellaneous Writings: H. P. Lovecraft*, ed. S. T. Joshi (Sauk City, WI: Arkham House, 1995), 253–5.
5 Joshi, *Lovecraft: A Life*, 133.
6 DeCamp, *Lovecraft: A Biography*, 99.
7 H. P. Lovecraft, "Americanism," in *Miscellaneous Writings*, ed. Joshi, 264–5.
8 H. P. Lovecraft, "In a Major Key," in *Miscellaneous Writings*, ed. Joshi, 424–5.
9 Lovecraft, *Selected Letters I*, xxi.
10 Joshi, *Miscellaneous Writings*, 491.
11 Lovecraft, *Selected Letters I*, 17.

12 H. P. Lovecraft, *Selected Letters III: 1929–1931*, ed. August Derleth and Donald Wandrei (Sauk City, WI: Arkham House, 1971), 207–8.
13 Lovecraft, *Selected Letters II*, 64–5.
14 Ibid., 67.
15 Lovecraft, *Selected Letters IV*, 248–9.
16 Ibid., 257.
17 Ibid., 252.
18 H. P. Lovecraft, *Selected Letters V: 1934–1937*, ed. August Derleth and James Turner (Sauk City, WI: Arkham House, 1976), 77–8.
19 Lovecraft, *Selected Letters II*, 314–15.
20 H. P. Lovecraft, "De Triumpho Naturae," in *The Ancient Track: The Complete Poetical Works of H. P. Lovecraft*, ed. S. T. Joshi (San Francisco, CA: Night Shade Books, 2001), 13–14.
21 H. P. Lovecraft, "On the Creation of Niggers," in *The Ancient Track*, ed. Joshi, 393.

6 Arthur Jermyn (1920)

1 Lovecraft, *Selected Letters I: 1911–1924*, 294.
2 S. T. Joshi puts forth two very odd claims in his analysis of "Arthur Jermyn," as published in *Lovecraft: A Life*, which require brief commentary here. First, Joshi, taking up a stray passage in the first paragraph of "Arthur Jermyn"—"if separate species we be"—makes the claim that Lovecraft may be asserting that the human species is not separate from the other species. Joshi, also, argues that the inhabitants of Sir Wade's lost city represent "missing links" between apes and humans, and that this city, in turn, may be "the ultimate source for all white civilization" (236). Needless to say, these claims are not supported by any of the Lovecraft texts. As we have seen in our analysis of Lovecraft's two racist poems in Chapter 4, Lovecraft *did be*lieve that humans, Blacks, and apes are separate species. Also, in "Arthur Jermyn," Lovecraft makes it very clear that the inhabitants of the lost city are an aberrant group of hybrids, not missing links. And they illustrate Lovecraft's contention that whites who have sexual relations with members of the lower species will eventually suffer negative repercussions—the hybrids end up being exterminated by neighboring tribes.
3 Rolland, *The Curious Case of H. P. Lovecraft*, 73.
4 De Camp, *Lovecraft: A Biography*, 143.
5 H. P. Lovecraft, "Arthur Jermyn," in *Dagon and Other Macabre Tales*, ed. August Derleth (Sauk City, WI: Arkham House, 1965), 49.
6 Ibid., 48.
7 Ibid.
8 Ibid., 55.

9 Ibid., 49.
10 Ibid.
11 Ibid.
12 Ibid., 49–50.
13 Ibid., 51.
14 Ibid., 47, 51.
15 Ibid., 54.

7 Herbert West—Reanimator (1922)

1 H. P. Lovecraft, "Herbert West—Reanimator," in *H. P. Lovecraft: Tales*, ed. Peter Straub (New York: Library of America, 2005), 54.
2 Mary Shelley, *Frankenstein* (New York: Bantam Books, 1981), 42.
3 Lovecraft, "Herbert West—Reanimator," 54.
4 Ibid., 27.
5 Ibid., 33–4.
6 Ibid., 37.
7 Ibid., 39.
8 Ibid., 42.
9 Ibid., 44.
10 Ibid.
11 Ibid., 49.
12 Ibid., 25.
13 Ibid., 41.
14 Ibid., 46.
15 Ibid., 54.
16 Ibid.

8 The Lurking Fear (1923)

1 Lovecraft, *Selected Letters I*, 201.
2 Ibid., 181.
3 Ibid., 198.
4 Callaghan Gavin, *H. P. Lovecraft's Dark Arcadia: The Satire, Symbology and Contradiction* (North Carolina: McFarland, 2013), 155–8.
5 Sara Williams, "'The Infinitude of the Shrieking Abysses': Rooms, Wombs, Tombs, and the Hysterical Female Gothic in 'The Dreams in the Witch-House,'" in *New Critical Essays on H. P. Lovecraft*, ed. Simmons, 66–9.

6 Ibid., 69.
7 Lovecraft, *Selected Letters V*, 418.
8 H. P. Lovecraft, "The Lurking Fear," in *H. P. Lovecraft: Tales*, 66–7.
9 Ibid., 67.
10 Ibid.
11 Ibid., 58.
12 Ibid., 60.
13 Ibid., 62.
14 Ibid., 65.
15 Ibid., 69–70.
16 Ibid., 74.
17 Ibid., 75–6.
18 Ibid., 55.
19 Ibid., 60, 65–6.
20 Ibid., 70, 71.
21 Ibid., 75.
22 Joshi, *Lovecraft: A Life*, 287–8.

9 The Rats in the Walls (1924)

1 Barton Levi St. Armand, *The Roots of Horror in the Fiction of H. P. Lovecraft* (Elizabethtown, NY: Dragon Press, 1977), 3.
2 Joshi, *Lovecraft: A Life*, 301.
3 Lovecraft, *Selected Letters I*, 258.
4 H. P. Lovecraft, "The Rats in the Walls," in *H. P. Lovecraft: Tales*, 80.
5 Ibid.
6 Ibid., 80, 87.
7 Ibid., 94.
8 Ibid., 80.
9 Ibid., 80–1.
10 Ibid., 81.
11 Ibid., 86, 88.
12 Ibid., 81.
13 Ibid.
14 Ibid., 95.
15 St. Armand, *The Roots of Horror*, 28.
16 Lovecraft, "The Rats in the Walls," 95–6.

17 Ibid., 95.
18 Joshi, *Lovecraft: A Life*, 302.
19 Lovecraft, "The Rats in the Walls," 93.

10 The Horror at Red Hook (1925)

1 Joshi, *Lovecraft: A Life*, 366.
2 H. P. Lovecraft, "The Horror at Red Hook," in *H. P. Lovecraft: Tales*, 128–9.
3 Ibid., 133.
4 De Camp, *Lovecraft: A Biography*, 241.
5 Lovecraft, "The Horror at Red Hook," 136.
6 Ibid., 137.
7 Ibid.
8 Ibid., 135.
9 Ibid.
10 Ibid., 139.
11 Ibid., 126.
12 Ibid., 143–4.
13 Ibid., 145.
14 Maurice Lévy, in *Lovecraft: A Study in the Fantastic*, makes a similar observation: "We think those strangers ... the monsters, fruit of repugnant matings of humans with 'outsiders,' represent the ultimate level of degeneracy that lies in waits for American civilization if it continues to encourage, or simply tolerate, the mixture of bloods and races." Translated by S. T. Joshi (Detroit, MI: Wayne State University Press, 1988), 61–2.
15 H. P. Lovecraft, "He," in *H. P. Lovecraft: Tales*, 147, 148.

11 Critical Commentaries

1 Sederholm and Weinstock, "Introduction," 36–7.
2 Simmons, "A Certain Resemblance," 13.
3 Interestingly, Toni Morrison, in *Playing in the Dark*, creates her own American aesthetic signifier and this is very similar to Simmons' continental version. Morrison calls this the "Africanist persona" and, in describing it, makes it clear that white American writers and artists respond to it in much the same way as Lovecraft does to the homogeneous, abject Other: "artists—and the society that bred them—[transfer] internal conflicts to a 'blank darkness,' to conveniently bound and violently silenced black bodies ... the image of reined-in, bound, suppressed, and repressed darkness become objectified" (Cambridge, MA: Harvard University Press, 1992), 38–9.

4   Simmons, "A Certain Resemblance," 19.
5   Julia Kristeva, *Powers of Horror: An Essay on Abjection* (New York: Columbia University Press, 1982), 1–3, 200.
6   H. P. Lovecraft, "Imprisoned with the Pharaohs," in *The Transition of H. P. Lovecraft: The Road to Madness* (New York: Del Rey Books, 1996), 185.
7   Mayer, "Race, Species, and Others," 120.
8   Ibid., 123.
9   Sederholm and Weinstock, "Introduction," 37.
10 Mayer, "Race, Species, and Others," 119.
11 Lovecraft, *Selected Letters II*, 290.

12 Lovecraft's Later Weird Tales

1   H. P. Lovecraft, "The Dunwich Horror," in *H. P. Lovecraft: Tales*, 385.

13 *The Case of Charles Dexter Ward* (1927)

1   H. P. Lovecraft, *The Case of Charles Dexter Ward*, in *H. P. Lovecraft: Tales*, 228, 233.
2   Ibid., 226.
3   Ibid., 303–4.
4   Ibid., 318.
5   Ibid., 309.
6   Ibid., 288.
7   Ibid., 312–13.
8   Lovecraft, "On the Creation of Niggers," 393.
9   Shapiro and Barnard, *Pentecostal Modernism*, 131.

14 The Whisperer in Darkness (1930)

1   H. P. Lovecraft, "The Whisperer in Darkness," in *H. P. Lovecraft: Tales*, 416.
2   Ibid., 443, 447.
3   Ibid., 447.
4   Ibid., 467–8.
5   Ibid., 466.
6   Ibid., 442.
7   Ibid., 475.

8 Ibid., 441, 442, 444.
9 Ibid., 448.

15 The Shadow Over Innsmouth (1931)

1 H. P. Lovecraft, "The Shadow Over Innsmouth," in *H. P. Lovecraft: Tales*, 646.
2 Ibid., 616.
3 H. P. Lovecraft, "The Call of Cthulhu," in *H. P. Lovecraft: Tales*, 177.
4 Lovecraft, "The Shadow Over Innsmouth," 597–8.
5 Ibid., 651.
6 Ibid., 653.
7 Tracy Bealer, "'The Innsmouth Look': H. P. Lovecraft's Ambivalent Modernism," *The Journal of Philosophy: A Cross—Disciplinary Inquiry*, Vol. 6, No. 14 (2011): 45, quoted in Mayer, "Race, Species, and Others," 124.
8 Shapiro and Barnard, *Pentecostal Modernism*, 137.
9 S. T. Joshi, "H. P. Lovecraft: The Decline of the West," in *The Weird Tale* (Austin: University of Texas Press, 1990), 225.
10 F. Scott Fitzgerald, *The Great Gatsby* (New York: Charles Scribner's, 1925), 13.

16 *At the Mountains of Madness* (1931)

1 S. T. Joshi, *A Dreamer and a Visionary: H. P. Lovecraft in His Time* (London: Liverpool University Press, 2001), 300.
2 H. P. Lovecraft, "At the Mountains of Madness," in *H. P. Lovecraft: Tales*, 499.
3 Ibid.
4 Ibid., 543.
5 Ibid., 576.
6 Ibid., 541–2.
7 Ibid., 546.
8 Ibid.
9 Ibid., 547.
10 Ibid., 555.
11 Ibid., 581.
12 Ibid.
13 Edgar Allan Poe, "The Narrative of Arthur Gordon Pym of Nantucket," in *Edgar Allan Poe: Poetry and Tales* (New York: Library of America, 1984), 1179.

14 Kenneth Silverman, *Edgar Allan Poe: Mournful and Never-Ending Remembrance* (New York: HarperCollins, 1991), 136.
15 Shapiro and Barnard, *Pentecostal Modernism*, 127–8.
16 Ibid., 127.
17 Joshi, *A Dreamer and a Visionary*, 301.

17 The Shadow Out of Time (1934)

1 Ibid., 345.
2 Ibid., 344.
3 H. P. Lovecraft, "The Shadow Out of Time," in *H. P. Lovecraft: Tales*, 736, 742.
4 Ibid., 736–7.
5 Ibid., 751.
6 Ibid., 745–6.
7 Ibid., 739.
8 Ibid., 720.
9 Ibid., 768–9.

18 Critical Commentaries (II)

1 W. Scott Poole, "Lovecraft, Witch Cults, and Philosophers," in *The Age of Lovecraft*, ed. Carl H. Sederholm and Jeffrey Andrew Weinstock, 222.
2 Ibid., 226.
3 Graham Harman, *Weird Realism: Lovecraft and Philosophy* (Winchester: Zero Books, 2012), 4–5.
4 Lovecraft, *Selected Letters II*, 266–7.
5 Harman, *Weird Realism*, 254–5.
6 Lovecraft, "The Call of Cthulhu," 194.
7 Lovecraft, "The Dunwich Horror," 389.
8 MacCormack, "Lovecraft's Cosmic Ethics," 199.
9 Ibid., 201.
10 Gina Wisker, in "'Spawn of the Pit': Lavinia, Marceline, Medusa, and All Things Foul: H. P. Lovecraft's Liminal Women" (2013), attempts to do the same sort of thing as MacCormack. Wisker uses a character, Marceline Bedard, in a story that Lovecraft revised but didn't actually write ("Medusa's Coil," written by Zealia Bishop in 1930) to bolster her claim that Lovecraft's so-called "liminal women"—Lavinia Whateley, Keziah Mason, and Asenath Waite—are more than merely abject characters in Lovecraft tales; they are empowered by their association with cosmic forces and with black magic

practitioners [*New Critical Essays on H. P. Lovecraft*, ed. David Simmons, 31–54]. This claim certainly applies to Marceline, but it does not apply to the women characters that Lovecraft actually created. All of the Lovecraft women are abject victims, used by either the trans-dimensional entities or the male black magic practitioners to accomplish the latter's nefarious goals.

11   MacCormack, "Lovecraft's Cosmic Ethics," 204.
12   Ibid., 207.
13   Sederholm and Weinstock, "Introduction," 33.

19 Conclusion

1   S. T. Joshi, *The Rise and Fall of the Cthulhu Mythos* (Poplar Bluff, MO: Mythos Books, 2008), 254.
2   Joshi, *Lovecraft: A Life*, 586, 588.
3   Jeffrey Andrew Weinstock, "An Interview with China Miéville," in *The Age of Lovecraft*, ed. Sederholm and Weinstock, 241.
4   Sederholm and Weinstock, "Introduction," 38.
5   Lovecraft, *Selected Letters V*, 367.
6   Lovecraft, *Selected Letters IV*, 102.
7   William Schnabel, in *Lovecraft's Racial Values*, holds a similar view. As he writes: "Numerous studies dealing with the biographies of authors and artists tend to show that conflicts, traumatisms and failure stimulate artistic creativity. Suffering seems to act as a catalyst, with artistic creation functioning as a 'deferred revenge,' a means of repairing a traumatic experience and source of torment" (France: Le Diable Ermite, 2021), 43–4.
8   Shapiro and Barnard, *Pentecostal Modernism*, 121.
9   The pertinent passage in Houellebecq is: "So the central passion animating [Lovecraft's] work is much more akin to masochism than to sadism; which only underscores its dangerous profundity … cruelty toward another can only produce a mediocre outcome; cruelty conferred upon oneself, on the other hand, is of an altogether different order of interest" (*H. P. Lovecraft: Against the World, against Life*), 109.
10   J. Gerald Kennedy and Liliane Weissberg, *Romancing the Shadow: Poe and Race* (Oxford: Oxford University Press, 2001), xiv.

Appendix—Lovecraft, *Lovecraft Country*, and Afrofuturism

1   Matt Ruff, *Lovecraft Country* (New York: HarperCollins, 2016), 102.
2   Lovecraft, *Selected Letters II*, 150.

3 Mark Dery, "Black to the Future: Interviews with Samuel R. Delany, Greg Tate, and Tricia Rose," in *Flame Wars: The Discourse of Cyberculture* (Durham, NC: Duke University Press, 1994), 180.
4 Kodwo Eshun, "Further Considerations on Afrofuturism," CR: *The New Centennial Review*, Vol. 3, No. 2 (2003): 298–9. doi:10.1353/ncr.2003.0021.
5 Ibid., 300.
6 Ibid., 298.
7 Victor LaValle, *The Ballad of Black Tom* (New York: Tom Doherty Associates, LLC, 2016), 66.

BIBLIOGRAPHY

Airaksinen, Timo. *The Philosophy of Lovecraft: The Route to Horror.* New York: Peter Lang, 1999.
Callaghan, Gavin. *H. P. Lovecraft's Dark Arcadia.* Jefferson, NC: McFarland Press, 2013.
Chamberlain, Houston Stewart. *The Foundations of the 19th Century.* 2nd ed. Translated by John Lees. Great Britain: Bodley Head, 1912.
De Camp, L. Sprague. *Lovecraft: A Biography.* New York: Doubleday, 1975.
Dery, Mark. "Black to the Future: Interviews with Samuel R. Delany, Greg Tate, and Tricia Rose." In *Flame Wars: The Discourse of Cyberculture.* New York: Duke University Press, 1994, 179–222.
DiAngelo, Robin. *White Fragility: Why It's So Hard for White People to Talk about Racism.* Boston, MA: Beacon Press, 2018.
Eshun, Kodwo. "Further Considerations on Afrofuturism." *CR: The New Centennial Review*, Vol. 3, No. 2 (2003), 287–302. doi: 10.1353/ ncr.2003.0021.
Harman, Graham. *Weird Realism: Lovecraft and Philosophy.* Winchester: Zero Books, 2012.
Houellebecq, Michel. *H. P. Lovecraft: Against the World, against Life.* Translated by Dorna Khazeni. Great Britain: Gollancz, 2008.
Joshi, S. T. *A Dreamer and a Visionary: H. P. Lovecraft in His Time.* Liverpool: Liverpool University Press, 2001.
Joshi, S. T. *H. P. Lovecraft: A Life.* West Warwick, RI: Necronomicon Press, 1996.
Joshi, S. T. *The Rise and Fall of the Cthulhu Mythos.* Poplar Bluff, MO: Mythos Books, 2008.
Joshi, S. T. *The Weird Tale: Arthur Machen, Lord Dunsany, Algernon Blackwood, M. R. James, Ambrose Bierce, H. P. Lovecraft.* Austin: University of Texas Press, 1990.
Kennedy, J. Gerald, and Liliane Weissberg, eds. *Romancing the Shadow: Poe and Race.* Oxford: Oxford University Press, 2011.
Kristeva, Julia. *Powers of Horror: An Essay on Abjection.* Translated by Leon S. Roudiez. New York: Columbia University Press, 1982.
LaValle, Victor. *The Ballad of Black Tom.* Edited by Ellen Datlow. New York: Tom Doherty Associates, LLC, 2016.
Lévy, Maurice. *Lovecraft: A Study in the Fantastic.* Translated by S. T. Joshi. Detroit, MI: Wayne State University Press, 1988.
Lovecraft, H. P. *The Ancient Track: The Complete Poetical Works of H. P. Lovecraft.* Edited by S. T. Joshi. San Francisco, CA: Night Side Books, 2001.

Lovecraft, H. P. *At the Mountains of Madness and Other Novels*. Selected by August Derleth. Sauk City, WI: Arkham House, 1964.

Lovecraft, H. P. *The Best of H. P. Lovecraft: Bloodcurdling Tales of Horror and the Macabre*. New York: Del Rey Books, 1982.

Lovecraft, H. P. *Dagon and Other Macabre Tales*. Selected by August Derleth. Sauk City, WI: Arkham House, 1965.

Lovecraft, H. P. *The Horror in the Museum and Other Revisions*. Sauk City, WI: Arkham House, 1970.

Lovecraft, H. P. *H. P. Lovecraft: Tales*. Edited by Peter Straub. New York: The Library of America, 2005.

Lovecraft, H. P. *Miscellaneous Writings: H. P. Lovecraft*. Edited by S. T. Joshi. Sauk City, WI: Arkham House, 1995.

Lovecraft. H. P. *Selected Letters I: 1911–1924*. Edited by August Derleth and Donald Wandrei. Sauk City, WI: Arkham House, 1965.

Lovecraft, H. P. *Selected Letters: II: 1925–1929*. Edited by August Derleth and Donald Wandrei. Sauk City, WI: Arkham House, 1968.

Lovecraft, H. P. *Selected Letters III: 1929–1931*. Edited by August Derleth and Donald Wandrei. Sauk City, WI: Arkham House, 1971.

Lovecraft, H. P. *Selected Letters IV: 1932–1934*. Edited by August Derleth and James Turner. Sauk City, WI: Arkham House, 1976.

Lovecraft, H. P. *Selected Letters V: 1934–1937*. Edited by August Derleth and James Turner. Sauk City, WI: Arkham House, 1976.

Lovecraft, H. P. *Something about Cats and Other Pieces*. Collected by August Derleth. Sauk City, WI: Arkham House, 1949.

Lovecraft, H. P. *The Transition of H. P. Lovecraft: The Road to Madness*. New York: Del Rey Books, 1996.

Morrison, Toni. *Playing in the Dark: Whiteness and the Literary Imagination*. Cambridge, MA: Harvard University Press, 1992.

Nelson, Dana D. *The Word in Black and White: Reading "Race" in American Literature*, 1638–1867. Oxford: Oxford University Press, 1992.

Poe, Edgar Allan. *Edgar Allan Poe: Poetry and Tales*. New York: The Library of America, 1984.

Rolland, Paul. *The Curious Case of H. P. Lovecraft*. London: Plexis, 2014.

Ruff, Matt. *Lovecraft Country*. New York: HarperCollins, 2017.

Schnabel, William. *Lovecraft's Racial Values*. Brixey-Aux-Chaniones, France: Le Diable Ermite, 2021.

Sederholm, Carl H., and Jeffrey Andrew Weinstock, eds. *The Age of Lovecraft*. Minneapolis: University of Minnesota, 2016.

Shapiro, Stephen, and Philip Barnard. *Pentecostal Modernism: Lovecraft, Los Angeles, and World-Systems Culture*. New York: Bloomsbury Academic, 2017.

Shelley, Mary. *Frankenstein*. New York: Bantam Books, 1981.

Silverman, Kenneth. *Edgar Allan Poe: Mournful and Never-Ending Remembrance*. New York: HarperCollins, 1991.

Simmons, David, ed. *New Critical Essays on H. P. Lovecraft*. New York: Palgrave Macmillan, 2013.

Spengler, Oswald, *The Decline of the West: Perspectives of World History*. Vol. II. Translated by Charles Francis Atkinson. (2007). http://archive.org/ details/ declineofwest02spenof/page/n5/ mode/2up (accessed April 20, 2023).

St. Armand, Barton Levi. *The Roots of Horror in the Fiction of H. P. Lovecraft.* Elizabethtown, NY: Dragon Press, 1977.
Thacker, Eugene. *In the Dust of This Planet: Horror of Philosophy.* Vol. 1. Winchester: Zero Books, 2011.
Woodard, Ben. *Slime Dynamics: Generation, Mutation, and the Creep of Life.* Winchester: Zero Books, 2012.

INDEX

"'A Certain Resemblance': Abject Hybridity in H. P. Lovecraft's Short Fiction" (Simmons) 8, 124–8
Adamite Order of the Ancient Dawn (AOAD) 218, 220
aesthetic signifier 124, 126, 233, 11, n.3
Africanist persona 233, 11, n. 3
Afrofuturism 10, 217, 221-4, 225, 227
Age of Lovecraft, The (Sederholm and Weinstock) 9, 123–4, 129, 130
Ahu-Y'hloa 164
Airaksinen, Timo 198
Akeley, Henry Wentworth 5, 22, 63, 151, 152, 153, 154, 155, 156, 157–9, 160
Alhazred, Abdul 174
Alice (Elizabeth Toldridge's maid) 35, 59
Allen, Zadok 162, 163, 166, 169
"Ancient Track, The," 55
Anderson, Sherwood 68, 69
"Americanism," 48–50
Appleton, John Howard 16
Argosy 46, 65, 100
Arkham House 51, 67, 207
"Arthur Jermyn," 8, 52, 64, 67–76, 86, 88, 92, 94, 95, 97, 101, 124, 125–6, 127, 130, 230, 6, n.2
Aryan Myth 36–7, 40, 47–9, 51, 52, 53, 54, 57
Asimov, Isaac 189
Astounding Stories 136, 171, 184
At the Mountains of Madness 4, 9, 17, 89, 136, 159, 171–81, 187, 188, 192, 193, 208, 211, 212, 219, 222
Augustan poetry 55

Baird, Edwin 67, 100
Ballad of Black Tom, The (LaValle) 224–5
Barlow, R. H. 183
Barnard, Philip 8, 9, 148, 168, 169, 179–80, 213–14
Bealer, Tracy 168
"Beast in the Cave, The," 89
Beckford, William 15
Bennett, George 92–3, 95
Béraud, Henri 183
Berkley Square (film) 183
Berry, George 217–19, 220
Berry, Hippolyta 220
"Beyond the Wall of Sleep," 63
Beyond Re—Animator 78
Black Atlantic Mythos 222–3
Black Book, The (Joseph) 113
"Black Stone, The" (Howard) 113
"Black to the Future: Interviews with Samuel R. Delany, Greg Tate, and Tricia Rose" (Dery) 221
Bloch, Robert 4
Book of Black Magic and of Pacts, The (Waite) 116–17
Book of Revelation, The (Joseph) 113
Bodley Head, The 37
Boyle, E. M. 192
Braithwhite, Caleb 217–19, 220, 225
Braithwhite, Christina 225
Braithwhite, Samuel 217–18
Braithwhite, Titus 218

Bride of Re—Animator 78
Brooklyn Heights 30, 36, 111
Brooklyn Hospital 29
Brown, Charles Brockden 15
Brown University 23, 24, 31
Burleson, Donald R. 7
Burroughs, Edgar Rice 69, 70
Bush, David Van 29
Butler Hospital 14, 18, 25, 29

"Call of Cthulhu, The," 135, 201
Callaghan, Gavin 89–90
Cannes Film Festival 78
Carter, Randolph 63, 89, 204
Case of Charles Dexter Ward, The 114, 117, 135, 136, 139–51, 157, 171, 190, 210
"Cats of Ulthar, The," 63
Cavalier, The 65
Chamberlain, Houston Stewart 36, 37–40, 42, 47, 48, 57, 64, 69, 193
Chambers, Robert W. 161
Clapham-Lee, Sir Eric Moreland 80, 83–4, 85
Clark, Lillian D. 14, 30, 35, 36, 89
Cobb, Irwin S. 161
Cole, Edward D. 46
Conservative, The 46–7, 50, 63
"Cool Air," 211
Crawford, William 161
"Crime of the Century, The," 38, 47–8, 52
Cthulhu Mythos 135, 197, 208
Cultes Des Goules (Comte d' Erlette) 191
Curious Case of H. P. Lovecraft, The (Roland) 46, 68
Curwen, Joseph 114, 117, 136, 140–4, 145, 146, 148, 149–50, 157

Daas, Edward F. 46
Dagon and Other Macabre Tales 67
Dandridge, Letitia 217
Danford, Paul 172, 173, 176, 177, 178, 219, 222
Darwin, Charles 58
Davis, Robert H. 100

de Camp, L. Sprague 17, 30, 32, 45, 48, 50–1, 69, 70, 114
de la Poer, Gilbert 104
de la Poer, Lady Margaret Trevor 106, 198
de la Poer, Mary 106
de la Poer, Walter 100–1, 106–7
"De Triumpho Naturae," 56–7, 193
Decline of the West, Perspectives of World History. Vol II, The (Spengler) 36, 40
Delapore, Alfred 106, 107
Delapore, Randolph 106
Delapore, Thomas 5, 22, 74, 100–1, 102, 103, 105, 106–9, 110, 120–1, 167, 220, 224
Deleuze, Gilles 203, 204
Delilah (Lillian Clark's maid) 35
Derleth, August 40, 51, 65, 67, 135, 183, 207, 220
Dery, Mark 10, 221–2
Descent of Man, The (Darwin) 58
Devil Worship: The Sacred Books and Traditions of the Yezidiz (Joseph) 113
DiAngelo, Robin 1–2, 35
"Doom that Came to Sarnath, The," 63–4, 161
Dracula (novel) 100
Drake, H. B. 183
Dream-Quest of Unknown Kadath, The 204
Dubois, W. E. B. 223, 224
Dudley, Jervas 63
"Dunwich Horror, The," 137–8, 143, 202
Dwyer, Bernard Austin 24
Dyer, William 5, 171, 172, 173, 176, 177, 178, 192, 219, 222

Edgar Allan Poe: Mournful and Never-Ending Remembrance (Silverman) 179
Einstein, Albert 199
Eshun, Kodwo 10, 222–4
Esoteric Order of Dagon 162, 164
Exham Priory 64, 100, 101, 103, 104, 106–7, 108, 110

INDEX

"Facts Concerning the Late Arthur Jermyn and his Family" *see* "Arthur Jermyn"
"Facts in the Case of M. Valdemar, The" (Poe) 121
"Festival, The," 89, 128
Fischer, Harry O. 90
"Fishhead" (Cobb) 161
Fitzgerald, F. Scott 170
Foundations of the Nineteenth Century, 2nd Ed, The (Chamberlain) 36, 37–8, 47–8, 57–8
Frankenstein (novel) 78–9
Freud, Sigmund 89–90, 97, 100
"From Beyond," 63
Fungi From Yuggoth 55
"Further Considerations on Afrofuturism." (Eshun) 222–4

Gamwell, Anne 14, 207
Gerritsen, Cornelia 117
G'll-hoo 164
Gobineau, Arthur de 36–7, 38
Gordon, Stuart 77–8
Great Gatsby, The (Fitzgerald) 170
Green, Misha 225
Greene, Sonia Haft 18, 26, 28–32, 42
Grimm's Fairy Tales 15
Guattari, Felix 203, 204
Guiney, Louise Imogen 13–14

H. P. Lovecraft: Against the World, Against Life (Houellebecq) 205, 213, 214, 227, Int., n.3, 237, 19, n.9
H. P. Lovecraft: A Life (Joshi) 39, 96, 230, 6, n.2
H. P. Lovecraft's Dark Arcadia (Callaghan) 89–90
Halsey, Dr. Allan 80, 81–2, 85, 95
"The Harbor Master" (Chambers) 161
Harman, Graham 9, 195, 198–203, 206
Harris, Woodburn 131
"Haunter of the Dark, The," 207
Hawthorne, Nathaniel 15

"He," 121
Heidegger, Martin 198–9
Henneberger, J. C. 127
"Herbert West—Reanimator," 64, 74, 77–86, 87, 94, 97
Hess, Clara 25
Hitler, Adolf 38, 54, 84
Hölderlin, Frederick 198
Holmes, Oliver Wendell 13
Home Brew 77, 87
"Horror at Red Hook, The," 30, 64, 89, 97, 99, 111–21, 141, 149, 165, 197, 224
Houdini, Harry 127–8
Houellebecq, Michel 205, 213, 214, 227
  Int. n. 3, 237, 19, n. 9
Houtain, George Julian 77, 87
Howard, Robert E. 23, 113, 114
Howie Award 6
Husserl, Edmund 198–9
Hutchinson, Edward 141, 145
Huxley, Thomas Henry 47–8

"Imprisoned with the Pharaohs," 8, 124, 126–8
"In a Major Key," 50, 52
In a Minor Key (Isaacson) 50
In the Dust of This Planet: Horror of Philosophy, Vol. I (Thacker) 198
Inequality of the Races, The (Gobineau) 37–8
"'Infinitude of the Shrieking Abysses': Rooms, Wombs, Tombs, and the Hysterical Female Gothic' in 'The Dreams in the Witch-House'" (Williams) 90
Innsmouth Look 129, 162, 166, 167
"'Innsmouth Look': H. P. Lovecraft's Ambivalent Modernism, The'" (Bealer) 168
Irigaray, Luce 203
Isaacson, Charles D. 50

Jackson, Fred 46
Jane Brown Memorial Hospital 207
Jermyn, Alfred 70, 73–4, 126

Jermyn, Arthur 5, 22, 68, 70, 71, 72, 74–5, 86, 95, 121, 125, 126, 129, 167, 220, 224
Jermyn, Nevil 70, 73
Jermyn, Philip 70, 72, 126
Jermyn, Robert 70, 72–3, 75
Jermyn, Sir Wade 64, 68, 69, 70, 71–2, 73, 76, 125, 126, 128
Journal of the American Psychological Society: 1928–9 191
Joseph, Isya 113, 114
Joshi, S. T. 7, 18, 21, 23, 24, 27, 28, 39, 48, 51, 96–7, 100, 110, 111, 114, 169, 171, 180–1, 183, 208, 209, 228, 2, n.2, 230, 6, n.2

Kaiser, Wilhelm II 38
Kalem Club 28, 31
Kant, Immanuel 199
Keezar, Alice 190
Kennedy, J. Gerald 214
Kleiner, Reinhart 23, 24, 28, 46, 52, 88
Kristeva, Julia 126

La of Opar 70
Lancaster, John 219
Lane, John 37
LaValle, Victor 224–5
Last Angel of History, The (Tate) 224
Lazarus (Beraud) 183
Leavitt, Robert 80, 83
LeFanu, Joseph Sheridan 15
Lewis, Matthew "Monk," 15
Long, Frank Belknap 28, 30, 31, 100, 102, 199
Lord Dunsany 63
Lovecraft: A Biography (de Camp) 48
Lovecraft: A Life (Joshi) 39, 96–7
Lovecraft Country (novel) 10, 217–21, 224, 225
Lovecraft Country (HBO series) 255
Lovecraft Debate 8–9, 206
Lovecraft, H. P.
 life
  amateur journalism 46–7, 63

  atheism 57–8
  birth 13
  childhood 13–19
  death 50–1, 207
  divorce 31–2
  education 22–4
  finances 18, 29, 30
  marriage 28–31
  philosophy 199–201, 203
  phobias 10, 27, 90–1, 211–12, 197
 residences
  Auburndale, MA 13–14
  Dorchester, MA 13
  New York, NY 18, 28–31
  Providence, RI 18, 30–3
 works
  essays 46–50
  letters 50–5
  poetry 55–9
  revisions and collaborations 204, 207
Lovecraft Paradox 124, 129, 130–2
Lovecraft, Susie 13–14, 15, 18, 19, 22, 24–7, 29, 50
Lovecraft, Sonia *see* Greene, Sonia Haft
"Lovecraft, Witch Cults and Philosophers" (Poole) 9, 195, 196–8
Lovecraft, Winfield Scott 13–14
"Lovecraft's Cosmic Ethics" (MacCormack) 8, 195, 198, 203–6
Loveman, Samuel 28, 30, 46
"Lurking Fear, The," 64, 87–97

MacCormack, Patricia 8, 9, 195, 198, 203–6
Mackenzie, Robert B. F. 192
MacLeod, Fiona 109
Malone, Thomas F. 5, 112–13, 115, 116, 118–20, 225
Marsh, Obed 162, 164, 166, 169
Martense, Gerrit 64, 91–2
Martense, Jan 94, 96
Mask of Cthulhu, The (Derleth) 65
Mather, Cotton 139

Maturin, Charles Robert 15
Mayer, Jed 8, 124, 128–32
Melanochroi 48
"Messenger, The," 55
Metamorphoses of Science Fiction: On the Poetics and History of a Literary Genre (Suvin) 130
Miéville, China 209–10
Miskatonic University 78, 80, 82, 151, 171, 177, 178, 184, 190, 191, 192, 202
Mnar 63
Moe, Maurice 24
Morrison, Toni 233, 11, n. 3
Morton, James Ferdinand 46, 50, 53
"MS Found in a Bottle" (Poe) 214
Munroe, Arthur 93, 95, 96
Murray, Margaret Alice 119, 139, 197
"Music of Erich Zann, The," 63

Narrative of Arthur Gordon Pym, The (Poe) 179–80, 214
Necronomicon (Alhazred) 174, 191, 202
New Critical Essays on H. P. Lovecraft (Simmons) 8, 124–8, 132, 233, 11, n.3
Nigger Man (Lovecraft's cat) 35
Norrys, Captain 101, 105, 106, 107, 108, 109, 110

O'Brien, Kid 82
Olmstead, Robert Martin 5, 22, 74, 85, 108, 128, 129, 135, 161–3, 165–7, 192, 220, 224
"On the Aryan Question" (Huxley) 48
"On the Creation of Niggers," 57–9, 102, 123, 147, 181, 193
"On the Methods and Results of Ethnology" (Huxley) 48
On the Origin of Species (Darwin) 58
"On the Supernatural in Poetry" (Radcliffe) 99
Orne, Simon 141, 145

"Outsider, The," 9, 89, 205, 206
Outsider and Others, The 207

Pabodie, Frank H. 171, 176, 177
Paris Festival of Fantasy, Science Fiction and Horror 78
Pawtuxet Valley Gleaner 16
Peaslee, Hannah 190
Peaslee, Jonathan 190
Peaslee, Nathaniel Wingate 5, 22, 63, 85, 130, 184, 186, 188, 190–3, 219, 222, 224
Peaslee, Robert K. 190
Peaslee, Wingate 184, 190, 191
Pentecostal Modernism: Lovecraft, Los Angeles, and World-Systems Culture (Shapiro and Barnard) 8, 9, 148, 168, 179–80, 213–14
Phillips, Annie Emeline *see* Gamwell, Annie
Phillips, Jeremiah W. 14
Phillips, Lillian Delora *see* Clark, Lillian
Phillips, Robie 14, 17, 18
Phillips, Sarah Susan "Susie" *see* Lovecraft, Susie
Phillips, Whipple Van Buren 2, 13–15, 17–18, 21, 25, 145
Philosophy of Lovecraft: The Route to Horror, The (Airaksinen) 198
"Pickman's Model," 112
Playing in the Dark (Morrison) 233, 11, n. 3
Plunkett, John Moreton Drax *see* Lord Dunsany
Pluto *see* Yuggoth
Poe, Edgar Allan 15, 63, 121, 179–80, 214
Poe, Eliza 179
Poole, W. Scott 9, 195, 196–8
Pope, Alexander 55, 56
Powers of Horror: An Essay on Abjection (Kristeva) 126
Price, E. Hoffman 204
Providence Tribune 16

Quadruple Object 200, 202
Quest, The (Eshun) 223

"Race, Species, and Others: H.
    P. Lovecraft and the Animal"
    (Mayer) 8, 124, 128–32
Radcliffe, Ann 15, 99, 100
"Rats in the Walls, The," 64, 74,
    89, 99–110, 112, 116, 130,
    131, 197
Re-Animator 77–8
Renshaw, Anne Tillery 26–7, 30
Return of Tarzan The (Burroughs) 69
*Rhode Island Journal of
    Astronomy, The* 16
*Rise and Fall of the Cthulhu Mythos,
    The* (Joshi) 208
Rise of the Colored Empires, The
    (Stoddard) 170
R'lyeh 165, 201, 225
Robinson, Buck 80, 82–3, 95
Rolland, Paul 46, 68
Romancing the Shadow: Poe and Race
    (Kennedy and Weissberg) 214
*Roots of Horror in the Fiction of H. P.
    Lovecraft, The* (St. Armand)
    99–100, 107–8
Ruff, Matt 10, 217–21, 224, 225
Russell, John 46

Sargent, Joe 165, 166
Sarnath 63–4, 161
Scott, Winfield Townley 25–6, 27
Seaton, Samuel 73, 75
Sederholm, Carl H. 7, 9, 123–4, 129,
    130, 206, 210
Segregation Era 6–7
Selwyn and Blount Imprint 112
Serres, Michel 203
"Shadow Out of Time, The," 4, 17, 85,
    89, 130, 136, 160, 174, 183–93,
    207, 211, 219, 222
"Shadow Over Innsmouth, The," 52,
    64, 69, 74, 85, 89, 108, 128–9,
    135, 136, 161–70, 192, 210–12,
    223, 224
Shadowy Thing, The (Drake) 183
Shapiro, Steven 8, 9, 148, 168, 169,
    179–80, 213–14
Shea, J. Vernon 2, 16, 18, 42–3, 54
Shelley, Mary 78

Shrewsbury, Labian 220
"Silver Key, The," 204
Silverman, Kenneth 179
Simmons, David 8, 124–8, 132
"Sin Eater, The" (MacLeod) 109
Smith, Clark Ashton 87, 183
Smith, William Benjamin 56
"Something About Cats," 46
Speciesist theories 128
Spengler, Oswald 36, 40–3
Sons of Adam 225
St. Armand, Barton Levi 99–
    100, 107–8
"Statement of Randolph Carter, The,"
    63, 89, 204
Stoddard, Lothrop 170
Stoker, Bram 100
Summers, Montague 139
Sully, Helen 24
Suvin, Darko 130
Supernatural Horror in Literature
    4, 30, 46
Suydam, Robert 112–14, 115, 116,
    117–18, 119, 120, 121, 141,
    149, 150, 198, 224–5

Tanglewood Tales (Hawthorne) 15
Tate, Greg 10, 223, 224
Tarzan and the Jewels of Opar
    (Burroughs) 69
Tarzan and the Lost Empire
    (Burroughs) 69
Tarzan the Invincible (Burroughs) 69
Tarzan the Terrible (Burroughs) 69
Tekeli-li 178, 179–80
Tekeli; or The Siege of Montgatz
    (Hook) 179
Tester, Tommy 224–5
Thacker, Eugene 198
"Thing on the Doorstep, The" 183
Thompson, Christine Campbell 112
"Through the Gates of the Silver Key"
    (Price) 204
Thuum-ha 63–4
Tillinghast, Dutee 144
Tillinghast, Eliza 144
Tobey, William 92–3, 95
"Tomb, The," 63

Toldridge, Elizabeth 35, 55–6, 59
Trail of Cthulhu, The (Derleth) 65, 220
Tremaine, F. Orlin 184
Turner, Atticus 217, 218, 219, 220
Turner, Montrose 217, 218

Unaussprechlichen Kulten (Von Junzt) 191
"Under the Pyramids" *see* "Imprisoned with the Pharaohs"
United Amateur Press Association (UAPA) 46–7
Utpatel, Frank 161

Valdemar, M. 121
Verhaeren, M. 71, 75

Waite, Arthur Edward 116–17, 139
Wandrei, Donald 51, 183
Ward, Charles Dexter 5, 22, 63, 114, 117, 135, 136, 139, 140, 142, 144–8, 149, 150, 157, 191, 192, 213
Ward, Charles Dexter Sr 145, 146, 147
Weinstock, Jeffrey Andrew 9, 123–4, 129, 130, 206, 210
Weird Realism: Lovecraft and Philosophy (Harman) 9, 195, 196, 198–203
Weird Tales 4, 28, 29, 46, 65, 67, 87, 100, 111, 113, 127, 136, 139, 151, 161, 171, 183, 207, 221
Weissberg, Liliane 214
West, Herbert 5, 22, 78, 79–80, 81–6, 95, 121

"Whisperer in Darkness, The," 4, 69, 136, 151–60, 161, 166, 180, 211
White Fragility: Why It's So Hard for White People to Talk About Racism (DiAngelo) 1, 35
Whateley, Wilbur 202
Whitman, Walt 50
Williams, Sarah 90
Willett, Marinus Bicknell 140, 141–2, 143, 145, 146, 147–8
Wilmarth, Albert N. 151, 152, 153, 155, 156, 157, 158–9, 166
Winesburg, Ohio (Anderson) 68
Witch Cult in Western Europe, The (Murray) 119, 197
Wonder Book, A (Hawthorne) 15
Wooley, Natalie 55
Wright, Farnsworth 136, 151, 161, 171, 221

Xanthochroi 47–8

Y'ha-nthlei 129, 164, 167
You'll Need a Nightlight (Thompson) 112
Yezidis 113–14
Yith 185, 187
Young Chemist, The (Appleton) 16
Yuggoth 45, 152, 154, 156, 157
Yuzna, Brian 78

Zahed, Eliphas Levi 139